Maryland Real Estate: Practice & Law

TENTH EDITION

DONALD A. WHITE

Dearborn™
Real Estate Education

This publication is designed to provide accurate and authoritative information in regard to the subject matter covered. It is sold with the understanding that the publisher is not engaged in rendering legal, accounting or other professional service. If legal advice or other expert assistance is required, the services of a competent professional person should be sought.

Vice President and General Manager: Roy Lipner
Publisher and Director of Distance Learning: Evan M. Butterfield
Associate Development Editor: Michael J. Scafuri
Editorial Production Manager: Bryan Samolinski
Creative Director: Lucy Jenkins

Published by Dearborn™ Real Estate Education,
a division of Dearborn Financial Publishing, Inc.®
30 South Wacker Drive
Suite 2500
Chicago, IL 60606-7481
(312) 836-4400
http://www.dearbornRE.com

Library of Congress Cataloging-in-Publication Data

White, Donald Allen, 1931-
    Maryland real estate : practice & law / Donald A. White.-- 10th ed.
        p. cm.
    Rev. ed. of: Maryland real estate / H. Warren Crawford. 9th ed. 1998.
    Includes index.
    ISBN 0-7931-4845-6
        1. Real estate business--Law and legislation--Maryland. 2. Vendors and
    purchasers--Maryland. 3. Real property--Maryland. I. Crawford, H. Warren.
Maryland   real estate. II. Title.

KF2042.R4 G34 2001 Maryland
346.75204'37--dc21
                                                                2001054829

Contents

Preface   v

1 Maryland Real Estate License Law and Related Regulations   1

2 Real Estate Agency   33

3 Real Estate Brokerage   49

4 Listing Agreements and Buyer Representation Agreements   60

5 Interests in Real Estate   74

6 How Ownership Is Held   76

7 Legal Descriptions   88

8 Real Estate Taxes and Other Liens   91

9 Real Estate Contracts   98

10 Transfer of Title   114

11 Title Records   118

12 Real Estate Financing   122

13 Leases   128

14 Environmental Issues and Real Estate Transactions   141

15 Fair Housing   151

16 Closing the Real Estate Transaction   162

Appendix A Maryland Real Estate License Examinations   164

Appendix B Complaint Procedure   172

Appendix C Useful Real Estate-Related Web Sites   174

Appendix D Documentation Required in Maryland Residential
            Real Estate Sales Transactions   177

Answer Key   178

Index   179

Preface

As a student entering a real estate course you face exciting challenges. You must learn a large body of theory and then apply it in practice. You will want to know legal principles and real estate theory so well that when you get your license you will be able to do the right thing almost automatically.

If you fail to understand and appreciate law and theory, you can suffer devastating financial and legal consequences. On the other hand, if you build your educational foundation in real estate well, you should be able to make the money you want and to not lose the money you make through costly mistakes.

The purpose of this book is to present clearly many of the laws and operating requirements for real estate brokerage in the State of Maryland. It builds on basic information presented in Dearborn™ Real Estate Education's real estate principles texts. The author has made a serious effort to avoid duplicating, in the present book, information presented in the principles texts. Therefore, you should study each subject area in *both the basic text and in this book* (see the table on page vii). Online information can be accessed using the Web addresses available throughout the text and in Appendix C in the back of the book.

Following most chapters are review questions. They are useful both for evaluation and learning. As you finish each chapter, and before you go on to the next, be certain that you are able to answer *and understand* each question presented. An answer key for all of the tests is included at the end of the book.

You will want to make frequent use of *Appendix C Useful Real Estate-Related Web Sites*. It contains several carefully chosen "hub" sites that give you access to many official sources for real estate law and regulation at various levels of government.

While the author exercised care in providing information about the laws governing the practice of real estate in Maryland, he urges the reader to consult legal counsel regarding any statutory enactment. The reader should not rely solely on this publication as legal authority for compliance with any statute.

Throughout your real estate course, you will be studying and taking tests in preparation for the Maryland Real Estate Licensing Examination. That examination is prepared and administered for the Maryland Real Estate Commission by an independent testing service, Psychological Services, Inc., (PSI), of Glendale, California. *Maryland*

Real Estate: Practice & Law has been designed to familiarize you with the subject matter you will find on that examination. The questions at the end of each chapter are prepared in a multiple-choice format similar to those in the licensing examination.

Throughout the text you will find Internet Web sites of particular value to students entering Maryland real estate brokerage. Some have several links to related sites. Even though Web sites come and go and change their addresses (URLs) with surprising frequency, you are urged to choose the most useful links and bookmark them for future use.

Students and teachers will find updates to this book at the Dearborn™ Web site shown below.

http://www.dearbornRE.com

Scroll down to find, under the first black bar, "Real Estate Educators." Find the words *Instructor Resources*. At the end of that line, click on **here.** On the next screen, ignore the call for a PIN number and scroll down to the list of state books.

About the Author

Maryland Real Estate: Practice & Law, Tenth Edition, is written by Donald A. White, DREI, of Bowie, Maryland. Mr. White has been a Maryland real estate licensee since 1967, and has held an associate broker license since 1972. He holds degrees in music (BsMusEd), religious education (MRE), and in business (MA). He has taught real estate licensing courses at Prince George's Community College continuously since 1972. He served several terms as Chair of the Education Committee of the Prince George's Association of REALTORS®. A past-President of the Maryland Real Estate Educators Association, he is presently a member of the Educational Advisory Committee to the Education Committee of the Maryland Real Estate Commission.

The author holds the DREI (Distinguished Real Estate Instructor) designation from the Real Estate Educators Association of which he is a charter member. He has taught frequently in REALTOR® continuing education seminars. He also was the principal author of *Questions and Answers on Maryland Real Estate* and coauthor, with Maurice Boren, of the *Study Guide to Maryland Real Estate License Examinations*.

Countless students and teachers of Maryland real estate subjects owe a debt of gratitude to H. Warren "Buck" Crawford, author or coauthor of the preceding nine editions of this book. His life of educational service and legal example has inspired them and helped equip them for their careers.

The author appreciates the constructive suggestions on the updating and revision of this text provided by Harold Gordon, Senior Instructor, Weichert Real Estate School; Professor Darlene Mallick, J.D., L.L.M., Anne Arundel Community College; Emily M. Mintz, GRI, RECS of Long & Foster Real Estate, Inc.; and by staff of the Office of the Maryland Attorney General. He also extends thanks to Michael Scafuri, Associate Development Editor at Dearborn™ Real Estate Education Company, who diligently shepherded this work to completion.

HOW TO USE THIS BOOK

The conversion table below provides a quick and easy reference for using *Maryland Real Estate: Practice & Law* in conjunction with various principles books. For instance, *Maryland Real Estate's* Chapter 16, "Closing the Real Estate Transaction," may be read in conjunction with Chapter 22 in *Modern Real Estate Practice*, Chapter 17 in *Real Estate Fundamentals,* Chapter 12 in *Mastering Real Estate Principles,* and Unit 22 in *National Real Estate Principles (Software)*.

Maryland Real Estate: Practice and Law, 10th Edition	*Modern Real Estate Practice*	*Real Estate Fundamentals*	*Mastering Real Estate Principles*	*National Real Estate Principles (Software)*
1. Maryland Real Estate License Law and Regulations	—	—	16	—
2. Real Estate Agency	4	9	13	4
3. Real Estate Brokerage	5	9	13	5
4. Listing and Buyer Representation Agreements	6	7	15	6
5. Interests in Real Estate	7	3	7	7
6. How Ownership Is Held	8	5	9	8
7. Legal Descriptions	9	2	6	9
8. Real Estate Taxes and Other Liens	10	3, 10	5, 25	10
9. Real Estate Contracts	11	7	14	11
10. Transfer of Title	12	4	10	12
11 Title Records	13	6	11	13
12. Real Estate Financing	14, 15	12,13	Unit VII	14, 15
13. Leases	16	8	8	16
14. Environmental Issues and the Real Estate Transaction	21	16	3	21
15. Fair Housing	20	15	17	20
16. Closing the Real Estate Transaction	22	17	12	22

1

Maryland Real Estate License Law and Related Regulations

OVERVIEW

In this chapter students will learn some of the history of brokerage regulation in Maryland; be introduced to the location of the statutory and regulatory documents that govern the industry today; come to understand the structure, duties, and powers of the Maryland Real Estate Commission; and come to appreciate the mechanics of obtaining, maintaining, and upgrading a brokerage license. They will delve into the various requirements and prohibitions that guide the everyday life of a real estate licensee.

HISTORY AND SOURCES OF MARYLAND LICENSE LAW

The Maryland Real Estate Brokers Act, a law designed to protect the public interest, first became effective on June 1, 1939. Since then there have been frequent revisions. All the work of real estate licensees is affected by this statute, and it is therefore the basis of much of this chapter.

The "Maryland Real Estate Brokers Act" appears as Title (Chapter) 17 in the

Business Occupations and Professions Article of the Annotated Code of Maryland. In this book, the author refers to this statute as the "Brokers Act" and as "Title 17".

Real estate brokerage is governed both by statutes, like the Brokers Act mentioned above, and by administrative law, i.e., regulations. The "Maryland Real Estate Brokers Act," was enacted by the General Assembly. Therefore, it is an example of *legislative (statutory)* law.

In addition to statutes and regulations, ***common law*** governs real estate brokerage. Common law, often—and unfortunately—called *the unwritten law*, is in actuality recorded in print. Many, many volumes contain lengthy *written* decisions by courts of appeal. The decisions were delivered in situations where no relevant statute existed, a contract did not address an important issue, or a statute was unclear and needed clarification. On occasions, laws no longer seemed to make sense to the judges writing the opinion. This last instance, in which judges modernize a law, is called *judicial activism.*

Decisions based on taking statutes at their face value and on the original intention of the legislators writing them, are examples of *strict construction*. For the U.S. Supreme Court to decide, in 1965, that the Civil Rights Act of 1866 meant exactly what it said and was still applicable in 1965, is an example of strict construction.

Statutes are *written* by bodies within the legislative branch of government; common law is *rendered* from the judicial bench.

Decisions made by courts of appeal become binding on lower courts within their judicial area. The higher the court of appeal making a decision, the more numerous the courts in which that decision becomes the standard—the *precedent*—for decisions made later in those lower courts.

The Maryland Real Estate Commission in the Department of Licensing and Regulation makes and enforces regulations to implement the Brokers Act. These regulations are *administrative law*. Administrative law seeks to apply statutes to particular situations.

A copy of the Brokers Act, in a booklet that also contains relevant portions of the regulations, is available at the Commission Offices, 500 North Calvert Street, 3rd Floor, Baltimore, MD 21202-2272, or from a local Board or Association of licensees such as the REALTORS® or Realtists. The two most recent versions of this important booklet were dated November 1996 and October 2000 respectively. Many college and public libraries can give you information about changes in the *statutes* passed since the most recent booklet. The information is

usually found in the Legal Reference section of the library.

The *Maryland Register,* a biweekly publication, reports, among many other things, both proposed and finalized changes in *regulations*. Months later the changes appear on new pages of the looseleaf volume of COMAR, the Code of Maryland Regulations.

The State Government Legislative Reference service, (301) 858-3810, can provide copies of proposed new or changed statutes. Copies of pending legislation can also be found and downloaded from the Web page of the Maryland General Assembly on the Internet at:

---

http://mlis.state.md.us/

There click "Bill Information and Status"; then, under "Bill Indexes," click "One or Two Subjects."

The statutes and regulations contained in this book are those in force at the time of its publication, including changes taking effect on October 1, 2001.

DEFINITIONS OF TERMS

As used in Title 17, certain words have special definitions unless the context requires otherwise. For example, **a real estate broker** is defined as an individual who provides **real estate brokerage services.** These services are defined as any of the following activities:

- For consideration, and for another person: selling, buying, exchanging, or leasing any real estate; or collecting rent for the use of any real estate

- For consideration, assisting another person to locate or obtain for purchase or lease any residential real estate

- Engaging in a business of regularly buying and selling real estate or leases or options on real estate

- Engaging in a business that promotes the sale of real estate through a listing in a publication issued primarily for that purpose

- Engaging in the business of subdividing land and selling the subdivided lots

- For consideration, serving as a consultant for any of the activities in this list

Although the law defines **persons** as "individuals, receivers, trustees, guardians, personal representatives, fiduciaries, or representatives of any kind and any partnership, firm, association, or other entity," only **natural persons (individuals)** may hold licenses. Licenses are also issued that show trade names under which licensed individuals deliver brokerage services.

In the statute and in this volume, **Commission** refers to the State Real Estate Commission. When the term **licensed** is used, it refers to the status of an individual licensed by the Commission.

LICENSES ISSUED BY THE COMMISSION

The Commission issues three levels of license: broker, associate broker, and salesperson. In mid-2001 it reported approximately 30,000 current resident licenses. These included 4,100 broker, 2,750 associate broker, and more than 23,000 salesperson licenses.

Individuals who go to work for brokers enter into either an employee or nonemployee contractual relationship with them. Throughout this book, the term **affiliate** refers either to a licensed associate broker *or* a licensed salesperson. Associate brokers are individuals who have met educational and testing requirements for becoming real estate brokers but whose licenses authorize them only to provide real estate brokerage services *on behalf of* brokers with whom they are affiliated. Their duties and authority are no greater than those of salespersons. Salespersons are individuals who aid the brokers with whom they are affiliated in providing real estate brokerage services.

Real estate salespersons and associate brokers affiliate with real estate brokers by entering into employee or into nonemployee relationships with them. The vast majority of salespersons and associate brokers are in a nonemployee relationship with their brokers.

When affiliates meet the Internal Revenue Service requirements for nonemployee status, their broker does not withhold federal or state income taxes, Social Security, or Medicare assessments. Moreover, the broker does not make any contribution to the affiliates' Social Security tax. The affiliates' paychecks are "net" to them; they are responsible for all their own taxes.

Section 3508 of the IRS Code specifies that to be classified for tax treatment as *self employed*, affiliates must

- be licensed real estate agents;

- receive substantially all of their brokerage remuneration based on production rather than upon hours worked; and

- have a written contract with their brokers stating that the affiliates will not be treated as employees for Federal tax purposes.

Real estate, as used in the Brokers Act, is defined as an interest in real property anywhere. It includes, but is not limited to, interests in condominiums, time-share estates, and time-share licenses, as those terms are defined in the *Real Property* Article.

In the Brokers Act, the term **state** refers to any state in the United States, its territories, possessions, or the District of Columbia. In this book when **State** is capitalized, it refers to the State of Maryland. In the statute, **Department** refers to the Department of Labor, Licensing, and Regulation under whose authority the Commission operates. **Secretary** refers to the Secretary of Labor, Licensing, and Regulation, the executive officer of the Department.

SCOPE OF THE BROKERS ACT

Certain persons who perform real estate activities are not governed by the Brokers Act. They are

- persons acting under a judgment or order of a court;

- public officers performing the duties of office;

- persons engaging in a single transaction that involves the sale or lease of any real estate, if they are acting under a power of attorney executed by the owner of the real estate;

- licensed auctioneers selling any real estate at public auction;

- owners or lessors of any real estate, unless the primary business of the owner or lessor is providing real estate brokerage services; and

- persons acting as receivers, trustees, personal representatives, or guardians.

In contrast, certain other persons, when performing acts of real estate brokerage, must conform to the relevant requirements of the Brokers Act, although they need not hold real estate licenses. They are

- financial institutions in the leasing or selling of property they have acquired through foreclosure or by receiving a deed or an assignment in lieu of foreclosure;

- lawyers not regularly engaged in the business of providing real estate services and who do not communicate to the public that they are in such business;

- home builders in the rental or initial sale of homes they have constructed;

- agents of a licensed real estate broker or of an owner of real estate, while managing or leasing that real estate for that broker or owner;

- persons who negotiate the sale, lease, or transfer of businesses when the sale does not include any interest in real property other than the lease for the property where the business operates; and

- owners who subdivide and sell not more than six lots of their own unimproved property in a calendar year. If they or their family have owned the property for ten years or more, there is no limit on the number of lots they may sell.

THE MARYLAND REAL ESTATE COMMISSION

The Maryland Real Estate Commission is one of several commissions within the Department of Labor, Licensing, and Regulation. It consists of nine members, five of whom are licensees chosen, one each, from the Eastern Shore, Baltimore Metropolitan Area, Baltimore City, Southern Maryland, and Western Maryland. They must have held Maryland real estate licenses at least ten years and have resided in the areas from which they are appointed for at least five years, both immediately prior to their appointment. Four others are consumer members who may not have had an ownership interest in or received compensation from an entity regulated by the Commission in the year just before their appointment.

Members are appointed by the Governor with the advice of the Secretary and the advice and consent of the Senate. Membership terms, which are staggered to ensure continuity, begin on June 1 and end four years later, either with reappointment or upon the appointment of a qualified replacement. Members may be removed before the end of their terms by the Governor in cases of incompetence or misconduct.

Each year members of the Commission elect a chairperson to preside at its meetings. This officer is covered by a surety bond. The Commission holds a public meeting each month with a majority of the members then under appointment constituting a quorum.

The Commission has adopted bylaws for the conduct of its meetings and regulations for the conduct of hearings and for issuance of licensing applications. With ten days' advance written notice a member of the public may address the Commission.

The Commission's Executive Director, who is appointed by and serves at the pleasure of the Secretary, is not one of its members and is different from its Chairperson. The Executive Director, a State employee, directs the day-to-day operations of the Commission and its office staff and field inspectors between monthly meetings.

Duties and Powers of the Commission

The Commission's basic duty is the administration and enforcement of the Brokers Act through the licensing process. To carry out this duty, the Commission is empowered to:

- investigate complaints about licensee behavior;

- conduct hearings and administer oaths;

- issue subpoenas for attendance of witness or production of evidence;

- take depositions; and

- seek injunctions (in certain circum-stances).

The Commission adopts, maintains, and enforces a Code of Ethics and General Regulations that set forth standards of conduct for all individuals licensed under the Act. The Code of Ethics and the General Regulations are part of COMAR–the Code of Maryland Regulations. This code addresses licensees' relations with the client, the public and with other licensees. It is quite different from the Code of Ethics of the National Association of REALTORS®.

The Commission must conduct an investigation relating to any complaint received in writing, under oath, alleging that an unauthorized person has provided real estate brokerage services. Effective October 1, 2001, the Commission received statutory authority to hold hearings on such a complaint and to impose a financial penalty not to exceed $5,000 for each proven violation. [An *unauthorized person* would be an individual who does not hold the required license and is not exempt from the license requirement.]

As of that same date, the Commission was empowered to hold hearings and assess fines as much as $5,000 per violation not only on licensees, but on any persons (individuals or business entities) who violate sections of the Brokers Act listed below ("§" indicates a section number).

§17-502 Handling of Trust Money

§17-525 Discriminatory real estate practices in Baltimore City

§17-526 Discriminatory real estate practices in Montgomery County

§17-527 Improper Solicitation of listings in Baltimore City and Baltimore County

§17-601 Providing real estate brokerage services without a license

§17-602 Misrepresentation: falsely repre-senting oneself as licensed to provide real estate brokerage services.

§17-603 Lending a license or acting under such a license

§17-604 Paying brokerage compensation to persons not licensed to receive it

§17-605 Offering to pay for referrals from (unlicensed) lawyers

§17-606 Posting a sign on a property without including facts about that property's being under ground rent

§17-607 Requiring the use of specified settlement and title companies, financial institutions and title lawyers

§17-608 Blockbusting (a misdemeanor, whether or not for monetary gain)

§17-609 Systematic solicitation of listings to change the racial composition of a neighborhood

§17-610 False statements involving a Guaranty Fund claim

§17-611 Violation of an order involving a conservation area

§17-612 Violating or causing any other person to violate the prohibitions and requirements of §17-322 and §17-328

Enforcement of the above portions of the statute is a *significant* increase in the powers and duties of the Commission.

Other Powers

The Commission already has many other powers and duties. In the course of its operation, it routinely

- issues, renews, suspends, or revokes licenses;

- orders investigations and holds hearings as needed;

- reprimands and/or fines licensees who have violated law or regulation;

- collects license fees and pays them into the General Fund of the State;

- collects fines and pays them into the General Fund of the State;

- submits an annual report of its activities to the Secretary;

- certifies, upon request of any person and payment of the required fee, the licensing status and qualifications of any person who is the subject of the request;

- approves the content of educational courses for licensing and for continuing education;

- appoints hearing boards (panels) of three members, at least one of whom must be a consumer member and one a **professional member** (licensee) from among the commissioners; and

- administers a **Guaranty Fund** to reimburse members of the public as much as $25,000 for actual losses caused by licensees and employees.

LICENSING AND LEVELS OF LICENSURE

Before providing real estate brokerage services in the State, individuals generally must be licensed by the Commission as real estate brokers, or as associate brokers, or as salespersons affiliated with and working under licensed brokers. Licenses are granted for a two-year term from their date of issuance.

Brokers

To qualify for the real estate broker license, applicants must:

- be of good character and reputation, and be at least 18 years old;

- have completed a 135-hour course in real estate approved by the Commission for real estate brokers;

- have been licensed as real estate salespersons actively and lawfully for at least three years; and

- have passed the broker prelicense examination.

If applicants are qualified to practice law in the State, the Commission waives the education and experience requirements. Broker education requirements are not interchangeable with those for salespersons. An individual who has been engaged in real estate practice as a licensed real estate broker in another state for at least three of the five years immediately preceding submission of application is considered to have satisfied the educational requirements.

Associate Brokers

To qualify for the associate real estate broker license, applicants must meet the basic requirements for the real estate broker license described above and also obtain from a licensed real estate broker a commitment providing that they shall become affiliated with that real estate broker when they become licensed.

Salespersons

To qualify for issuance of the salesperson license, an applicant must:

- be of good character and reputation;

- be at least 18 years of age;

- successfully complete a basic 60-hour course in real estate approved by the Commission;

- pass the required examination; and

- obtain from a licensed real estate broker a commitment to become affiliated with that broker as a real estate salesperson when licensed.

General Licensing Rules

Applicants must successfully complete pre-licensing education requirements before they are permitted to take exams. After passing both parts of each exam, they must apply for licensure **within one year** or be subject to reexamination. They must apply on the Commission's application forms—and pay the required fees as shown in Figure 1.1.

Applicants who are not residents of the State must submit to the Commission their *irrevocable consent.* This consent allows the licensee to be served with official documents without the server's having to travel to a foreign (out-of-state) jurisdiction to present them. Applicants are required to submit any additional documentation that

Figure 1.1 Fees

The proper fees must accompany every application. These fees are established by statute and as such are subject to change by the General Assembly. Total fees payable to the Commission are

	Original License Fee	Guaranty Fund Assessment*	Total Original Fees	Renewal or Exchange of License Fee
Broker	$95	$20	$115	$95
Associate Broker	$65	$20	$85	$65
Salesperson	$45	$20	$65	$45

Applicants are also required to pay the testing service a $46 examination fee to register to take or retake any real estate examination. Standard examination registration fees, which are neither refundable nor transferrable, may be paid by check, money order, company check, or cashier's check. Cash is not accepted.

Fees for other services:

Taking a broker examination	$10
Taking a salesperson examination	10
Change of office or place of business	5
Change of name on licensee's records	5
Transfer of salesperson license to new broker	10
Issue duplicate license (when original is lost or destroyed)	5
Issue duplicate pocket card (when original is lost or destroyed)	1
Return checks for lack of funds	25
Certify licensure	10
Issue Branch Office Certificate	5
Reissue license (when it has been on inactive status)	10
Reinstate license (when it has not been timely renewed)	100

*This assessment is paid upon issuance (but not renewal) of any license.

the Commission requires in order to determine their professional competence or good character and reputation. Broker applicants must also submit or pay for a credit report.

Reciprocity

The Commission may waive any requirement for individual licenses for applicants who hold comparable or equivalent licenses granted by another state if those applicants pay the required application fees, meet the relevant requirements, and submit certification of license history from the other state. If applicants are seeking broker licenses based on their comparable licenses in another state, they must provide adequate evidence of actively maintaining brokerage offices there.

Pocket Cards and License Certificates

License certificates and pocket cards that the Commission issues show

- the names of licensees;

- the names of the licensed real estate brokers with whom they are affiliated, as those names appear on their brokers' licenses;

- the date each license will expire; and

- the registration numbers of the licensees.

Although issued to affiliates, the certificates and pocket cards are sent to the broker. The pocket cards are detached and given to affiliates, but the licenses are maintained and conspicuously displayed in the office out of which the licensees operate.

Although no such requirement is explicitly stated anywhere in the Broker Act or any regulation, the Commission has informed the author that licensees are expected to carry their pocket cards whenever they engage in real estate brokerage activity.

Real estate brokers' licenses authorize them to provide real estate brokerage services to the public. Associate brokers' and salespersons' licenses, however, authorize those individuals to provide such services only on behalf of the licensed real estate brokers with whom they are affiliated, and never in their own names or on behalf of brokers with whom they are not affiliated.

Exchange of Licenses and Additional Licenses and Affiliations

Licensed real estate brokers may also obtain real estate salesperson or associate broker licenses and become affiliated with other licensed real estate brokers. To do so they are required to submit proper applications and payment of additional license and Guaranty Fund fees. They must also obtain a commitment for such affiliation from any other broker with whom they may affiliate. Moreover, each such broker must be informed of all other licenses and affiliations. Brokers may also operate more than one real estate company, but, for each additional real estate brokerage company, they must obtain a separate real estate broker's license and pay an additional Guaranty Fund fee.

Licensees who hold salesperson, associate broker, or broker licenses may exchange those licenses for other levels of license by complying with procedures established by the Commission and paying the required additional fees.

Affiliates may obtain additional licenses and become affiliated with additional Maryland brokers by obtaining a commitment from each additional broker, paying the required additional licensing fees and Guaranty Fund assessments, and giving notice of such multiple relationships to all their brokers.

Reinstatement requires that the applicant show proof of meeting all applicable continuing education requirements for the period since expiration and pay past-due renewal fees as well as the $100 reinstatement fee. They must also meet the requirement of good character and reputation. Neither timely nor late renewal of a license affects the power of the Commission to bring charges for prior acts or conduct.

Affiliates may apply to the Commission to transfer their affiliation from one broker to another after obtaining from the new broker a commitment stating that, on cancellation of the current affiliation and issuance of new license certificates and pocket cards, they will become affiliated with the new broker. They shall also submit a statement confirming termination of their prior relationship, either from their former brokers or from themselves, with their transfer applications. It is advisable in every case, although not clearly required by law or regulation, that the former broker be informed of the details of the transfer.

Dishonored Checks

In the event of a dishonored check, licensees are not considered to have properly renewed their licenses until they pay both the original amount of the renewal fees and a collection fee of $25 for each dishonored check.

Continuing Education

Continuing education for license renewal is measured in *clock hours* with credit allowed only for individual courses of not less than one and one-half—and not more than six—hours in length. 15 clock hours are required for each renewal.

Term, Renewal, and Transfer of Licenses

Not later than one month before their licenses expire, the Commission mails to licensees renewal application forms and notices that state

- current license expiration dates;

- the dates by which the Commission must receive the renewal applications—when licensees use hard-copy (paper) applications for renewal; and

- the amount of the renewal fees.

The Commission continues to process hard-copy applications. The preferred mode of application for renewal is online—a method designed to produce instantaneous processing.

When licensees are real estate brokers, the Commission mails the renewal application forms and notices to their main offices. Notices of the need to renew are mailed to the residences of affiliates. It is essential that licensees keep the Commission updated on any changes in their home addresses.

Renewal must be accomplished before licenses expire. Those renewing must pay to the Commission the required renewal fees and affirm that they have completed the required number of hours of continuing education. Those not completing the required number of hours until after the expiration date are renewing late and are no longer licensed to provide brokerage activities. They may, however, apply for reinstatement at any time within four years after the expiration date.

There are several categories of subject matter approved for these courses:

A - Federal, State or local legislative and regulatory changes
B - Antitrust law
C - Fair Housing law
D - Real estate ethics or professional standards
E - Disclosure
F - Professional enhancement for practicing licensees
G - Technology relating to real estate brokerage services (Not more than three hours per renewal)

To be approved by the Commission, all continuing education course subject matter must relate to real estate.

Approved courses may be presented by the Maryland Association of REALTORS® or its member boards, the Real Estate Brokers of Baltimore City, Inc., or any similar professional association, or by an educational institution approved by the State Board of Higher Education.

Continuing education courses must be taught by qualified instructors who are experienced in the real estate industry.

The Commission's guidelines require continuing education instructors to have experience and expertise in the area or activity about which they are teaching.

When licensees complete each unit of study, the training institution that conducted the course issues certificates of completion to each student stating the

• number of clock hours;

• name and date of the course taken;

• code letter of the subject category; and

• the names of the teacher and/or the organization presenting the training.

The education provider also reports these data to the Commission.

The Commission may waive continuing education requirements for licensees who show good cause for being unable to meet the requirement.

Special Requirement for Experienced Licensees: Residential and Commercial

Individuals who have been licensed for ten years or more need complete only six hours of continuing education for each license renewal. The six hours must consist of four and one-half hours of Legislative Update and one and one-half hours of Fair Housing.

Such individuals who practice exclusively in the area of commercial real estate and do not—and will not—perform any residential transactions, may take six hours of Legislative Update and no Fair Housing.

Inactive Status

The Commission will place the licenses of associate real estate brokers and real estate salespersons into inactive status when they are no longer affiliated with licensed real estate brokers and their license certificates and pocket cards are returned to the Commission.

A licensee whose license is on inactive status may not provide real estate brokerage services through that license. This prohibition includes accepting fees for referrals. There are referral *companies* but there is no referral *license status*.

The placement of a license on inactive status does not affect the power of the Commission to suspend or revoke the license or to take any other disciplinary action against the licensee.

Unless a license is reissued (reactivated), the license expires four years after the date it is placed on inactive status. A licensee whose license is on inactive status remains responsible for renewing that license during the period of inactive status as required. Such renewal does not constitute reactivation. Subject to the four-year limitation, a licensee may renew a license while it is on inactive status without complying with the continuing education requirements.

The Commission will reactivate the license of real estate brokers on inactive status and reissue license certificates and pocket cards to such brokers if they request reactivation and pay to the Commission the $10 reissuance fee. They must also meet the continuing education requirements that would have been necessary for renewal of licenses had they not been on inactive status. Salespersons and associate brokers returning from inactive status must meet the same requirements and must also submit an affiliation commitment, contingent on their reactivation, from a broker.

Display of License Certificates; Loss or Destruction

Licensed real estate brokers are required to display their license certificates at all times in a conspicuous place in their office. The license certificates of licensees who are affiliated with a real estate broker must be displayed at the office location out of which each usually works.

The Commission must immediately be notified of the loss or destruction of a license certificate or pocket card. Upon receipt of an affidavit of loss or destruction and payment of the required fee, ($1 for a lost or destroyed pocket card; $5 for a license certificate) the Commission will issue appropriate duplicates.

Change of Name

When a licensee or a firm takes a new name, on receipt of the required application fee ($5), the old certificate, pocket card, and any required documentation, the Commission issues to the licensee a new license certificate and pocket card that reflect such change.

Licensure and the Deceased Broker

On the death of a licensed real estate broker, any adult member of the family may carry on the brokerage for up to six months to close and terminate the business. To do this, the certificate and pocket card of the deceased broker must be surrendered to the Commission. Any information required by the Commission must also be submitted.

Before the end of the six-month period for carrying on the business of a deceased real estate broker, an individual doing so may qualify for and receive from the Commission the license of the deceased broker, if the individual

- is a member of the immediate family of the decedent;

- has been continuously licensed as a real estate salesperson for the immediately preceding three years;

- passes the real estate broker examination required by this subtitle; and

- surrenders his or her real estate salesperson license certificate and pocket card to the Commission.

There must also have been compliance with the conditions for carrying on the business as stated in the first paragraph of this section.

A person receiving the reissued license of a deceased real estate broker may hold and use that license for as long as four years without meeting the 135-hour educational requirement. However, if the requirement has not been met within four years, the license automatically expires.

Return of Licenses to Commission and Termination of Affiliation

The license certificates and pocket cards of affiliates must be returned to the Commission by their broker

- upon the request of a real estate salesperson or associate real estate broker;

- upon the death of the affiliate; or

- after a hearing before the Commission, and upon a finding that the license of a real estate salesperson or associate broker should be suspended or revoked.

Real estate brokers are required to surrender to the Commission, promptly on demand, any such person's license that may be in their possession or control. Failure to do so is grounds for disciplinary action.

In the event of an affiliate's termination (discharge) a broker must

- immediately mail to the licensee, at the last known address of that individual, notice of such termination;

- submit written notice to the Commission, including a copy of the notice mailed to the licensee; and

- return the license certificate of the licensee to the Commission.

Licensing of Out-of-state Applicants

The Commission will issue licenses only to nonresident applicants who file with the Commission a signed statement of **irrevocable consent.** By submitting this statement, applicants agree that suits and actions may be commenced against them without their actually being served papers notifying them of a forthcoming suit. They are consenting that official delivery of papers to the executive director of the Commission shall bind applicants in any action, suit, or proceeding brought against them, in any county in which the cause of action arose or the complaining party resides.

When serving process on the executive director of the Commission, persons filing must immediately send a copy of the filing, by certified mail, to the principal office of the person against whom the action is directed.

NOTE: The signature block on license examination applications contains these words: "If the address of this registration is not within the State of Maryland, I do hereby irrevocably consent that suits and actions may be commenced against me in the proper courts of the State of Maryland as required by the Maryland Annotated Code."

Maryland law states that if any nonresident real estate broker or other such licensee participate in any real estate transaction, divide fee(s), and/or hold deposits from any such transaction in Maryland, that very act, is construed (considered) to give irrevocable consent.

PROCESSING COMPLAINTS

The Commission's Web site provides a form to be downloaded on which complaints against licensees may then be submitted. Upon the Commission's receipt of a properly completed complaint form, it sends a copy of the complaint to the broker of the company involved together with a letter from the Commission's executive director, stating that the broker must respond in writing with a full explanation of the allegations and what action the broker recommends. A broker's failure to respond to this inquiry may be considered grounds for disciplinary action. A chart indicating the steps in handling a complaint against a licensee is found in Appendix B of this book.

A copy of the executive director's letter is also sent to the complainant. Then, upon receipt of the broker's response, a reply is sent to the complainant from the Commission, along with a copy of the broker's reply.

The Commission commences proceedings on a complaint made by a Commission member or by other persons who must make them under oath. Complaints must be in writing, state specifically the facts on which the complaint is based, and may be accompanied by documentary or other evidence.

After review of the content of the complaint, it may be referred for investigation, if it appears an infraction has occurred. A complaint not referred for investigation is considered dismissed. Within 30 days of such dismissal, any member of the Commission may file an exception to the dismissal. If such exception is taken, the full Commission will hold a hearing to weigh proceeding with an investigation.

If an exception is not filed, the dismissal is considered a **final decision** of the Commission, which means that any party aggrieved by the decision may appeal to the appropriate court. Decisions may not be appealed until they are final.

If the Commission or its designee, after an investigation, determines that grounds exist for disciplinary action, the matter is referred for a hearing. Complaints not referred for a hearing after investigation must be dismissed. This has the same effect as a final decision: any party aggrieved by that dismissal may make judicial appeal.

Hearings and Notices

Except as otherwise provided in the State Government Article (as in situations where summary action is needed), before the Commission takes any final action, it gives the individual against whom the action is contemplated an opportunity for a hearing before the Commission or a hearing board.

At least ten days before the hearing, the hearing notice is served personally on the individuals against whom complaint has been made, or sent by certified mail to their last known addresses. If the individuals are licensees other than a broker, at least ten days before the hearing the Commission shall serve notice of the hearing to each real estate broker with whom the licensees are affiliated.

The individuals may have attorneys represent them at hearings. If the individuals against whom the action is contemplated fail or refuse to appear, the Commission may proceed to hear and determine the matter without their presence. These hearings are open to the public.

Real Estate Hearing Board

The Commission establishes two or three real estate hearing boards—often called panels—each consisting of three Commission members. At least one member of each panel must be a professional member, and at least one must be a consumer member. From among each hearing board's members, the Commission designates a chairperson.

Referral of Cases; Procedures Before Hearing Board

The Commission may order a hearing for any complaint that has been filed with the Commission and any other matter for which a hearing may be required.

Before deciding to hold a hearing, a panel will meet privately to

- review complaints and consider whether they provide a reasonable basis for disciplinary hearings, and

- review claims against the Guaranty Fund to determine what further action to take.

They meet in public to

- hear licensees' responses to and defenses against complaints, and then

- decide whether to authorize punitive actions against them.

Hearing boards exercise the same powers as, and conduct hearings for, the Commission. They report their decisions and actions to the Commission. Panels specifically advise the Commission of any action they take against licensees involved in monetary loss, misappropriation of funds, or fraud.

Hearing Regulations

COMAR—The Code of Maryland Regulations—provides for four types of hearings:

1. Judicial Hearings

2. Applications for Licensure

3. Revocation or Suspension of Licenses

4. Claims Against the Guaranty Fund

Hearings are conducted under several levels of overlapping hearing regulations.

The decision of a hearing board is regarded as a *final decision* of the Commission. This means that any aggrieved party may then make a judicial appeal.

Upon dismissal of a complaint, the complainant and the licensee are notified in writing. The dismissal of a complaint after investigation is not reviewable further. Other complaints substantially based on the same facts are usually similarly dismissed.

Summary Actions

Summary actions are those taken before holding a hearing.

Revocation after Actions of Other Agencies

The Commission may summarily order the revocation of the license of any licensee. If the licensee is convicted of a violation of this title, the conviction is final and the period for appeal has expired.

The license of any nonresident licensee may be revoked if the real estate regulatory agency of the state where the licensee is a resident revokes the license issued by that state and certifies the order of revocation to the Commission.

When the Commission orders a summary revocation under this section, it gives licensees written notice of the revocation and the finding on which it was based. After the revocation is effective, the Commission grants them an opportunity to be heard promptly either before the Commission or before a hearing board.

Rather than summarily order revocation of a license under this section, the Commission may elect not to revoke the license until after the licensee is given an opportunity for a hearing. If the Commission elects to give the licensee an opportunity for a hearing before revoking the license, the Commission gives notice and holds the hearing in the same manner as required for other hearings.

In any hearing held because of conviction or revocation by other agencies, the Commission considers only evidence of whether or not the alleged conviction or revocation in fact occurred. However, in such hearings a licensee may present matters in mitigation of the offense charged.

Summary Suspension of Licenses for Trust Fund Violations

The Commission may—but is not required to—summarily order the suspension of a license if the licensee fails to

- account promptly for any funds held in trust; or

- on demand, fails to display to the Commission all records, books, and accounts of any funds held in trust.

The Commission gives the licensee notice and supporting reasons for its action and offers the opportunity to be heard later.

A summary suspension may start immediately, or at any later date set by the order, and shall continue until the licensee complies with the conditions set forth by the Commission in its order or until the Commission orders a different disposition after a hearing held under this section.

Judicial Review

When parties strongly disagree with a final decision of the Commission they may appeal to the circuit court. Upon the filing of a bond by the licensee, a circuit court may grant licensee stay (delay) of the suspension or revocation. The court may set the required bond in any amount up to $50,000. The bond money would be for the use and benefit of any member of the public who might suffer financial loss because of any violation of the Brokers Act by the licensee.

Notice of Revocation or Suspension

Whenever a licensee's license is revoked or suspended and a stay is not ordered by the Commission or a court, the Commission notifies

- the licensee,

- the real estate broker with whom the licensee is affiliated,

- the Maryland Association of REALTORS®, and

- the local Board or Association of REALTORS®, and the Realtist organization in the area of the licensee's office.

If the Commission revokes or suspends the license of a nonresident licensee, the Commission also notifies the Real Estate Commission or other licensing authority in the state where the licensee is a resident, reporting the cause for the revocation or suspension of the license.

Figure 1.2 describes some confusing terms used in licensing procedures.

Figure 1.2 License Procedures Often Confused

Process	Occasion
Renewal	At end of every two-year term
Reissuance (Reactivation)	Returns license to active from inactive status
Reinstatement	Revives license which expired for lack of renewal, or restores license after suspension.

REAL ESTATE GUARANTY FUND

The Guaranty Fund exists to reimburse members of the public for actual financial losses at the hands of real estate licensees and their unlicensed employees. The maximum reimbursement for any claim is $25,000.

Use of Monies Collected

The Commission deposits all money collected for the Guaranty Fund with the State treasurer, who invests it with the investment earnings credited to the Fund.

Initial Assessment for Fund

Before granting initial licenses to applicants, the Commission requires them to pay a $20 assessment that is credited to the Guaranty Fund. Regardless of how many times an individual applies to the Commission for one level of license, the Commission makes only one such assessment. An exception is the situation in which a licensee is granted overlapping multiple licenses of the same or different levels, and may have to pay multiple assessments.

If the amount in the Guaranty Fund falls below $250,000, the Commission assesses all the individuals then holding licenses a fee—typically payable at renewal—sufficient to return the Guaranty Fund to that level.

Claims Against the Fund

A person may recover compensation from the Guaranty Fund only for actual financial losses. Claims must be based on acts or omissions that occurred in the provision of real estate brokerage services by licensees or unlicensed employees of a licensed real estate broker. Claims must involve transactions that relate to real estate located in the State and be based on acts or omissions in which money or property is obtained from a person by theft, embezzlement, false pretenses, forgery, or an act that constitutes fraud or misrepresentation.

A claim against the Guaranty Fund must

- be in writing and under oath,

- state the amount of loss claimed,

- state the facts on which the claim is based, and

- be accompanied by documentation or other evidence that supports the claim.

At any claim hearing, the burden of proof shall be on the claimant to establish the validity of the claim.

A person may not recover from the Guaranty Fund any loss that relates to

- the purchase of any interest in a limited partnership that invests in real estate,

- a joint venture that is promoted by a real estate licensee for the purpose of investment in real estate, or

- the purchase of commercial paper secured by real estate.

A claim under the Guaranty Fund may not be filed by the spouse or by the personal representative of the spouse of the individual alleged to be responsible for the act or omission giving rise to the claim.

Any claim must be filed with the Commission within three years of the loss or discovery of the loss.

Notice to Buyer

Real estate brokers must include in each sales contract a written notice that buyers are protected by the Guaranty Fund in an amount not exceeding $25,000. Although only buyers are mentioned in this notice, sellers may also submit claims.

Action by Commission on a Claim

The Commission must act promptly upon receiving claims by:

• forwarding copies to licensees and/or unlicensed employees alleged to be responsible and to their brokers;

• requiring a written response, within ten days, from each of those individuals concerning the allegations set forth in the claim (This ten-day period is shorter than the 20 days required for response to other inquiries from the Commission);

• reviewing the claim and any responses to the claim; and

• conducting an investigation.

On the basis of its review of a claim and any investigation it conducts, the Commission either schedules a hearing or dismisses the claim.

Special Disposition of Smaller Claims

If the claim is $3,000 or less, the Commission, through a designated staff member such as the executive director, may issue a ***proposed order*** either to pay or to deny the claim. Both the claimant and the licensee receive a copy of this proposed order.

Within 30 days either the claimant or licensee may request a hearing or file written exceptions to the order. If either happens, the Commission must schedule a hearing on the claim. If no hearing is requested and no exceptions taken, the proposed order becomes a final order of the Commission.

Other Claims

The Commission gives notice of the hearing and opportunity to appear before the Commission both to the claimants and the licensees or unlicensed employees alleged to be responsible. The Commission must send the required notices to every party involved before conducting the hearing.

When the persons alleged to be responsible are licensees, the Commission combines this hearing with disciplinary proceedings against licensees arising from the same facts alleged in a claim. Claimants can be *party* to that portion of the proceedings about the claim, but may be only a *witness* in the disciplinary portion.

The misdemeanor penalty for knowingly making a false statement or material misstatement of fact about a Guaranty Fund matter is a fine of not more than $5,000 or imprisonment not exceeding one year or both.

Payments by the Guaranty Fund

If a claim proves valid, the Commission orders its payment by the Guaranty Fund. The amount of compensation recoverable from the Guaranty Fund is limited to the actual monetary loss incurred by the claimant. The payout may never be more than $25,000 for any one claim. The amount paid may not include:

- losses other than those from the original transaction;

- commissions owed to a licensee acting as either a principal or an agent in a real estate transaction; or

- any attorney's fees incurred in seeking money from the Fund.

Payment is not made until either the time for seeking judicial review is over or any judicial stay has expired. The Commission orders payment of claims in the order in which they were awarded.

Reimbursement of the Guaranty Fund

When payment is made from the Fund, the Commission immediately and without further proceedings suspends the licenses of the offending licensees. Licensees suspended in this way are not reinstated until the licensees repay the full amounts owed to the Fund, plus interest, and make formal application for reinstatement. Reimbursement of the Fund does not affect any disciplinary actions imposed on licensees.

After payment of a claim by the Guaranty Fund, the licensee responsible is required to reimburse the Fund in full for the amount paid and for interest of at least 10 percent. (General Regulation .23 presently sets the rate at 12 percent.) The licensees responsible for the claim are jointly and severally liable. Each does not bear a proportionate share; each is responsible for the entire amount until the entire amount is paid.

If licensees do not reimburse the Guaranty Fund as provided, the Commission may sue them for the amount that has not been reimbursed and seek liens against their real property.

PROHIBITED ACTS

After giving proper notice, conducting any needed investigation, holding the required hearing, and reaching its conclusions, the Commission is empowered to deny a license to any applicant, reprimand licensees, and to suspend or revoke the licenses of any licensees who:

- fraudulently obtain or attempt to obtain a license for themselves or others;

- fraudulently use licenses;

- directly or through other persons willfully make misrepresentations or knowingly make false promises;

- intentionally or negligently fail to disclose to any person with whom they deal a material fact that they know or should know that relates to property with which they deal;

- as affiliates, provide or attempt to provide real estate brokerage services on behalf of real estate brokers without informing in writing any other real estate broker under whom the affiliates are licensed;

- fail to follow the law concerning dual agency;

- retain or attempt to retain the services of any unlicensed individuals (in such a way as to evade the law prohibiting payment of a commission to an unlicensed individual);

- guarantee, authorize or permit other persons to guarantee future profits from the resale of real property;

- solicit, sell or offer to sell real property so as to influence or attempt to influence a prospective party to the sale of real property by offering prizes or free lots, conducting a lottery or contest, or advertising "free appraisals," unless prepared to appraise real estate free of charge for any person, for any purpose;

- accept a listing contract to sell real property that fails to provide a definite termination date that is effective automatically without notice from the buyer or the seller;

- accept a listing contract to sell real property that provides for a "net" return to a seller and leaves the licensees free to sell the real property at any price higher than the "net" price;

- knowingly solicit a party to an exclusive listing contract with another licensee to terminate that contract and enter a new contract with the licensees making the solicitation;

- solicit a party to a sales contract, lease, or agreement that was negotiated by other licensees to breach the contract, lease, or agreement for the purpose of substituting a new contract, lease, or agreement for which the licensees making the solicitation are either the real estate brokers or affiliated with those real estate brokers;

- for any transactions in which the licensees have served as or on behalf of a real estate broker, fail to furnish promptly to each party to the transaction copies of the listing contract to sell or rent real property, the contract of sale, or the lease agreement;

- for any transactions in which the licensees have served as or on behalf of a real estate broker, fail to keep copies of all executed listing contracts to sell or rent real property, contracts of sale, or lease agreements;

- whether or not acting for monetary gain, knowingly induce or attempt to induce persons to transfer real estate or discourage or attempt to discourage persons from buying real estate by making representations about the existing or potential proximity of real property owned or used by individuals of a particular race, color, religion, sex, handicap, familial status, or national origin; or by representing that the existing or potential proximity of real property owned or used by individuals of a particular race, color, religion, or national origin will or may result in: the lowering of property values, a change in the racial, religious, or ethnic character of the block, neighborhood, or area, an increase in criminal or antisocial behavior in the area or a decline in the quality of the schools serving the area;

- use any of the following material if it includes the name of an organization or association of which the licensees are not members: contract forms for the listing of real property for sale, rent, or exchange; contract forms for the sale, rent, or exchange of real property; or any advertising matter;

- as real estate brokers or affiliates, advertise the sale or rent of or an offer to buy real property while failing to disclose in the advertisement the name of the advertisers and the fact that the advertisers are real estate licensees;

- advertise in any misleading or untruthful manner;

- as affiliates, advertise the sale or rent of or an offer to buy real property in their names while failing to disclose in the advertisement the name of the real estate broker on whose behalf the affiliates are acting;

- for real estate brokerage services provided by associate real estate brokers or real estate salespersons, accept commissions or other valuable considerations from persons other than real estate brokers with whom they are affiliated;

- fail to account for or to remit promptly any money that comes into their possession;

- pay or receive a rebate, profit, compensation, or commission in violation of any provision of this Act;

- under the laws of the United States or of any state, are convicted of felonies or misdemeanors that are directly related to their fitness and qualification to provide real estate brokerage services; or a crime that constitutes a violation of any provision of the Brokers Act;

- engage in conduct that demonstrates bad faith, incompetency, or untrustworthiness or that constitutes dishonest, fraudulent, or improper dealings;

- with actual knowledge of the violation, associate with licensees in a transaction or practice that violates any provision of the Brokers Act;

- fail as real estate brokers to exercise reasonable and adequate supervision over the provision of real estate brokerage services by other individuals on behalf of the broker;

- provide to any parties contracts that do not contain a notice of a buyer's right of selection, as required by the Brokers Act;

- require a buyer to employ a particular title insurance company, settlement company, escrow company, or title lawyer in violation of this Act;

- fail to make the disclosure of representation as required by §17-528;

- violate any trust accounts provision of this Act that relates to trust money;

- violate any other provision of this Act;

- violate any regulation adopted under this Act or any provision of the Code of Ethics; or

- violate §17-320(d) by failing as branch office managers to exercise reasonable and adequate supervision over the brokerage work of sales agents or associate brokers in their offices.

Instead of, or in addition to, suspension or revocation, the Commission may impose a penalty not exceeding $5,000 for each violation. To determine the amount of the penalty imposed, the Commission considers:

- the seriousness of the violation;

- the harm caused by the violation;

- the good faith of the licensee; and

- any history of previous violations by the licensee.

The Commission pays any penalty collected into the General Fund of the State.

The Commission considers several facts when granting, denying, renewing, suspending, or revoking licenses, or reprimanding licensees, when the individuals concerned have been convicted of certain crimes. In the case of felonies *and* misdemeanors, they consider

- the nature of the crime, and

- the relationship of the crime to the activities authorized by the license.

In the case of *felonies* (crimes for which the maximum imprisonment could be more than one year), they consider:

- the relevance of the conviction to the fitness and qualification of the applicants or licensees to provide real estate brokerage services;

- the length of time since the conviction; and

- the behavior and activities of the applicants or licensees before and after their convictions.

The Drug Enforcement Act of 1990 authorizes the Commission to impose sanctions upon licensees for a controlled substance offense.

PROHIBITED ACTS PUNISHABLE BY IMPRISONMENT

In addition to the prohibitions and penalties enumerated above, the Brokers Act provides for fines not to exceed $5,000 and/or imprisonment not to exceed one year for the following acts. Note that the term *person* includes licensees, nonlicensees, individuals, and business entities such as corporations, partnerships, limited liability companies, etc. These are criminal offenses for which imprisonment is a possible penalty.

Although the Commission is empowered to pursue *all* violators of these provisions, *including nonlicensees*, and to impose monetary penalties of as much as $5,000, *only a court can try, convict, and sentence an offender to prison.*

1. Except as otherwise provided in the Brokers Act, a person may not provide, attempt to provide, or offer to provide real estate brokerage services unless licensed by the Commission.

2. Unless authorized under this Act to provide real estate brokerage services, a person may not represent to the public by use of the title *Licensed Real Estate Broker, Licensed Associate Real Estate Broker* or *Licensed Salesperson,* by other title, by description of services, methods, or procedures, or otherwise that the person is authorized to provide real estate brokerage services in the State.

3. Real estate brokers may not allow other licensees or any other unauthorized individuals to provide real estate brokerage services independently as real estate brokers. Real estate brokers may not retain unlicensed individuals to provide real estate brokerage services on their behalf. Licensed real estate brokers may not lend their license certificates or pocket cards to other individuals.

4. Licensees may not pay any form of compensation for the provision of real estate brokerage services to persons not licensed under the Brokers Act, except that payment may be made to individuals who are licensed in another state and who meet the requirements of this Act. A professional service corporation formed under this Act may also receive such compensation.

5. Except as otherwise provided, licensees may not pay or offer to pay commissions to lawyers simply for the referral of persons as possible parties to residential real estate transactions. Licensees may not solicit referral business from lawyers by a mass solicitation that offers to pay fees or commissions to the lawyers. This does not apply to payments or offers of payments to lawyers who hold a real estate broker license under this Act or are otherwise entitled to a commission. Other than the commissions expressly prohibited, the law does not prohibit the payment or the offer of a payment of a commission by a licensee to a lawyer for other services that relate to real estate transactions.

6. In a real estate transaction involving a single-family dwelling, licensees or lawyers acting as real estate brokers may not require buyers, as a condition of settlement, to employ particular title insurance companies, settlement companies, escrow companies, mortgage lenders, financial institutions, or title lawyers. However, a seller may make owner financing a condition of sale.

7. Whether or not acting for monetary gain, persons may not knowingly induce or attempt to induce other persons to sell or rent dwellings or otherwise transfer real estate or knowingly discourage or attempt to discourage other persons from purchasing real estate by making representations regarding:

    • the entry or prospective entry into a neighborhood of individuals of a particular race, color, sex, religion, or national origin;

- the existing or potential proximity of real property owned or used by individuals of a particular race, color, sex, religion, or national origin; or

- the existing or potential proximity of real property owned or used by individuals of a particular race, color, sex, religion, or national origin will or may result in: the lowering of property values; a change in the racial, religious, or ethnic character of the block, neighborhood or area; an increase in criminal or antisocial behavior in the area; or a decline in the quality of schools serving the area.

8. Persons may not provide financial assistance by loan, gift, or otherwise to other persons if they have actual knowledge that the financial assistance will be used in transactions that result from a fair housing violation.

9. If one of the purposes of the solicitation or attempted solicitation is to change the racial composition of a neighborhood, persons may not solicit or attempt to solicit the listing of residential properties for sale or lease by in-person door-to-door solicitation, telephone solicitation, or mass distribution of circulars.

10. A corporation, partnership, or any other association may not commit or cause any other person to commit any act that constitutes grounds for disciplinary action against a licensee under the Brokers Act. Violators are guilty of misdemeanors and, upon conviction, subject to a fine not exceeding $5,000.

11. In transactions involving residential property in Baltimore City:

- All real estate brokers shall break down the properties listed in the registry by price categories etablished by the Commission. If a prospective buyer requests to see the registry, they shall allow the prospective buyer to see the part of the registry for the price category in which the prospective buyer indicates interest. This does not require a real estate broker who is a member of a multiple-listing service to disclose properties that are obtained from multiple listing.

- Unless requested to do so by a prospective buyer or renter, real estate licensees may not fail or refuse to show any residential property that is available for sale, rent, or sublease to a prospective buyer or renter because of: the race, color, sex, religion, age, or national origin of the prospective buyer or renter; the racial composition or character of the neighborhood where the property is located.

- Licensees may not fail or refuse to show all available listed residential properties that are in a certain area and within a specified price range to a prospective buyer or renter who has requested to be shown all available properties that are in the area and within the specified price range.

- If the representation is made because of the race, color, sex, religion, age, or national origin of the prospective buyer or renter, or because of the racial composition or character of the area where the property is located, real estate licensees may not represent to a prospective buyers or renters that the available residential properties, prospective sites for a residence, or listings are limited to those already shown when, in fact, there is a residential property, a prospective site for a residence, or a listing that is available and within the price range specified by the prospective buyer or renter.

A licensee may charge a reasonable fee for showing a residential property to a prospective buyer or renter.

- In Baltimore City and Baltimore County, real estate licensees may not mass-solicit listings by using the name or address of a present or previous client without the written consent of both parties to the contract involving that client.

  The Commission enforces the provisions of this section concerning Baltimore City. For this purpose, it receives complaints, conducts investigations, issues subpoenas, administers oaths, and holds hearings.

12. In transactions involving residential property in Montgomery County:

- Real estate brokers shall maintain current and complete registries of all residential properties that they personally list for sale or rent in Montgomery County and, if members of a multiple-listing service, a registry of properties listed with the Montgomery County multiple-listing service.

- Licensees may not refuse to show any residential property or prospective site for a residence that is available for sale, rent, or sublease to a prospective buyer or renter because of the race, color, religion, sex, marital status, national origin, physical or mental handicap of the prospective buyer or renter, or because of the composition or character of the neighborhood in which the property is located.

  The Commission enforces the provisions of this section concerning Montgomery County. For this purpose it receives complaints, conducts investigations, issues subpoenas and holds hearings.

Maryland courts are required to report to the Commission, for appropriate action, all convictions of licensees for violation of this Act with respect to blockbusting and discriminatory real estate practices in Baltimore City or Montgomery County.

REAL ESTATE BROKERAGE PRACTICE IN BALTIMORE CITY

Although Baltimore City does not issue or require a separate real estate license to perform real estate activities there, local law does regulate the activities of licensees who practice in that city. Many of the prohibited acts are similar, if not identical, to State law. The Baltimore City real estate license law is found in §132 of Article 19 of the Baltimore

City Code under the title "Real Estate Practices."

MARYLAND SECURITIES ACT

The Maryland Securities Act requires licensing of persons engaged in the offer and sale of real estate-related securities, including limited partnership interests in real property. The Maryland Securities Commission regulates all activities construed to be securities-related business. To inquire if certain activities could be construed as securities-related business, contact the Maryland Securities Commissioner.

REAL ESTATE APPRAISERS ACT

Title 16 of the *Business Occupations and Professions* Article of the Annotated Code of Maryland establishes licensing and certification procedures for real estate appraisers and creates a nine-member State Commission of Real Estate Appraisers within the Department of Labor, Licensing, and Regulation to administer that act.

Individuals who are licensed to provide real estate brokerage services do not also need to be licensed as real estate appraisers when merely recommending a listing price or a purchase price for real estate, provided that the opinion is not called an appraisal. A **competitive market analysis (CMA)** is not an appraisal, and its preparation for a seller or purchaser does not require an appraisal license or certificate.

However, changes in the Commission *Code of Ethics,* effective since January 1, 2001,

require that licensees shall not prepare CMAs or render opinions of value of specific properties that are outside the field of their experience, unless they obtain the assistance of an expert on those types of properties, or disclose their lack of experience to their clients. If experts are engaged, licensees shall identify them to their clients and inform them of the experts' contribution.

When asked to render an *opinion of value* of a parcel of real property, the licensee shall make a careful physical inspection of the property and a thorough analysis of all factors affecting the value of the property in addition to meeting the requirements for use of experts described in the preceding paragraph.

To receive a real estate appraisers license or certification, an individual must complete mandated educational requirements, pass an examination developed by the State Commission of Real Estate Appraisers, and have accumulated 2,000 hours of acceptable appraisal work experience.

An individual may hold a real estate license and at the same time be a licensed or certified real estate appraiser. Such individuals should be extremely careful to avoid any conflicts of interest that could arise from providing real estate appraisal services in transactions in which they, their friends, relatives, or those employed by their broker are also agents or principals.

BUILDING INSPECTIONS

Licensees are not required to be experts in building construction, but they should be alert to **red flags** which exist in a property with which they are dealing. Red flags are physical indications that there may be a defect in the property not readily apparent to a layperson or an inexperienced home purchaser. Red flags suggest the presence of latent defects. Latent defects are material facts that must be brought to the attention of all parties entering into a transaction.

Parties should be formally advised to seek the expert advice of a licensed home inspector or a licensed structural engineer.

Since October 1, 2001, Title 16 of the *Business Occupations and Professions* Article has required individuals who provide home inspections to be licensed by the State Commission of Real Estate Appraisers and Home Inspectors. It is unlawful to provide such inspections for consideration without this license. The penalty for doing so is a fine of not more than $5,000 per violation. Exempt from this requirement are state and local government inspectors and building code enforcement officials acting within the scope of their employment, as well as licensed construction professionals acting within the scope of their licenses when their services may be required in the building or remodeling of real property as long as they are not claiming to be licensed home inspectors.

CHANGES IN THE LICENSE LAW AND REGULATIONS

Changes are occasionally made in the Brokers Act and the regulations of the Commission. The material included in this chapter is current as of the date of publication. However, readers are cautioned to ascertain whether changes have been made since publication of this book. See the first two sections of this chapter for sources of updated information.

The General Assembly makes any changes in the Brokers Act (Title 17) while the Commission can make changes in the Regulations (COMAR).

Before the Commission adopts, amends, or repeals regulations, it publishes notice of the proposed action in the *Maryland Register,* with an estimate of economic impact, a notice of opportunity for public comment on the proposal, and the text of the proposed changes. After 45 days, the Commission takes final action on the proposal. At that time, a report of final action is published in the *Maryland Register.* The final action takes effect 10 days after that notice appears, unless the Commission specifies a later date.

QUESTIONS

1. Licensed salespersons may represent

   a. any owners who directly employ them.
   b. not more than one owner at one time.
   c. only brokers under whom they are licensed.
   d. any broker who is duly licensed.

2. License certificates issued for salespersons must be

   a. carried by them at all times.
   b. displayed by their brokers in their brokerage offices.
   c. retained by the Commission.
   d. displayed by them in their homes.

3. Brokers need NOT notify the Commission when

   a. salespersons resign.
   b. changes occur in the locations of their offices.
   c. changes occur in the names of their firms.
   d. changes occur in commission sharing.

4. As a licensed salesperson, you receive a lead from a friend who is not a real estate licensee. You would like to split your commission with your friend.

   a. This is a violation of the license law.
   b. This is NOT a violation of the license law.
   c. This is a violation of the license law only if the seller is NOT informed.
   d. This is a violation of the license law only if your broker has NOT given written permission.

5. To satisfy the requirements of the IRS and to receive the advantages of "self-employed" status, licensees must do all the following EXCEPT

   a. have a written employment contract with the broker agreeing to their self-employed status.
   b. be free from their broker's control of how their work is done.
   c. earn substantially all income from the brokerage firm in commissions.
   d. hold a real estate license.

6. Which of the following fees is paid biennially?

   a. Guaranty Fund fee
   b. Broker's or salesperson's original license fee
   c. Broker's or salesperson's license renewal fee
   d. Guaranty Fund reassessment

7. In Maryland, the act of "blockbusting" is

   a. unethical but NOT prohibited by law.
   b. a felony.
   c. a misdemeanor.
   d. a legitimate sales technique.

8. Individuals found guilty of operating in the real estate business without a license may be fined by

   a. the district attorney.
   b. the Commission.
   c. the Board or Association of REALTORS®.
   d. the attorney general.

9. An unlicensed person improperly collecting a real estate commission is guilty of

   a. duress.
   b. a felony.
   c. a misdemeanor.
   d. fraud.

10. The Commission may revoke the license of any licensee who is found guilty of

    a. slandering competitors.
    b. intemperance.
    c. bad faith.
    d. violation of the motor vehicle code.

11. The maximum penalty for filing a false statement with the Commission in reference to the Guaranty Fund is

    a. NOT less than $200.
    b. NOT more than $200.
    c. $10,000 and up to two years' imprisonment.
    d. $5,000 and up to one year's imprisonment.

12. A license to provide real estate brokerage services can be issued only to a(n)

    a. corporation.
    b. limited liability company (LLC).
    c. partnership.
    d. natural person.

13. Members of the Maryland Real Estate Commission are appointed by the

    a. Maryland Senate.
    b. Governor
    c. House of Delegates.
    d. Executive Director of the Commission.

14. A salesperson license issued by the Commission on November 1 will expire

    a. one year from the date of issue.
    b. two years from the date of issue.
    c. April 30 of the next even-numbered year.
    d. March 1 of the next even-numbered year.

15. The main purpose of the Brokers Act is to

    a. raise revenue.
    b. protect the public interest.
    c. control salespersons.
    d. restrict competition.

16. The executive director of the Commission is

    a. appointed by the Governor.
    b. confirmed by the State Senate.
    c. appointed by the Secretary.
    d. selected from the Maryland State Employees Classified System.

17. Ads to buy or sell listed real estate placed by licensees must include the

    a. name and address of the property owner.
    b. name of the listing salesperson.
    c. trade name of the broker.
    d. location of the property.

18. The Guaranty Fund must be maintained at a minimum of

    a. $250,000.   c. $2,000.
    b. $25,000.   d. $200,000.

19. The Commission's Code of Ethics addresses relations with three groups. Which of the following is NOT one of those groups?

    a. Relations to the public
    b. Relations to the Commission
    c. Relations to the client
    d. Relations to fellow licensees

20. The Maryland Real Estate Commission is composed of

    a. five members.
    b. four persons who are not engaged in the real estate business as well as five licensees.
    c. four professional and four consumer members.
    d. brokers selected from real estate boards or associations throughout Maryland.

21. The Commission may refuse to issue a license to a Maryland resident who has filed a proper application and met the legal requirements

    a. after holding a hearing on the matter.
    b. if the applicant has been convicted of a traffic violation within the past year.
    c. without holding a hearing on the matter.
    d. if the applicant has not reached the age of 21 years.

22. License fees are established by the

    a. Commission in Regulations.
    b. Real Estate Broker Board.
    c. Secretary of the Department of Labor, Licensing, and Regulation.
    d. General Assembly in statutes.

23. Which of the following is an act of real estate brokerage that requires a real estate brokerage license?

    a. A mortgage loan institution sells real estate acquired through foreclosure.
    b. A person offers to guide friends in the sale of their home. The individual will charge a consulting fee of $150.
    c. An attorney-at-law, representing a spouse in a divorce action, helps sell a house the couple owns for 3 percent of the selling price.
    d. A property owner subdivides his land and sells five lots in one calendar year.

24. Fees paid for licenses finally go to the

    a. Maryland General Fund.
    b. testing service.
    c. Real Estate Board or Association active in the area.
    d. Comptroller of the State of Maryland.

25. Employees of the Commission

    a. include an executive director and field inspectors.
    b. must be licensed as brokers or salespeople while employed by the Commission.
    c. must have been licensed before being employed by the Commission.
    d. are permitted to perform acts of brokerage for which a license is required.

26. When brokers discharge salespersons, the licenses of the salespersons should be

    a. returned to the Commission by the brokers.
    b. returned to the Commission by the salespersons.
    c. removed from display but retained by the brokers.
    d. returned to the salespersons.

27. The Guaranty Fund protects a buyer for certain financial losses up to

    a. $250,000. c. $2,500.
    b. $25,000.   d. an unlimited amount.

28. Which of the following statements pertaining to Maryland real estate licenses is NOT correct?

    a. Their holders are regulated by authority of the *Business Occupations and Professions Article* of the Maryland Annotated Code.
    b. They are issued and administered by the Maryland Real Estate Commission.
    c. They are not issued to corporations or associations.
    d. They are required for every person who sells real estate for consideration.

29. To deliver real estate brokerage services, a licensed real estate salesperson must

    a. be associated with a licensed real estate associate broker.
    b. perform real estate acts only on behalf of a licensed broker.
    c. be associated with a REALTOR®.
    d. operate a real estate business under his or her own name or trade name.

2

Real Estate Agency

OVERVIEW

While most of this chapter emphasizes Maryland real estate law and practice, some basic general terms are here defined simply, even though many of those terms have already been defined in the students' principal textbook. On occasion, a brief explanation (in parentheses) may follow a technical term.

The topics addressed here include: the inter-relation between agency law and real estate brokerage; consumer confusion about agency; possible agency relationships; presumed buyer representation; various consent and disclosure forms; organization and management of brokerage firms, including advertising and the handling of funds.

BROKERAGE AND AGENCY: NOT ALWAYS THE SAME

Brokerage involves bringing parties together and helping them negotiate contracts in return for a fee. Many kinds of brokers—commodity brokers, for instance—often do not actually represent either buyers or sellers. They merely *facilitate transactions*. The student should understand that performing certain kinds of brokerage does not always and everywhere require the broker to represent, i.e., be an agent of either party.

AGENCY

Real estate agency and brokerage are closely intertwined. This book limits itself to brokerage that includes agency.

Agency Duties

One can find almost all the agency duties of real estate licensees in §528 to §535 of Title 17, the Maryland Real Estate Brokers Act, and Sections 1 through 8 of Title 11, Section 9 of the Code of Maryland Regulations—COMAR.

The statute—referred to throughout this book as the *Brokers Act*—is found in the *Business Occupations and Professions* Article of the Annotated Code of Maryland.

The Code of Maryland Regulations is published in looseleaf form, placed in libraries throughout the state, and is updated annually. Several parts of COMAR dealing with real estate brokerage are also published by the Real Estate Commission in a booklet together with Title 17—the Brokers Act.

Agency Relationships

Maryland real estate licensees, when serving as agents, owe their *clients* (the persons they represent) **fiduciary duties** as described in the principal text: Care, Obedience, Accounting, Loyalty, and Disclosure. Although they are fewer in number, these demanding duties are in addition to the longer list of duties also owed to *customers* (third parties).

Licensees owe *customers*, and other *third parties*, honest and fair dealing, due (appropriate) care, prompt presentation of all offers and counteroffers, honest answers to all questions (except those that are declared to be confidential by a client or otherwise forbidden by law), and affirmative (voluntary) disclosure of material facts. See Figure 2.1.

Important Terms: Assist versus Represent

Virtually all real estate brokerage companies in Maryland offer to *assist* purchasers as *customers* in finding properties to purchase without representing them as *clients*. They can represent purchasers as clients if requested. They also *represent* owners as *clients* in the sale of properties. Understanding the difference between *client-level service* and *customer-level service* is fundamental to effective and lawful provision of real estate brokerage

services. Licensees represent clients. They assist customers.

Figure 2.1 Agents' Duties and Services to Customers and Clients

Duty or Service	To Their Principals (Clients)	To Third Parties (Like Customers)
Care	✔	
Obedience	✔	
Accounting	✔	
Loyalty	✔	
Disclosure of All Facts	✔	
Magisterial Acts: The Exercise of Judgment	✔	
Honesty and Fair Dealing	✔	✔
Reasonable Care and Skill in Performance	✔	✔
Affirmative Disclosure of Material Facts	✔	✔
Presentation of All Written Offers	✔	✔
Ministerial Acts: Performing Servant Deeds	✔	✔

Evolution of Buyer Representation

Until the early 1980s, residential real estate brokers usually represented client-sellers. Although buyers were typically regarded by law as third parties, they often–sometimes to their harm–regarded the salesperson assisting them as *their* agent.

Since then, consumers have become better informed. Today they typically demand that their "agent" actually *be* their agent—be on their team and deliver client-level service. They want a knowledgeable professional who will be loyal to them; who will not only help them locate property to purchase, but who will also protect their interests, keep their confidence, and coach them in negotiations about price and many other matters throughout the transaction.

The Industry's Response to Buyer Representation

Most firms throughout Maryland, in response to this growing demand, now also offer to represent buyers—to give them client-level service. These firms were already providing representation for clients who listed their properties with them.

The following case illustrates a simple application of buyer representation.

Example 1

Salesperson Norman, formally representing buyer Elizabeth on behalf of his broker, shows her a property listed with another broker's, Eugene's, firm. Susan is the owner/seller of the property. Susan therefore, is Eugene's client; she is receiving client-level service from Eugene's company while Elizabeth is receiving client-level service from Norman's.

Both brokerage firms in this case are providing *single-agency* service. Each broker is the agent of one party.

Example 2

A more complex situation arises when a client-buyer, Elizabeth, asks Norman to show her a property, owned by John, that is listed with Norman's company. John is obviously a client of Norman's company.

At this moment, Norman's company is being asked to represent parties on opposite sides of the same possible transaction. How can it give client service to both seller, John, and buyer, Elizabeth?

Can *an individual* (a natural person) loyally represent opposing parties? Certainly not. It would be like a trial with one attorney who must both prosecute and defend a person accused of a crime.

Norman's company definitely wants both to sell its listings and also earn fees for representing clients like Elizabeth. In doing this, a company faces the possibility of conflict of interest.

The Maryland Solution: The Intra-Company Agent (ICA)

The situation described in Example 2 above has such potential for conflict of interest that Maryland has recently written into the Broker Act certain actions that Norman's company is required to take if it wishes to keep both Elizabeth and John as clients.

The firm must first have the written consent of all parties to such dual agency. Then

Norman's broker appoints two affiliates within the company to serve as **intra-company agents**. [The term *intra* means *within* as in *intra*-mural games—those played *within* the *walls* of an institution.]

So Norman's broker appoints two affiliates, Viola and Celeste, as intra-company agents (ICAs) of John and of Elizabeth respectively. Norman's broker is not permitted to appoint herself as one of the ICAs.

The firm—with the full knowledge and informed consent of both buyer and seller—can now serve as agent of both parties in the contemplated transaction.

To maintain each side's confidentiality, the broker backs away from the transaction personally, and lets the intra-company agents handle their respective clients. Each ICA will give her party full client treatment: care, obedience, accounting, loyalty, and disclosure.

If Norman's company were very small and had only its broker and one other licensee, it could not perform the dual agency allowed by Maryland law. The law requires the broker to appoint two persons **other** than the broker to be the ICAs. In a multi-office company, office managers, acting in the place of the broker and at the broker's direction, may *appoint* ICAs but not *serve as* ICAs.

Agency Options in Representation

Licensed real estate brokers in Maryland, as in other states, typically may choose to be either *single agency* or *dual agency* companies. Those operating as single agency

companies typically choose to act as one of the following:

- A *single agency* company offering to represent either buyers or sellers, but not both, in any given transaction

- An *exclusive seller agency* company, which offers to represent only sellers in all transactions

- An *exclusive buyer agency* company, offering to represent only buyers in all transactions

Single agency companies offer to represent sellers and treat prospective buyers as customers (not clients) of that brokerage. They also do this when prospective buyers for the property are brought to them by *cooperating* agents, as described in *Categories of Representation* below.

The same single agency companies may also offer to represent buyers in dealing with properties listed with other companies. What they will *not* do is offer to represent buyers and sellers *in the same property transaction*.

Companies that decide to engage in disclosed dual agency must make the adjustments Norman's company did in Example 2.

It is essential for each company to decide which agency service or services it will offer and present that policy and its associated procedures to everyone in the organization. All persons affiliated with the company should be trained in the proper performance of these services. It is the responsibility of licensees who manage offices to ensure that these services are being performed according to the detailed requirements of the Brokers Act.

Categories of Representation

The Brokers Act and the Real Estate Commission's *Agency Relationship Information Form* (seen in Figure 2.2) recognize and define several kinds of agency representation in real estate brokerage: seller's agent, cooperating agent, buyer's agent, presumed buyer's agent, dual agent, and intra-company agent.

- *Seller's agents* are licensees who are affiliated with or acting as the listing broker for real estate. They *represent* the seller and *assist* prospective buyers in the acquisition of that real estate.

- *Cooperating agents* are a sub-type of seller's agent. They are not affiliated with or acting as the listing broker for a property. Rather, they function as *subagents of the seller, representing the seller* through and under the seller's listing broker. They also *assist* prospective *buyers* in the acquisition of real estate.

The above has long been a typical arrangement in transactions that involve a listing brokerage firm and a selling brokerage firm assisting a customer. It remains a common practice.

- *Buyer's agents* are licensees who *represent* prospective buyers in the acquisition of real estate. When representing buyers in acquiring a property listed with another company, *buyer's agents are not subagents of the owner-seller*. Nor are they cooperating agents as described in the paragraph above.

There are two classes of *buyer's agents*. One class is the *presumed buyer agent* who has no express agreement to represent a prospect and who may make no claim for payment for this representation.

The other class is the *buyer agent by written agreement*. This type may receive compensation for performance of the task set forth in the written agreement.

- *Dual agents* are *firms* who represent not only sellers but also prospective purchasers in the same property transaction. All parties must sign the *Consent for Dual Agency* form, presented in Figure 2.3 if dual agency is to proceed.

- *Intra-company agents* are a sub-type under dual agents. They are pairs of licensees affiliated with a broker and designated by that broker (or by their office manager) to deliver client-level service (one to the seller and one to the buyer) in the sale of a specific parcel of real estate listed with their company. They are acting on behalf of their firm which is the dual agent. Both buyer and seller must have agreed to this arrangement for it to go forward.

Presumed Buyer's Agency Relationship: A Recent Development

The Maryland Brokers Act has stated since January 1, 1999, that a licensee who assists a prospective buyer in finding property to buy—and is neither affiliated with nor the broker of the listing company for the property shown—is *presumed by law* to be acting as agent of the purchaser. Either the licensee or the prospect may expressly decline this relationship.

Figure 2.2   Commission's Agency Relationship Information Form (Page 1 of 2)

January 1, 1999

State of Maryland
Real Estate Commission

Understanding Whom Real Estate Agents Represent

Before you decide to sell or buy or rent a home you need to consider the following information:

Agents Who Represent the Seller

Seller's Agent: A seller's agent works for the real estate company that lists and markets the property for the sellers, or landlords, and exclusively represents the sellers or landlords. That means that he or she may assist the buyer or tenant in purchasing or renting the property, but his or her duty of loyalty is only to the sellers or landlords. The seller pays the seller's agent's fees as specified in a written listing agreement.

Cooperating Agent: A cooperating agent works for a real estate company different from the company for which the seller's agent works. The cooperating agent can assist a buyer or tenant in purchasing or renting a property, but his or her duty of loyalty is only to the sellers or landlords. The cooperating agent's fees is paid by the sellers or landlords through the seller's agent's company.

Agents Who Represent the Buyer

Presumed Buyer's Agent (no written agreement): When a person goes to a real estate agent for assistance in finding a home to buy or rent, the agent is presumed to be representing the buyer and can show the buyer properties that are *not* listed by the agent's real estate company. A presumed buyer's agent may *not* make or prepare an offer or negotiate a sale for the buyer. The buyer does *not* have an obligation to pay anything to the presumed agent.

If for any reason the buyer does not want the agent to represent him or her as a presumed agent, either *initially* or *at any time,* the buyer can decline or terminate a presumed agency relationship simply by saying so.

Buyer's Agent (by written agreement): A buyer or tenant may enter into a written contract with a real estate agent which provides that the agent will represent the buyer or tenant in locating a property to buy or rent. The agent is then known as the buyer's agent. That agent assists the buyer in evaluating properties and preparing offers, and negotiates in the best interests of the buyer or tenant. The agent's fee is paid according to the written agreement between the agent and the buyer or tenant. If you as a buyer or tenant wish to have an agent represent you exclusively, you must enter into a written buyer agency agreement.

Dual Agents

The possibility of **dual agency** arises when the buyer's agent and the seller's agent both work for the same real estate company, and the buyer is interested in property listed by that company. The real estate company, or broker, is called the "dual agent." Dual agents do not act exclusively in the interests of either the seller or buyer, or landlord or tenant, and therefore cannot give undivided loyalty to either party. There may be a conflict of interest because the terms of the seller and buyer may be different or adverse.

If both seller and buyer, or landlord and tenant, agree to dual agency by signing a Consent For Dual Agency form, then the real estate company (the "dual agent") will assign one agent to represent the seller or landlord (the seller's "intra-company agent") and another agent to represent the buyer or tenant (the buyer's intra-company agent"). Intra-company agents may provide the same services to their clients as exclusive seller's or buyer's agents, including advising their clients as to price and negotiation strategy, provided the clients have both consented to be represented by dual agency.

Provided by the Maryland Real Estate Commission

Figure 2.2 Commission's Agency Relationship Information Form (Page 2 of 2)

If either party does not agree to dual agency, the real estate company may withdraw the agency agreement for that particular property with either the buyer or seller, or both. If the seller's agreement is terminated, the seller must then either represent him or herself or arrange to be represented by an agent from another real estate company. If the buyer's agreement is terminated, the buyer or tenant may choose to enter into a written buyer agency agreement with an agent from a different company. Alternatively, the buyer or tenant may choose not to be represented by an agent of his or her own but simply to receive assistance from the seller's agent, from another agent in that company, or from a cooperating agent from another company.

No matter what type of agent you choose to work with, you have the following rights and responsibilities in selling or buying or renting property:

➤Real estate agents are obligated by law to treat all parties to a real estate transaction honestly and fairly. They must exercise reasonable care and diligence and maintain the confidentiality of clients. They must not discriminate in the offering of properties; they must promptly present each written offer or counteroffer to the other party; and they must answer questions truthfully.

➤Real estate agents must disclose all material facts that they know or should know relating to a property. An agent's duty to maintain confidentiality does not apply to the disclosure of material facts about a property.

➤All agreements with real estate agents should be in writing and should explain the duties and obligations of the agent. The agreement should explain how the agent will be paid and any fee-sharing agreements with other agents.

➤You have the responsibility to protect your own interests. You should carefully read all agreements to make sure they accurately reflect your understanding. A real estate agent is qualified to advise you on real estate matters only. If you need legal or tax advice, it is your responsibility to consult a licensed attorney or accountant.

Any complaints about a real estate agent may be filed with the Real Estate Commission at 500 North Calvert Street, Baltimore, MD 21202. (410) 230-6200.

This notice is information required by law and is **NOT A CONTRACT**

We, the ❑ Sellers/Landlord ❑ Buyers/Tenants acknowledge receipt of a copy of this disclosure and that

_____((firm name)

and_____(salesperson) are working as:

❑   seller/landlord's agent
❑   cooperating agent
❑   buyer's agent
❑   dual agent (See Consent Dual Agency form)
(You may check more than one box)

_____   _____
Signature   Date   Signature   Date

I certify that on this date I made the required agency disclosure to the individuals identified below and they were unable or unwilling to acknowledge receipt of a copy of this disclosure statement.

_____
Signature of agent   Date

_____   _____
Name of individual to whom disclosure was made   Name of individual to whom disclosure was made

Figure 2.3 Commission's Consent for Dual Agency (Page 1 of 2)

January 1, 1999

STATE OF MARYLAND
REAL ESTATE COMMISSION

Consent For Dual Agency

(In this form, the word "seller" includes "landlord", "buyer" includes "tenant", and "purchase" or "sale" includes "lease.")

When Dual Agency May Occur

The possibility of dual agency arises when:

> ➤ The buyer is interested in a property listed by a real estate company; and

> ➤ The seller's agent and the buyer's agent work for that same real estate company.

Before the buyer and seller can proceed to be represented by a dual agent, they must both sign a Consent For Dual Agency. If they have previously signed a Consent For Dual Agency, they must affirm their consent for the sale of a particular property to a particular buyer.

**Important Considerations
Before Making a Decision
About Dual Agency**

☛ A dual agent does not exclusively represent either the seller or buyer and there may be a conflict of interest because the interests of the seller and buyer may be different or adverse.

☛ As a dual agent, the real estate company does not owe undivided loyalty to either the seller or buyer.

Your Choices Concerning Dual Agency

When a dual agency situation in fact arises, the buyer and seller have the following options:

1. **Consent in writing to dual agency.** If all parties consent in writing, the real estate company (the "dual agent") will assign one real estate agent from the company to represent the seller or landlord (the seller's "intra-company agent") and another agent from the company to represent the buyer or tenant (the buyer's "intra-company agent"). Intra-company agents may provide the same services to their clients as an exclusive seller's or buyer's agent, including advising their clients as to price and negotiation strategy.

2. **Do not consent to dual agency.** If either the buyer or the seller, or landlord or tenant, refuses to consent in writing to dual agency, the real estate company must terminate the agency agreement for that particular property with either the buyer or the seller, or both. If the seller's agreement is terminated, the seller must then either represent him or herself or arrange to be represented by an agent from another real estate company. If the buyer's agreement is terminated, the buyer or tenant may choose to enter into a written buyer agency agreement with an agent from a different company. Alternatively, the buyer or tenant may choose not be represented by an agent of his or her own but simply to receive assistance from the seller's agent, from another agent in that company, or from a cooperating agent from another company.

Figure 2.3 Commission's Consent for Dual Agency (Page 2 of 2)

Duties of a Dual Agent and Intra-Company Agent

Like other agents, dual agents and intra-company agents must keep confidential information about a client's bargaining position or motivations unless the client gives consent to disclose the information. For example, a dual agent or intra-company agent may not tell the other party, or the other party's agent, without consent of the client:

> ➢ anything the client asks to be kept confidential*,
> ➢ that the seller would accept a lower price or other terms,
> ➢ the reasons why a party wants to sell or buy, or
> ➢ that a party needs to sell or buy quickly

- However, like all agents, a dual agent and intra-company agent must disclose any material facts about a property to the other party.

How Dual Agents Are Paid

Only the dual agent receives compensation on the sale of a property listed by that company.

If a financial bonus is offered to an agent who sells property that is listed with his company, this fact must be disclosed in writing to both the buyer and seller.

I have read the above information, and I understand the terms of the dual agency. I understand that I do not have to consent to a dual agency, and that if I do not consent, there will not be a dual agency. I hereby voluntarily consent to have

_____act as dual agent for me as the:
(Firm Name)

❑ seller in the sale of the property at:_____.

❑ buyer in the purchase of any property listed for sale with the above-referenced firm.

_____   _____
Signature   Date   Signature   Date

AFFIRMATION

The undersigned Seller(s) hereby affirms consent to Dual Agency:

_____   _____
Signature   Date   Signature   Date

The undersigned Buyer(s) hereby affirms consent to dual agency:

_____   _____
Signature   Date   Property Location

_____
Signature   Date

Prior to the above date, the statute presumed just the opposite—that the prospect was a customer. This reversal has caused some confusion among long-time agents who have not gotten the word, or, just don't believe the change happened, pointing out the necessity for required continuing education.

In the past, most prospective homeseekers *thought* that the salesperson working with them was *their* agent and was "on their side." Now the law *requires* the salesperson to be on the prospect's team until either the prospect or the licensee expressly declines to continue this presumed relationship.

Fiduciary Duties to a Presumed Client

During the period of presumed buyer representation, the licensee and that licensee's firm, owe the potential buyer full fiduciary duties. One of those duties—loyalty—includes *confidentiality*. This means that whatever the presumed client says to the licensee must be treated as confidential from then on.

This is true even if the presumed client (buyer prospect) walks away and never comes back. It is also true if the presumed client later refuses both presumed representation and contractual, formal representation. Confidentiality continues—even if the presumed client dies!

Even the termination of presumed agency does not end the confidentiality owed to the disclosures of the presumed client. Any facts learned from prospects during the period of presumed buyer representation must be kept confidential by the licensee and not be used to that client's disadvantage in any later negotiations.

To avoid this potential conflict-of-interest problem, some firms make it their policy for affiliates to decline presumed buyer representation very early in their contacts with prospects. This refusal to engage in presumed buyer representation can be made orally or in writing. Some firms leave it up to the individual licensee.

When Presumed Representation (Agency) Ends

Other than by entering into a formal written buyer representation agreement, *presumed agency representation* of buyers *only* ends when one of these three things occurs:

1. The licensee or the buyers reject the presumed relationship. (This can be done orally.)

2. The buyers either begin negotiations or cause an offer to be presented for the purchase of a specific property.

3. The buyers wish to be shown a property listed with the licensee's own company.

In the first instance, the rejection can be made at any time before either the second or third instance occurs.

Agency Disclosure

Either upon first contact or during the first scheduled face-to-face meeting with prospects, the licensee will present them with the Real Estate Commission's form *Understanding Whom Real Estate Agents Represent,* seen in Figure 2.2.

The prospects' acceptance of the form—with or without signing it—does not end their presumed client status. The fact that the form may show that the licensee represents sellers, buyers, or whomever, does not end the presumed buyer representation. Nor does the prospects' signing the form create a contractual buyer representation relationship in which the licensee could be compensated for representing the buyer.

The form is not a contract form; it is an information piece on which signatures of prospects and licensee are requested. The prospects' signatures are not required for the presentation of the form to be effective. There is provision for only the licensee to sign it and to state that the prospects could, or would, not sign. Dates shown on the signatures show that the disclosure was made in a timely way so as to satisfy the law.

On this form, the buyers can see in which of the four categories of agent their salesperson is working when dealing with them. It is basically an information form about how real estate agents in general may work and how the broker's salesperson, in particular, is working.

Buyers are free to reject any kind of representation and continue to be assisted in seeking a property to buy. They will receive customer-level service.

But if they voice no preference and the licensee does not reject presumed representation at this point, the presumed representation continues until one of the three events happens required by law to end it.

If the buyers want formal buyer representation with its client-level service, they must enter into a written agreement with the licensee's firm for its broker to represent them as purchasers. Details of this form are found in Chapter 4.

On the *Buyer Representation Agreement* form, the buyers should also indicate whether they are willing to consider any property that will require dual agency. Dual agency would arise if client-purchasers want to be shown a property listed with their buyer broker's firm. The company can only show a buyer client those of its listings whose owners also have consented to the possibility of dual agency when their properties were listed.

Buyers' consent to dual agency, with respect to a particular property, is made on another form provided by the Real Estate Commission—*Consent for Dual Agency* (Figure 2.3). The sellers must confirm their willingness to proceed to negotiations by signing a *Consent for Dual Agency* form naming this particular buyer.

Mere disclosure of the existence of presumed buyer representation does not bring it to an end. A decision to end presumed buyer representation must be voiced either by the prospect or by the licensee.

Once made, however, a decision—either to enter into a written buyer representation agreement with the company or to reject representation—would end the *presumed* buyer representation.

A firm that chooses to avoid presumed buyer representation may require its affiliates to make immediate disclosure of the agency alternatives available to prospects and to refuse to continue in the presumed buyer representation role.

However, before the licensee working with them can prepare a written offer on their behalf or even show them a property listed with the licensee's firm, presumed representation must end and prospects must make a written choice about representation—whether to sign a formal representation agreement and receive client-level service or to reject representation and receive customer-level assistance.

Affiliates acting under presumed buyer representation may lawfully show prospects properties listed with other firms. If prospects have not agreed to contractual buyer representation, they are free to walk away and later buy through another firm any or all property they have been shown by the first firm.

Presumed clients may walk away at any time when an affiliate continues in the role of presumed buyer representative. They have all the freedom of customer-prospects and also the right to expect client-level service—all without any financial responsibility to the firm that is serving them! They may even go to other firms to try to buy the properties shown them by the first firm.

Of course, prospects being assisted as customers have always been free to walk away from the company that has been assisting them. But they have had no claim to fiduciary duties—to client-level service.

Brokers should periodically reexamine and, where necessary, revise their policy and procedure manuals, office standard operating procedures, and all representation agreement forms to take into account the categories of representation in the present law including, of course, presumed buyer representation.

Confidentiality—A Right of All Clients

Whatever confidential information a licensee learns from individuals while representing them—either by agreement or as presumed buyer representatives—such as information about their personal finances, bargaining strategy, and motivations to buy or to sell, must of course be kept confidential throughout the conduct of the entire transaction. Moreover, the confidentiality continues even after the agency terminates, a transaction is completed, and after a written agency agreement expires.

Information that had previously been confidential may be disclosed with the written permission of the former client or when the information has become public knowledge by the former client's publication of it.

Agents are forbidden to reveal confidential information to other clients whom they may later represent—or to other agents in their own company who may represent parties negotiating with the previous clients—or to use such "inside information" to the disadvantage of the previous clients.

If they are working with a new client in a transaction involving the former client, they must disclose to the new client that they cannot disclose to them things they previously learned about the old client.

Because it is very confusing, the subject of confidentiality requires repeated explanation in company training programs. Awareness of the need for greater confidentiality should reduce or end casual office conversation about cases, clients, and customers.

Brokerage offices that practice dual agency must provide locked files, or other security arrangements, so that confidential information about buyers or sellers in the same transaction can be kept segregated and not fall into the hands of the intra-company agent representing the wrong party.

The broker (on behalf of the firm, the actual dual agent) has full access to all this information but is forbidden by law to share it with adverse parties in any transaction unless required by court order or by the requirement to disclose material facts.

Agency Relationship and Payment of Fees

Maryland law now clearly states that agency relationships and responsibilities are not determined by which party pays for brokerage services.

For example, when sellers pay a licensee the brokerage fee charged by a buyer broker, that payment does not make that broker the sellers' agent.

Now this concept is *counterintuitive*; it goes against conventional wisdom and also against what many students have actually heard in previous classes. So, study it; learn it!

Worse yet, it is not necessary for a brokerage fee to be promised or paid to *create* an agency relationship with a licensee. Certain behaviors and statements of a licensee, however, may properly be construed (interpreted) by a member of the public—and perhaps later, a jury—to indicate that the licensee is indeed their agent, even without a formal agreement.

Consider this example: A licensee who says to a customer, "Trust me; I'll get you a great deal," has asked the customer to regard him or her as trustworthy and loyal, i.e., as the customer's agent.

When this occurs while the licensee is already serving as agent or subagent for the sellers in the same transaction, an undisclosed (probably unintended and certainly unlawful) dual agency is created that may later prove to be the basis for rescission of sales contract, loss of commission, suit for damages, and disciplinary action by the Commission.

Last, but unfortunately not least, the person to whom the licensee owed loyalty (because of a careless remark) owes the licensee nothing for his or her trouble! This *implied agency,* like presumed representation, can amount to all work and no pay.

No individual licensee can *directly* and *personally* represent both parties to a residential transaction. The broker of a company properly involved in a dual agency situation is the *dual agent* but does not directly and personally deal with the parties;

the broker appoints intra-company agents to do so.

Disclosure and Fairness

According to the Code of Ethics and the Regulations of the Commission, the obligation of absolute fidelity to the client's interest is primary, but it does not relieve licensees from the obligation to deal fairly with all parties to a transaction.

Statutory attempts to guarantee fairness by requiring disclosures often miss their mark because members of the public can receive so many and such complex disclosures that they have no clue about much of what is being disclosed!

Disclosures To Be Clear

The Brokers Act requires all licensees who are representing sellers to disclose to buyers, or to the agents of the buyers, the fact that they (the licensees) are representing sellers.

When they represent buyers, they are similarly required to disclose that fact to sellers.

Under the Brokers Act, this disclosure must be made *not later than the first scheduled face-to-face meeting* with such parties. The author believes it is wiser to make the disclosure *at first contact*. This is, in fact, required of REALTORS® by their national organization, the National Association of REALTORS® (NAR) in its Code of Ethics.

Perhaps one-third of all licensees in Maryland are not REALTORS® and are only subject to the Real Estate Commission's authority. Nevertheless, the author believes the REALTORS® have it right. Disclose early and often.

The form that the Commission requires *all licensees* to use in this disclosure is presented in Figure 2.2.

QUESTIONS

1. Real estate brokers' principals are their

   a. managers.
   b. clients.
   c. prospects.
   d. customers.

2. In handling a transaction involving any purchase and sale of residential real property, a real estate broker

   a. is the agent of the owner of the property being sold.
   b. may not act as the agent of the buyer.
   c. may not represent both buyer and seller in the same transaction without designating two intra-company agents.
   d. may not personally represent both buyer and seller unless both parties agree.

3. Arthur has been assigned by his broker, Marie, to work with Tony to provide buyer representation for the purchase of a property listed by Charise, a salesperson with Marie's company. Marie has named Charise to represent the seller. In this situation, which of the following is true?

   a. Tony is a prospect; Arthur is his intra-company agent; Marie is a single agency broker; Charise is the intra-company agent for the seller.
   b. Tony is a client; Arthur is his intra-company agent; Marie is a disclosed dual agent; Charise is the intra-company agent of the purchaser.
   c. Tony is a customer; Arthur is his salesperson; Marie is an intra-company agent; Charise represents the seller.
   d. Tony is a client; Arthur is his intra-company agent; Marie is not a single agency broker; Charise is the intra-company agent for the seller.

4. Brokers who represent buyers of real estate

   a. are regarded by the law as dual agents in such transactions.
   b. must disclose this agency relationship to sellers.
   c. are in violation of the Brokers Act.
   d. will not be compensated.

5. Which of the following statements is true concerning *presumed buyer representation?*

   a. Presumed buyer representation begins when a licensee shows a prospective purchaser a property listed by another brokerage firm.
   b. Presumed buyer representation ends when a licensee shows a prospective purchaser a property listed with another brokerage firm.
   c. A prospective purchaser who declines to enter into a buyer representation agreement is no longer owed confidentiality for matters discussed with the licensee who had been providing presumed buyer representation up to that point.
   d. A licensee is no longer the presumed buyer representative of a purchaser who makes an offer on a property.

6. Which statement concerning agency is true?

   a. A broker is the agent of the party who is paying for his services.
   b. A broker is allowed to be a dual agent in a transaction if no harm is done.
   c. A salesperson may personally act as dual agent if both buyer and seller agree in writing.
   d. A broker who represents both buyer and seller in the same transaction must appoint two intra-company agents.

7. Agent's duties to their principals include

   a. disclosure of all facts.
   b. loyalty.
   c. presentation of all written offers.
   d. all of the above.

8. Under the Brokers Act, licensees who are representing sellers must disclose this fact to buyers, or the agents of the buyers,

   a. at first contact.
   b. when an offer is made.
   c. not later than the first scheduled face-to-face meeting.
   d. when the buyer or agent of the buyer asks.

3

Real Estate Brokerage

OVERVIEW

In this chapter, students will be introduced to a great many new words and ideas that relate to real estate brokerage. They will also find explanations of the concepts those new words stand for. This information is basic to students' passing the state licensing examination.

BROKERAGE

The Brokers Act defines *real estate brokerage* as performing certain services *for another person in return for consideration.* These services are

- selling, buying, exchanging, or leasing real estate;

- collecting rent for the use of any real estate;

- giving assistance in locating or obtaining any residential real estate for purchase;

- regularly dealing in real estate or in leases or options on real estate;

- promoting the sale of real estate by listing it in a publication issued primarily for promoting real estate sales;

- subdividing land and selling the divided lots; and

- acting as consultant in any of these activities.

The Code of Maryland Regulations— COMAR recites the numerous specific ways that the Brokers Act is to be applied to every aspect of providing brokerage services. Although relevant sections of COMAR have long been published in the same bound booklet with the Brokers Act, they come from a different source.

COMAR consists of regulations created by the Real Estate Commission with the guidance of the Department of Labor, Licensing, and Regulation and under the authority of the Brokers Act. For licensees, these regulations have *the force of law,* although they are "only" regulations.

ORGANIZATION OF BROKERAGE FIRMS: PRACTICE THROUGH CORPORATIONS, PARTNERSHIPS, OR LIMITED LIABILITY COMPANIES

Brokers may provide real estate brokerage services through any of the forms of business organization mentioned in the headlines above if they are employed by or have another contractual relationship with that business organization and have been designated by it as broker, personally responsible for the provision of real estate brokerage services through it.

Brokers must also submit notice to the Commission stating their intention to do so. The notice must include

- the name of the real estate broker submitting the notice;

- a statement that the named individual has been designated as the broker of the firm;

- the address of the firm's principal place of business and of each proposed branch office;

- any trade or fictitious name that the firm intends to use while conducting the business of the firm; and

- a list of all the licensed associate real estate brokers and licensed real estate salespersons who will be affiliated with the broker of the firm and any other information that the Commission may require by regulation.

The Commission maintains current information regarding any corporation or partnership through which real estate brokerage services are provided.

An individual who assists in providing brokerage services for a firm while associated with the firm as a partner, officer, shareholder, or in any other capacity, must hold either a salesperson's or an associate broker's license.

Company officers, shareholders, etc., who do not provide brokerage services do not need to be licensed.

A corporation, partnership, or limited liability company (LLC) that provides real estate brokerage services is not, by its compliance with the requirements for so doing, relieved of any responsibility that it may have for any acts or omissions of its officers, partners, employees, or agents.

An individual who provides real estate brokerage services through a corporation or partnership is not, by reason of employment or other relationship with the corporation, partnership, or limited liability company, relieved of any individual responsibility regarding those services.

Limitation on Interests Held by Affiliates

Not more than 50 percent of ownership control in any form of business organization providing real estate brokerage services may be held directly or indirectly by salespersons or associate brokers or any combination thereof. Otherwise, affiliates might become able to control their principal, the broker, rather than the other way around.

Affiliation Arrangements

Brokers may provide brokerage services only personally or through real estate salespersons or associate brokers licensed under them. Such affiliates typically act as independent contractors or as employees. Any individual, including a licensed associate real estate broker, who provides real estate services on behalf of a real estate broker shall be considered a real estate salesperson with respect to the provision of those services.

SUPERVISION (Effective Since September 17, 2001)

Supervision means direction and review of professional real estate activities. Commission Regulation 5 requires brokers to supervise all licensees affiliated with them whether they are employees or "independent contractors," i.e., classified by the Internal Revenue Service as *self-employed*.

Brokers are also to direct and review the supervisory activities of each branch office manager.

Branch office managers are charged with responsibility to supervise the professional real estate activities of associate brokers and salespersons registered to their office.

Factors to be considered in determining reasonable and adequate supervision, include but are not limited to availability of:

- regular training or education sessions held at least once every two months;

- experienced supervisory personnel to review and discuss contracts provisions, brokerage agreement provisions, and advertising;

- written procedures which give clear guidance for handling deposit monies and other funds;

- compliance with all fair housing laws and regulations;

- advertising requirements for real estate transactions;

- review of all contracts which have been signed by all parties;

- use and limitations of unlicensed personal assistants;

- disclosure of agency relationships by licensees in real estate transactions;

- obligation of all licensees to comply with the Broker Act, the Commission's Code of Ethics, and all applicable local, State, and federal laws and regulations;

- restrictions on the sale or lease of a licensee's real property and the purchase or leasing of real property by licensees for their personal use; and

- the unauthorized practice of law by a licensee.

In addition, the firm must have evidence of

- attendance at sales meetings;

- review of all executed contracts;

- review of all advertisements placed by any affiliate;

- compliance with firm's written procedures and policies and distribution to affiliates of those written policies and procedures; and

- procedures for informing affiliates of new or changed real estate laws and regulations.

Brokers who are charged with failure to supervise properly but cannot show evidence of meeting these requirements bear the burden of proof that their supervision has been reasonable and adequate.

PERSONAL ASSISTANTS

Some salespersons and associate brokers use personal assistants to help them in the conduct of their work. Some of these assistants hold real estate licenses while others do not.

A 1994 memorandum from the Commission states, in pertinent part,

> . . . licensees should be extremely careful in delegating responsibilities to others. They should also be aware that, under the Internal Revenue Code, a person whom they hired to assist them would most likely be considered an employee of the licensee who retained him or her and the licensee would be liable for complying with all IRS requirements on record keeping and payroll deduction, as well as being responsible for carrying workmen's compensation insurance.

Referring to those acting as personal assistants, the publication continues:

> . . . [U]nlicensed persons, *as well as licensed agents employed by associate brokers or salespersons* (emphasis added) may not provide real estate brokerage services.

It urges seeking legal counsel for specific situations.

What Personal Assistants May and May Not Do

The Commission's guidelines list acts that personal assistants may and may not perform. Note that the word *licensee* as it appears in the guidelines means a licensed associate broker or salesperson affiliated with and acting under the supervision of a broker.

A personal assistant may

- answer the telephone and forward calls to a licensee;
- submit listings and changes to a multiple listing service;
- follow up on loan commitments after a contract has been negotiated;
- assemble documents for closing;
- secure documents (public information) from courthouse, public utilities, etc;
- have keys made for company listings;
- write ads for approval of licensee and supervising broker and place advertising;
- type contract forms at the direction of and for approval by licensee and supervising broker;
- compute commission checks;
- place signs on property;

- arrange the date and time of home inspection, termite inspection, mortgage application, well or septic inspection, presettlement walk-through or settlement;
- prepare flyers and promotional information for approval by licensee and supervising broker;
- act as courier service to deliver documents, pick up keys, etc;
- schedule an open house;
- schedule appointments for licensee to show listed property; and
- accompany a licensee to an open house or showing:
  1. for security purposes; and
  2. to hand out preprinted materials.

A personal assistant may not

- prepare promotional materials or ads without the review and approval of licensee and supervising broker;
- show property;
- answer any questions on listings, title, financing, closing, etc.;
- discuss or explain a contract, listing, lease, agreement, or other real estate document with anyone outside the brokerage;
- be paid on the basis of real estate activity, such as a percentage of commission, or any amount based on listings, sales, etc.;
- negotiate or agree to any commission, split, management fee or referral fee on behalf of a licensee;
- solicit property owners to list their property for sale, either in person or by telephone;
- solicit purchasers or lessees for the purchase or lease of real property;

- discuss with prospective purchasers or lessees the attributes or amenities of a property, whether at an open house or under any other circumstances;
- discuss with the owner of real property the terms and conditions of the real property offered for sale or lease;
- collect, receive, or hold deposit monies, rent, other monies, or anything else of value received from the owner of the real property or from a prospective purchaser or lessee;
- provide owners of real property or prospective purchasers or lessees with any advice, recommendations, or suggestions as to the sale, purchase, exchange, or leasing of the real property to be listed or real property presently available for sale or for lease; and
- hold himself or herself out in any manner, orally or in writing, as being licensed or affiliated with a particular company or real estate broker as a licensee.

A Possible Alternative

Some companies require that all personal assisting be done by licensees who work on the "buddy system" with the licensee they are assisting. Remuneration is paid by the firm's broker on an agreed-upon apportionment of all commissions earned with the assistant's help. Thus the assistant remains self-employed; and the "buddy" being helped has no Human Resources (Personnel Department) duties to perform because of the assistant. The broker remains the employer of both and disburses all compensation.

WORKERS' COMPENSATION

Some real estate salespersons and associate real estate brokers may be exempt from the workers' compensation requirements if they are on a commission-only basis under a written agreement with the broker and otherwise qualified as self-employed for federal tax purposes. The IRS has three requirements that qualify a person as *self-employed* or "qualified real estate agent" status:

1. The individual is a licensed real estate agent.

2. Substantially all the remuneration for services performed as a real estate agent by the individual is directly related to sales output, rather than to number of hours worked.

3. The individual performs services under a written contract with the individual's broker stating that the individual will not be treated as an employee for Federal tax purposes.

If all three requirements are met, the IRS will not treat the individual as an employee or the person for whom the services are performed as an employer. Reference Title 26, Subtitle C, Chapter 25, Section 3508 of the Internal Revenue Code. Companies should seek the advice of competent counsel in this matter.

SALES COMMISSION DISPUTES

The licensing law does not provide for the Real Estate Commission to arbitrate disputes between brokers or between brokers and salespersons over distribution of commissions. Such disputes should be submitted for arbitration to the respective Board or Association of REALTORS® if the parties to the dispute are members of the same board or to the Maryland Association of REALTORS® if the parties to the dispute are members of different boards or associations. Arbitration may be pursued through other agencies. To prevent commission disputes, the percentage and distribution of commissions should be in writing, especially those setting forth the agreement between brokers and their salespersons.

PLACES OF BUSINESS—OFFICES

Each licensed real estate broker who is a nonresident of the State shall also maintain an office in Maryland if the state in which the nonresident broker resides requires a resident of this State who is licensed in the other state to maintain an office in that state.

The place of business in Maryland required by this Act for all broker licensees must be an office or headquarters where they and their employees and/or affiliates regularly transact real estate business. Records of the brokerage's transactions, including the records of the broker's escrow account, must be kept in a secured location at this office. A commercial answering service, a mechanical recording device, or a mail drop, singly or in combination, do not meet the requirements for an office. Brokers must display in their main offices their own licenses and the licenses of all their affiliates who work at that location.

The *Americans with Disabilities Act* requires places of public accommodation to make reasonable modifications to meet the needs of handicapped members of the public. Real estate offices are such places. Access for the public should be barrier free, and employees should be alerted to assist any challenged persons who visit an office. Moreover, every firm with 15 or more employees—and this includes affiliates—must make reasonable accommodation to the needs of any handicapped person working for the firm.

Office Signs

A real estate broker must display a sign clearly visible to the public at each office and branch office that the real estate broker maintains; the sign must include the words *Realty, Real Estate* or, where authorized by the respective trade associations, *REALTOR*® or *Realtist*.

Change in Location of Offices

Within ten days of changing the location of any office, a real estate broker must submit: written notice on a form provided by the Commission of such change in the address of the principal office or any branch office of the broker; the license certificate and pocket card of the broker or, for the branch office, its certificate; and the required fee. Upon receipt of these things, the Commission shall issue a new certificate and card to the broker for the unexpired period of the broker's license or branch office certificate. If a real estate broker changes the address of the principal office or a branch office of the broker and fails to submit the required notice, the license of the broker is automatically suspended until the broker submits the required notice.

Branch Offices

Licensed real estate brokers may maintain branch offices in the State. They must appoint managers for each branch office who are either associate brokers or salespersons with three years of active experience. These managers must exercise reasonable and adequate supervision over the provision of real estate brokerage services by all affiliates working out of their branch office. This responsibility is in addition to, and not in lieu of, the responsibility of the broker. Licenses of all licensees working out of a branch office are displayed in that branch office together with a branch office certificate that shows, among other things, the name of the broker as registered with the Commission and the address of the main office.

Branch office certificates renewed in early 1998 were given staggered expiration dates. Upon their next renewal, they will be good for a two-year period. Newly issued certificates—as contrasted with renewals—are for a two-year period. There is a $5 fee for each certificate. Applications for branch office certificates must identify the individuals appointed as managers of the branch offices and be accompanied by payment of the required fees.

ADVERTISING

Both the Brokers Act and COMAR require all licensees to show in all advertising the fact that they are licensees. This disclosure must be made even when the licensees are selling their own real property. Licensees affiliated with a broker who use their own names and/or phone numbers in advertisements must clearly identify the broker under whom they are licensed. Licensees may not advertise the listings of other brokerage firms without their approval.

Licensees using a *trade name* (for example, the name of a franchise) on a "for sale" sign, business card, office sign, sales contract, listing contract, or other document are required to clearly and unmistakably include their own name or trade name as registered with the Commission. The same rule applies to telephone and face-to-face conversations. The broker's name as registered with the Commission must be made clear in each encounter.

A broker's outdoor advertisements or for sale signs posted on any property that is subject to *ground lease* must state the annual ground rent and capitalization if the price of the leasehold property is shown on the sign. The capitalization is the sum for which the property could be purchased *in fee*. The lettering showing the ground rent and capitalization must be at least as large as the lettering showing the property sale price. Maryland ground rents are discussed in Chapter 13 of this book.

COMAR requires that a licensee obtain an owner's permission before placing signs on a property. Licensees should check local laws regarding the use of for sale, directional, and open house signs on public property. They should also honor any restrictions imposed by cooperatives, condominiums, and homeowner associations. Licensees should familiarize themselves with HUD guidelines and rules concerning the use of the Equal Housing Opportunity logo or slogan to avoid giving even the appearance of discriminatory practices.

FUNDS OF OTHERS HELD IN TRUST

Trust money is defined as a deposit, payment, or other money that a person entrusts to a real estate broker to hold for the benefit of the owner or beneficial owner of that money and for a purpose that relates to a transaction involving real estate in this State.

The beneficial owner of funds in a trust account is that person, other than the owner (source) of the trust money, for whose benefit a licensee holds the money. In summary, **the owner** of an earnest money deposit is the purchaser while **the beneficial owner** is the seller.

Depositing Earnest Money

The Brokers Act requires that when brokers receive trust money, such as earnest money deposits, and are not directed in writing to the contrary by the money's owner and beneficial owner, they must *promptly* deposit that money in a non-interest-bearing checking account, a non-interest-bearing savings account, or any combination of these accounts they maintain for that purpose in authorized financial institutions in Maryland.

Brokers are required to report the bank's name and the account's number to the Commission as soon as they start depositing trust monies there. If a licensee establishes another non-interest-bearing or special escrow account, changes an escrow account number, or transfers the account to another bank, the broker must notify the Commission in writing within ten days of such action. Trust monies from many or all of a broker's transactions may be held in any single trust money account.

Recent legislation has clarified the maximum definition of the term *promptly* in this matter: a maximum of *seven business days*. This time frame accommodates very large, multioffice companies where funds must be transported to a remote headquarters for processing and deposit. *Promptly* still means *as soon as possible*. Deposits are not to be delayed just because more time now seems to be allowed.

In 1986, the Commission agreed to a procedure whereby language contained in the sales contracts authorizes delaying deposit of earnest monies until the seller executes and accepts the contract.

Associate real estate brokers or real estate salespersons who obtain trust money while providing real estate brokerage services shall promptly submit that money to the broker they are representing.

Real estate brokers may not use trust money for any purpose other than that for which it is entrusted to them.

Authorized Financial Institution

Except when directed to the contrary, brokers must deposit all trust money in a financial institution located in the State whose deposits are insured by the Federal Deposit Insurance Corporation, the Federal Savings and Loan Insurance Corporation, the National Credit Union Administration,

the State of Maryland Deposit Insurance Fund Corporation, or the Maryland Credit Union Insurance Corporation.

Maintenance and Disposition of Trust Money

Legislation passed in 2001 offers an additional option brokers may choose when left holding a deposit from a failed transaction. (It is highlighted in bold type below.) The problem usually has been that buyer and seller will not agree on who gets the earnest money deposit when a deal collapses.

The Brokers Act requires real estate brokers to maintain trust money in an authorized account until one of four things happens:

1. The real estate transaction is consummated or terminated.

2. The real estate broker receives proper written instructions from the owner and beneficial owner directing withdrawal or other disposition of the trust money.

3. A court directs disposition of funds after a broker's interpleader.

4. The owner or beneficial owner of the trust money fails to complete the real estate transaction for which the trust money was entrusted.

In the fourth case, prior to distributing the trust money, real estate brokers shall notify both the owner and the beneficial owners (from here on the author will call them *the buyer* and *the seller*) that they intend to distribute the trust money to the persons who, in the good faith opinion of the brokers, are entitled to receive it in accordance with the terms of the real estate contract.

This notification shall state whether the trust money will be paid to the buyer or the seller and tell them both that either of them may prevent distribution of the trust money by submitting a protest within 30 days.

If neither party submits a protest within that time, the trust money will be distributed in accordance with the real estate broker's notice.

All notices and responses in this matter must either be hand-delivered to both the buyer and seller, or to the broker; or sent by certified mail, return receipt requested, and regular mail to all the parties involved.

If the buyer and/or seller wish to protest the distribution of the trust money, they must submit the protest in writing to the broker holding the trust money within 30 days from the date the notice to them was delivered or mailed.

Brokers who receive a letter of protest shall distribute the trust money in accordance with one of the other three alternatives. If no written protest is received, real estate brokers shall distribute the trust money in accordance with the terms of the notice sent earlier.

When the duty of real estate brokers to maintain trust money in an account terminates, they must promptly account for all trust money. Real estate brokers may invest trust money as the owners and beneficial owners of the trust money instruct in writing or as the real estate brokers, owners and beneficial owners make written agreement.

Licensees must maintain, in a secured area within their office, adequate records of all real estate transactions engaged in by them as licensees. The records of transactions, including bank accounts or deposits referred to in these regulations, are to be available during usual business hours for inspection by the Commission, its field representatives, or its other employees.

The firm's real estate broker must be the signer, or at least one of the signers, on checks drawn on escrow accounts that the broker is required to maintain. The broker may designate an alternate signer to sign checks. This designated alternate signer, however, must be a licensee. A nonlicensee may be a cosigner on the broker's escrow account, provided all checks are also signed by a designated licensee.

QUESTIONS

1. Any outdoor sign or advertisement displayed on property for sale subject to ground rent

   a. must, if price is shown, also show the annual ground rent but need not show any other details until inquiry is made by a prospective purchaser.
   b. must, if price is shown, show ground rent and cost of capitalization in lettering no smaller than the lettering used for the price.
   c. need show only leasehold price.
   d. need show only leasehold price and the phrase *plus GR*.

2. When licensees advertise real property they have listed for sale,

   a. the name of the salesperson may not be included in the advertisement unless the identity of the broker is also included.
   b. only the broker's name is permitted in advertisements.
   c. the price of the property must be included in all advertisements.
   d. members of multiple-listing services may advertise any of the services' listings.

3. The designated place of business for a real estate broker's office required by law may properly be a

   a. telephone answering service.
   b. post office box.
   c. van or recreational vehicle registered with the Motor Vehicle Administration.
   d. definite office location.

4. A real estate brokerage firm performing activities for which a real estate license is required may be operated by

   a. real estate salespersons.
   b. an associate broker.
   c. any person holding a valid real estate license issued by the State Real Estate Commission.
   d. a licensed real estate broker.

5. Advertising by a broker must include the

   a. trade name of that broker as registered with the Commission.
   b. name of the broker's REALTOR® board or association or Realtist organization.
   c. name of the licensed real estate broker.
   d. name of the licensee who listed the property.

6. In Maryland, the person primarily responsible for the real estate brokerage services provided through a corporation is the

   a. president of the corporation.
   b. licensed real estate broker of the firm.
   c. chairman of the board.
   d. majority stockholder of the corporation.

7. Salespersons may use their own names and phone numbers in advertising listed property if

   a. their broker affiliation is clearly shown.
   b. their office manager's name is shown in letters at least half the size of the salespersons'.
   c. different colors for the broker's and salespersons' names are used.
   d. the broker gives permission.

8. When there are no instructions to the contrary from their owner and beneficial owner, the Brokers Act states that earnest money deposits

   a. may be commingled with the broker's funds.
   b. may be deposited in an insured and approved financial institution in Maryland.
   c. are to be placed in an interest-bearing account.
   d. may be withdrawn at any time prior to settlement as long as a licensee's signature appears on the escrow check.

4

Listing Agreements and Buyer Representation Agreements

OVERVIEW

Maryland recognizes representation agreements between broker licensees and buyers and between broker licensees and sellers. (References to buyers and sellers should be understood to apply to tenants and landlords whenever the sense allows.)

Listings are agency agreements in which brokers agree to help sellers sell, and sellers agree to compensate them for their service. These agreements may be either exclusive-right-to-sell, exclusive-agency, or open agreements as these terms are explained in the student's principal text.

The process of persuading a property owner to enter into such an agreement with a broker is also called *listing* a property.

Buyer representation agreements are agency agreements in which brokers agree to help buyers find property. They may be either *exclusive*, *exclusive agency*, or *open* buyer agency agreements.

CONTENT OF RESIDENTIAL BROKERAGE AGREEMENTS

Although there is no standard form provided by either statute or regulation either for listing contracts or for buyer representation agreements, the law has some specific requirements and prohibitions.

For example, all residential agency agreements—whether representing buyers or sellers, and whether open or exclusive—must be in writing and be signed by the parties to the agreement.

Each agreement must state the duties and authority of the agent, the compensation to be paid to the agent, and the performance that will call for such payment. It also must state a definite date upon which the agreement will end without further notice from either party.

It must set forth whether the agent is authorized to receive compensation from persons other than the client. Also, it must state whether the agent is authorized to cooperate with other brokers and share compensation with them. It must also reveal the amount of the shared compensation if other brokers are to be involved. The parties to an agency agreement may not waive any of the above requirements.

Listings may not take the form of "net" agreements under which brokers retain all amounts in excess of minimum sales prices.

Contrasting Effects of *Silence* in a Contract

The Brokers Act states that *when there is no express agreement to the contrary in the brokerage agreement*,

- listing brokers are *not* required to seek additional offers when the listed property becomes subject to a contract of sale; but

- listing brokers *are* required to present additional offers and counteroffers to the sellers of property already subject to such a contract.

The distinction is important: In the first case, brokers are not required to *seek* offers; in the second, they are required to *present* offers that are made, typically through other firms, after a property is sold (under contract).

Other Provisions

Many firms have chosen to incorporate in their agency agreements authorization from the client to perform ministerial acts on behalf of third parties. The law states that when such permission is given, brokers' ministerial acts for nonclients cannot be construed (interpreted) to be in violation of loyalty to their clients. The Brokers Act also states that a licensee's performing

ministerial acts for a nonclient may not be construed (interpreted) to form an agency relationship between the nonclient and the licensee performing the ministerial act.

Licensees must give copies of agency agreements to principals before beginning to carry out the tasks assigned in the agreements. Licensees must also keep copies of all agency agreements indefinitely.

At the time of listing a property for sale, brokers are to present the Residential Property Disclosure and Disclaimer Statement to sellers for their completion and signature together with a warning that neither disclosure or disclaimer removes the legal requirement that sellers reveal to any purchaser all material defects in a listed property.

In most agency agreements, seller-principals make choices with respect to dealing with buyer agents, subagents, and dual agents. These choices are indicated on the completed listing forms together with such routine issues as offering price, date of availability, acceptable forms of financing, and help with purchasers' closing costs.

Buyer-clients also indicate in their agency agreement whether they are open to negotiations that involve dual agency.

Licensee Responsibilities

Licensees representing either a seller or a buyer must, at the first scheduled face-to-face meeting with the opposing party, disclose in writing to that party their agency relationship using the Agency Relationship Information Form mandated by the

Commission. See Figure 2.2 in Chapter 2 of this book.

In addition, a licensee serving in the capacity of presumed buyer agent must disclose that fact at least orally to any seller or the agent of any seller being contacted.

Licensees provide all prospective buyers of a listed property a copy of the previously prepared Property Condition Disclosure and Disclaimer Statement at the time of showing that property. See Figure 4.1.

They also provide the federal lead paint disclosure form for property built before January 1, 1979, that is under consideration. There is a form for rentals and a different one for sale properties. It is vitally important to use the correct one.

Failure to provide required disclosures may enable buyers to rescind contracts. Maryland Real Estate Commission regulations state that creating such potential situations by failing to see to it that sellers present disclosure forms is a breach of fiduciary duty for which a licensee can be disciplined.

LISTING AGREEMENT PROPERTY INFORMATION

In agency agreements for the sale of a property, the age of the house, area of the lot, zoning of the property, taxes, and other detailed property information should appear in the portion of listing agreements that will be published. If accurate data are not available from the owner, the listing licensee should obtain correct data from public records or personal inspection.

Estimates of such information and "educated guesses" are totally unacceptable.

Listing licensees should also examine any existing house location survey of the property, notice what information it shows regarding property lines and improvements, and determine if it is thorough and up-to-date. Accurate information responsibly presented in the listing reduces chances for confusion and uncertainty when the property is shown and a contract offer prepared.

When describing the condition of the property in remarks distributed through the multiple listing service (MLS), licensees must be careful not to say anything that buyers may later consider misrepresentation. Licensees must also take care not to insert information into the MLS that betrays sellers' confidentiality. *This obligation of confidentiality does not extend to material facts.*

Material Facts

To prevent error and misrepresentation, the Commission's *Code of Ethics* requires that licensees make reasonable efforts to discover all *material facts* about each property they list. A material fact includes any negative information about a property that is not readily visible to or discoverable by a prudent purchaser and that would tend to discourage such a purchaser from going forward with a purchase. The Brokers Act requires that licensees disclose such information that they know, *or should know*, to each prospective buyer.

Figure 4.1 Property Disclosure and Disclaimer Statement (Page 1 of 4)

MARYLAND RESIDENTIAL PROPERTY DISCLOSURE AND DISCLAIMER STATEMENT

Property Address: _____

Legal Description: _____

NOTICE TO SELLER AND PURCHASER

Section 10-702 of the Real Property Article, *Annotated Code of Maryland*, requires the owner of certain residential real property to furnish to the purchaser either (a) a RESIDENTIAL PROPERTY DISCLAIMER STATEMENT stating that the owner is selling the property "as is" and makes no representations or warranties as to the condition of the property or any improvements on the real property, except as otherwise provided in the contract of sale, or (b) a RESIDENTIAL PROPERTY DISCLOSURE STATEMENT disclosing defects or other information about the condition of the real property actually known by the owner. Certain transfers of residential property are excluded from this requirement (see the exemptions listed below).

10-702. EXEMPTIONS. The following are specifically excluded from the provisions of §10-702:

1. The initial sale of single family residential real property:
    A. that has never been occupied; or
    B. for which a certificate of occupancy has been issued within 1 year before the seller and buyer enter into a contract of sale;
2. A transfer that is exempt from the transfer tax under §13-207 of the Tax-Property Article, except land installment contracts of sales under §13-207(a) (11) of the Tax-Property Article and options to purchase real property under §13-207(a)(12) of the Tax-Property Article;
3. A sale by a lender or an affiliate or subsidiary of a lender that acquired the real property by foreclosure or deed in lieu of foreclosure;
4. A sheriff's sale, tax sale, or sale by foreclosure, partition, or by court appointed trustee;
5. A transfer by a fiduciary in the course of the administration of a decedent's estate, guardianship, conservatorship, or trust;
6. A transfer of single family residential real property to be converted by the buyer into use other than residential use or to be demolished; or
7. A sale of unimproved real property.

MARYLAND RESIDENTIAL PROPERTY DISCLOSURE STATEMENT

NOTICE TO OWNERS: Complete and sign this statement only if you elect to disclose defects or other information about the condition of the property actually known by you; otherwise, sign the Residential Property Disclaimer Statement. You may wish to obtain professional advice or inspections of the property; however, you are not required to undertake or provide any independent investigation or inspection of the property in order to make the disclosure set forth below. The disclosure is based on your personal knowledge of the condition of the property at the time of the signing of this statement.

NOTICE TO PURCHASERS: The information provided is the representation of the Owners and is based upon the actual knowledge of Owners as of the date noted. Disclosure by the Owners is not a substitute for an inspection by an independent home inspection company, and you may wish to obtain such an inspection. The information contained in this statement is not a warranty by the Owners as to the condition of the property of which the Owners have no knowledge or other conditions of which the Owners have no actual knowledge.

How long have you owned the property? _____

Property System: Water, Sewage, Heating & Air Conditioning (Answer all that apply)

Water Supply	❑ Public	❑ Well	❑ Other _____		
Sewage Disposal	❑ Public	❑ Septic System approved for _____ (# bedrooms)			
Garbage Disposal	❑ Yes	❑ No			
Dishwasher	❑ Yes	❑ No			
Heating	❑ Oil	❑ Natural Gas	❑ Electric	❑ Heat Pump Age ____	❑ Other _____
Air Conditioning	❑ Oil	❑ Natural Gas	❑ Electric	❑ Heat Pump Age ____	❑ Other _____
Hot Water	❑ Oil	❑ Natural Gas	❑ Electric Capacity _____ Age ____		❑ Other _____

FORM: DLLR/REC/P/10-1-01Rev

Provided by the Maryland Real Estate Commission

Figure 4.1 Property Disclosure and Disclaimer Statement (Page 2 of 4)

Please indicate your actual knowledge with respect to the following:

1. Foundation: Any settlement or other problems?   ❑ Yes   ❑ No   ❑ Unknown
Comments:_____

2. Basement: Any leaks or evidence of moisture? ❑ Yes ❑ No ❑ Unknown ❑ Does Not Apply
Comments:_____

3. Roof: Any leaks or evidence of moisture?   ❑ Yes   ❑ No   ❑ Unknown
    Type of Roof:_____Age_____
Comments:_____
    Is there any existing fire retardant treated plywood? ❑ Yes ❑ No ❑ Unknown
Comments:_____

4. Other Structural Systems, including exterior walls and floors:
Comments:_____
    Any defects (structural or otherwise)? ❑ Yes ❑ No ❑ Unknown
Comments:_____

5. Plumbing system: Is the system in operating condition? ❑ Yes ❑ No ❑ Unknown
Comments:_____

6. Heating Systems: Is heat supplied to all finished rooms? ❑ Yes ❑ No ❑ Unknown
Comments:_____
    Is the system in operating condition? ❑ Yes ❑ No ❑ Unknown
Comments:_____

7. Air Conditioning System: Is cooling supplied to all finished rooms?❑Yes ❑ No ❑ Unknown ❑ Does Not Apply
Comments:_____
    Is the system in operating condition? ❑ Yes ❑ No ❑ Unknown ❑ Does Not Apply
Comments:_____

8. Electric Systems: Are there any problems with electrical fuses, circuit breakers, outlets or wiring?
    ❑ Yes   ❑ No.   ❑ Unknown
Comments:_____
    Will the smoke detectors provide an alarm in the event of a power outage? ❑Yes ❑ No ❑ Does Not Apply
Comments:_____

9. Septic Systems: Is the septic system functioning properly? ❑ Yes ❑ No ❑ Unknown ❑ Does Not Apply
    When was the system last pumped? Date_____ ❑ Unknown
Comments:_____

10. Water Supply: Any problem with water supply?   ❑ Yes   ❑ No   ❑ Unknown
Comments:_____
    Home water treatment system: ❑ Yes ❑ No ❑ Unknown
Comments:_____
    Fire sprinkler system: ❑ Yes ❑ No ❑ Unknown ❑ Does Not Apply
Comments:_____
    Are the systems in operating condition? ❑ Yes ❑ No ❑ Unknown
Comments:_____

11. Insulation:
    In exterior walls?   ❑ Yes   ❑ No   ❑Unknown
    In ceiling/attic?   ❑ Yes   ❑ No   ❑ Unknown
    In any other areas?   ❑ Yes   ❑ No   Where? _____
Comments:_____

12. Exterior Drainage: Does water stand on the property for more than 24 hours after a heavy rain?
    ❑ Yes   ❑ No   ❑ Unknown
Comments_____
    Are gutters and downspouts in good repair? ❑ Yes ❑ No ❑ Unknown
Comments:_____

Figure 4.1 Property Disclosure and Disclaimer Statement (Page 3 of 4)

13. Wood-destroying inspects: Any infestation and/or prior damage? ❑ Yes　　　　❑ No　　　　❑ Unknown
Comments:_____

| | Any treatments or repairs? ❑ Yes | ❑ No | ❑ Unknown |
| | Any warranties? ❑ Yes | ❑ No | ❑ Unknown |

Comments:_____

14. Are there any hazardous or regulated materials (including, but not limited to, licensed landfills, asbestos, radon gas, lead-based paint, underground storage tanks, or other contamination) on the property? ❑ Yes ❑ No ❑Unknown
If yes, specify below
Comments:_____

15. Are there any zoning violations, nonconforming uses, violation of building restrictions or setback requirements or any recorded or unrecorded easement, except for utilities, on or affecting the property? ❑ Yes ❑ No ❑ Unknown
If yes, specify below
Comments:_____

16. Is the property located in a flood zone, conservation area, wetland area, Chesapeake Bay critical area or Designated Historic District?
　　　　❑ Yes　　　　❑ No　　　　❑ Unknown　　　　If yes, specify below
Comments:_____

17. Is the property subject to any restriction imposed by a Home Owners Association or any other type of community association?　　❑
Yes　　　　❑ No　　　　❑ Unknown　　　　If yes, specify below
Comments:_____

18. Are there any other material defects affecting the physical condition of the property? ❑ Yes ❑ No ❑ Unknown
Comments:_____

NOTE: Owner(s) may wish to disclose the condition of other buildings on the property on a separate RESIDENTIAL PROPERTY DISCLOSURE STATEMENT.

The owner(s) acknowledge having carefully examined this statement, including any comments, and verify that it is complete and accurate as of the date signed. The owner(s) further acknowledge that they have been informed of their rights and obligations under §10-702 of the Maryland Real Property Article.

Owner _____　　Date _____

Owner _____　　Date _____

The purchaser(s) acknowledge receipt of a copy of this disclosure statement and further acknowledge that they have been informed of their rights and obligations under §10-702 of the Maryland Real Property Article.

Purchaser _____　　Date _____

Purchaser _____　　Date _____

Figure 4.1 Property Disclosure and Disclaimer Statement (Page 4 of 4)

MARYLAND RESIDENTIAL PROPERTY DISCLAIMER STATEMENT

NOTICE TO OWNER(S): Sign this statement only if you elect to sell the property without representation and warranties as to its condition, except as otherwise provided in the contract of sale; otherwise, complete and sign the RESIDENTIAL PROPERTY DISCLOSURE STATEMENT.

The undersigned owner(s) of the real property described above make no representations or warranties as to the condition of the real property or any improvements thereon, and the purchaser will be receiving the real property "as is" with all defects which may exist, except as otherwise provided in the real estate contract of sale. The owner(s) acknowledge having carefully examined this statement and further acknowledge that they have been informed of their rights and obligations under §10-702 of the Maryland Real Property Article.

Owner _____   Date_____

Owner_____   Date_____

The purchaser(s) acknowledge receipt of a copy of this disclaimer statement and further acknowledge that they have been informed of their rights and obligations under §10-702 of the Maryland Real Property Article.

Purchaser _____   Date_____

Purchaser _____   Date_____

Page 4 of 4

FORM: DLLR/REC/P/10-1-01Rev

Stigmatized Property

A licensee may not be held personally liable for failure to disclose that an owner or occupant of the property is, was, or is suspected of being infected with human immunodeficiency virus (HIV) or diagnosed with acquired immunodeficiency syndrome (AIDS).

Moreover, Maryland statutes declare that the occurrence of a homicide, suicide, natural death, accidental death, or felony on a property is not a material fact that sellers or their agents are required to disclose. Therefore, failure to disclose them is not a basis for disciplinary action by the Commission or for a civil suit.

A licensee needs the express permission of sellers to reveal any of these matters to prospective purchasers or their agents, because such disclosure might impede the sale of the listed property. Notice that, even when sellers have given permission to answer questions about these matters, under the Brokers Act, licensees need not volunteer the information as they would in the case of material facts. In order to meet the requirement of truthfulness, they must answer prospects' questions about these matters when given sellers' permission.

RESIDENTIAL PROPERTY DISCLOSURE AND DISCLAIMER

At the time a listing agreement is prepared and executed, another important document is completed *by the sellers*. This instrument affects all parties to a sales transaction. It is the Residential Property Disclosure and Disclaimer Statement, which was presented in Figure 4.1. On this form, sellers choose whether to disclose the condition of a large number of physical features of the listed property. If they choose to make such disclosure, they should *complete* the form.

A completed form is one in which sellers respond to every inquiry on the Statement, even if only to say "unknown" or "not applicable." A form with one missing response causes the seller not to meet the obligations imposed by law. It also enables the buyer to rescind the contract in the same way as if they had not been given any Disclosure/Disclaimer Form at all.

If they choose not to disclose, sellers complete the portion of the form that makes this refusal and state that they are selling the property "as is." Contrary to popular belief, use of the term *as is* does not free the sellers or their agents from the need to make *voluntary disclosure of material facts*.

Either disclosing or disclaiming may be more appropriate under certain market conditions—such as a "buyers' market" or a "sellers' market"—but licensees should not coach sellers in this choice. They should certainly not suggest use of the disclaimer as a means of withholding material facts.

The author strongly suggests that to avoid assuming unwarranted liability, the licensee not help the sellers complete the Disclosure and Disclaimer Statement. Rather, advise sellers to seek any guidance needed for this task from legal counsel and/or other technical professionals. The responses are to be the representations of the owners, not the licensee.

Listing agents should obtain from sellers completed Maryland Residential Property Disclosure and Disclaimer Statements at the time of taking listings. Listing licensees must inform sellers of their rights and obligations arising from this form, which is required in sales of residential properties of four or fewer single family units. (There are seven situations in which single-family properties being sold do not require the use of the form. These limited situations are listed on the preprinted Disclosure and Disclaimer Statement.)

Duty to Inform Buyers about Disclosure/ Disclaimer Form

When buyers are not represented by an agent, listing *licensees working with prospective buyers* must inform them of their rights and obligations with respect to the Property Disclosure and Disclaimer Statement.

The duty to make such disclosure falls upon *cooperating agents when listed properties are sold by other firms.* The rights and obligations of all parties are listed right in this form. The Broker Act requires the Commission to prepare this form and require its use by all brokerage firms in this State.

As of October 1, 2001, the Commission distributed a revised Disclosure/Disclaimer form that refers to hardwired and battery operated smoke detectors. This reference was mandated by the State Legislature in its Year 2001 Session. *Licensees are urged to use the most current form.* Failure to do so will likely expose seller-clients to the risk of rescission of sales contracts.

When listing licensees learn that prospective purchasers are planning to make an offer, they must make every effort to provide them with the Disclosure and Disclaimer Statement in a timely manner. This can be done personally or through the buyers' broker.

When listing agents do not know in advance that an offer is forthcoming, they should present the completed Disclosure and Disclaimer Statement to the purchasers or their agent immediately when an offer is produced. The purchasers can then reconsider their offer in the light of the Disclosure and Disclaimer Statement before releasing the offer for presentation.

If purchasers receive the Disclosure and Disclaimer Statement before or upon entering into the contract, they may not rescind the contract of sale based upon the information contained in the Disclosure and Disclaimer Statement.

Purchasers who do not receive this Disclosure and Disclaimer Statement before they enter into a sales contract retain the right to rescind the contract for five days after they do receive the form, until they apply for a loan, or until they occupy the property, whichever is earliest.

If purchasers never get a Disclosure and Disclaimer Statement and are never warned by a lender of the loss of their right to rescind, they can, in theory, rescind at any time before settlement or before presettlement occupancy.

TERMINATION OF AGREEMENT

The law sets no minimum or maximum time periods for agency agreements. The term of such an agreement is negotiable between client and broker. Every listing and every buyer representation agreement must contain a definite termination date on which it will end without further notice from either party. Automatic extension provisions violate this law.

Unless the agency agreement states to the contrary, licensees have no further obligations or duties to clients after termination, expiration, or completion of performance of the brokerage relationship except to account for all trust monies and to keep confidential all personal and financial information about the clients or other matters that clients request be kept confidential.

Death of an owner in severalty would normally terminate a listing agreement by operation of law. However, death of one owner, when a married couple has held title as tenants by the entirety, may not necessarily terminate a listing. It is prudent to have the language of a listing form reviewed by a firm's legal counsel in order to clarify whether such an agency agreement will be binding upon a deceased seller's estate.

Licensees may withdraw from representing either buyer-clients or seller-clients who refuse to consent to disclosed dual agency and to terminate brokerage relationships with them. However, the Brokers Act states that dual agents, simply by making required disclosures of the existence of dual agency, have not thereby terminated their brokerage relationships.

In this State, a trustee sale, foreclosure sale, tax sale, or condemnation proceeding will generally terminate a listing.

COMMISSIONS

Brokers (typically working through licensees affiliated with them) negotiate their compensation with the sellers in each transaction. The amount or rate of commission charged in a transaction is not set by any law, regulation, association, or board. Client and broker negotiate it. To suggest otherwise is a violation of federal and state antitrust laws and can bring severe penalties. Commission splits between and among brokers in cooperating situations are similarly negotiable. Commission schedules within brokerage firms are established by negotiation between the broker and the affiliates licensed under them.

The Brokers Act specifically states that payments or promises to pay compensation to licensees do not determine that brokerage (agency) relationships have been created or exist nor do they create brokerage relationships. Contrary to a long-held notion, *those who pay agents are not made clients of those agents just because of the payment.*

Sellers typically pay brokerage commissions at settlement, using proceeds arising from the settlement. Brokers and home owners may, however, agree at the time of listing that if settlement does not take place, no commission is due.

Maryland law indicates that, unless there is a previous agreement to the contrary, listing brokers have earned their commissions when sellers accept and sign enforceable contracts of sale. Recent court cases have debated the definition of the term *enforceable*.

According to the Brokers Act, persons performing brokerage services may not maintain an action (sue) for commission unless they had authority to provide those services at the time both of offering to perform and of performing the services.

THE DUAL AGENCY OPTION

Licensees procuring a listing should introduce the sellers to the possibility of a potential buyer also being represented by their company. They should explain the concept of "intra-company agents" as outlined in the Brokers Act and seek the sellers' decision as to whether they will accept dual agency. Their response can be reflected in the provisions of the listing agreement itself. The student should review the discussions in Chapter 2 of this book and the one earlier in this chapter.

BROKER COOPERATION

The Code of Ethics states that brokers shall cooperate with other brokers on property listed exclusively by their firms whenever it is in the interest of their clients. The cooperating companies may then share commissions on a previously agreed-upon basis. Negotiations concerning property subject to exclusive listings must be carried on solely through listing brokers.

In the listing interview, the broker must present to sellers the Agency Relationship Disclosure required by the Commission. See Chapter 2 of this book. At that time, the

sellers should decide what relationship(s) they are authorizing with cooperating real estate firms: cooperation with subagency, dealing with another brokerage without subagency—which occurs when a prospective purchaser is represented by a buyer broker—or whichever arises.

Sellers should be made to understand that licensees from other companies who represent a purchaser will not be representing them. Sellers should also decide if—and how—the commission they pay will be shared with another company if when dealing with another brokerage no subagency occurs. Many listing forms allow sellers to authorize their broker to work with and compensate buyer brokers by sharing part of the brokerage fee.

On the listing data form brokers submit to the multiple-listing service, they should show how sellers have decided to choose from among their representation options.

SIGNATURES

When all relevant data have been entered on the listing form, all persons who have an ownership interest in the property must sign it. Alternatively, persons who have proper authorization from the owners—such as attorneys-in-fact, acting under a properly drafted power of attorney—may sign the listing for them. Competent legal counsel should be consulted in such situations. It is the responsibility of the listing agent to make sure that the signatures of all required parties are on a listing. A listing becomes effective on the date of the last required signature.

When separated or divorcing couples holding title as tenants by the entireties wish to list property, the author recommends consultation with the attorneys representing the parties. Because divorced parties may each retain interests, both their signatures likely will be necessary for an enforceable listing.

When sellers are corporations, trustees, guardians of minors, or personal representatives, documentation of the authority of persons signing the listing is often required. A licensee faced with such situations is urged to seek competent legal guidance.

MULTIPLE-LISTING SERVICES AND COMMON SOURCE INFORMATION COMPANIES

The Brokers Act states that licensees who make use of common source information companies, such as multiple-listing services, are not considered to be agents of those services or companies simply by virtue of their use of data from those companies. Licensees who participate in such companies are not thereby considered to be the agents or subagents of any client of another broker by reason of such participation. These information services may not restrict access to their services to licensees based on the level of their licenses.

Several Boards and Associations of REALTORS® offer multiple-listing services serving specific geographical areas. Listing contract forms and numerous addenda are available from local real estate boards, associations, and multiple-listing services for the exclusive use of their members.

There are often special forms for different types of property, such as residential for sale; commercial/industrial for sale or lease; income property; farms; commercial office rental; residential lots; unimproved land; condominiums; cooperatives; and businesses. Although the brokerage industry has produced statewide standardized forms, licensees should be alert to differences that still exist between the standardized forms and the forms unique to certain brokerage firms.

The word REALTOR® and its related logo appear in the printed portion of many MLS listing and other contract forms. Licensees who use any form that bears the name of an organization of which they are not members violate the Brokers Act.

LOCAL REQUIREMENTS

Licensees should familiarize themselves with and conform to all relevant county and municipal requirements in areas where they provide real estate services. For instance, Baltimore County zoning regulations require "development plan notice and conveyances" to be provided to any purchaser of a home in any area covered by an approved development plan. In other counties, air traffic patterns are part of the information that prospective purchasers must receive. In 1998, Montgomery County greatly restricted the use of signs. That county has established special licensing requirements for persons who wish to post any signs in residential areas within that jurisdiction.

OUT-OF-STATE LISTINGS

Maryland licensees are not authorized to show out-of-state property properly listed and advertised in Maryland unless they also have valid licenses issued in the state where the property is located and comply with all laws of that state.

QUESTIONS

---

1. Broker use of which type of residential listing agreement is illegal in Maryland?

   a. "Net"
   b. Exclusive-agency
   c. Open
   d. Exclusive-right-to-sell

2. A seller should complete the Property Disclosure and Disclaimer Statement

   a. at settlement.
   b. when an offer is received.
   c. when the property is being listed.
   d. after a sales contract has been signed.

3. When purchasers receive no property Disclosure and Disclaimer Statement, either before, at, or after entering into a purchase agreement, the

   a. contract is void by action of law after three days.
   b. purchasers may rescind the contract before they apply for a mortgage loan.
   c. contract is voidable by the purchaser for five days.
   d. lender has five days to tell the purchaser of the right to void the agreement.

4. Sellers must receive a copy of their listing agreement

   a. if they request it.
   b. before the broker advertises the property or offers it for sale.
   c. within 15 days after acceptance by the broker.
   d. only when a buyer is found.

5. In order to show a property located in the State of Virginia which is multiple-listed with a Maryland brokerage, a Maryland licensee must

   a. hold a Virginia real estate license.
   b. be a member of Maryland's multiple-listing service.
   c. be a Maryland broker licensee.
   d. hold a multiple-state license certificate.

6. A listing agreement form published by a multiple-listing service may be used by any

   a. broker or salesperson licensed by the Commission.
   b. member of any Board or Association of REALTORS®.
   c. licensed member of the organization that operates that listing system.
   d. licensee.

7. A listing on Maryland residential property

   a. may contain an automatic renewal provision.
   b. may be parol.
   c. must be in writing and signed by all parties.
   d. may leave the commission fee to be negotiated at the time an offer is made.

8. Purchasers who receive the residential Disclosure and Disclaimer Statement before signing their contract offer may

   a. rescind the contract at any time up to three days after signing.
   b. rescind the contract at any time up to five days after signing.
   c. rescind at any time prior to settlement or to taking occupancy.
   d. not rescind the contract based on any facts the statement discloses.

9. The amount or rate of commission on a real estate sale

   a. must be stated in the listing agreement.
   b. is established by the Commission.
   c. is established by the local real estate Board or Association of REALTORS®.
   d. is established by law.

10. In Maryland, a residential listing agreement

   a. does not create an agency.
   b. may be oral.
   c. must be in writing.
   d. need not contain a definite termination date.

5

Interests in Real Estate

OVERVIEW

Freeholds in fee simple absolute, fee simple determinable, fee simple conditional, and life estates—as well as future interests, such as remainder and reversion—are recognized in Maryland.

Leasehold estates for years, from period to period, at will, and at sufferance are also recognized. In addition, a ground rent system, as described in Chapter 13 of this book, exists in some areas.

Concerning legal life estates, both dower and curtesy have been abolished, and there is no homestead exemption in Maryland.

EASEMENT BY PRESCRIPTION AND ADVERSE POSSESSION

An easement by *prescription* may be acquired in Maryland when an adverse user uses another's land for the required **(prescribed)** 20 years. Notice where the term *prescriptive* comes from. Similarly, adverse possession can also ripen into a claim for ownership after 20 years, not only of open, hostile, continuous, and notorious

occupancy, but also under *claim of right* or *color of title*.

By requiring such claim or color, Maryland rejects *squatters' rights*. Squatters have no claim to land other than squatting on it. Claim of right or color of title arises in a situation where an innocent buyer is deeded property by a person thought to be its owner but later is proved not to be. Such an innocent buyer is said to be a "BFP"—a *bona fide purchaser* for value. Consult competent legal counsel in cases involving related matters.

RIPARIAN RIGHTS

Owners of real estate bordering a navigable body of water in Maryland have the common-law right to make a landing, wharf, or pier for their own use or for the use of the public. The right to make such an improvement is also subject to state and federal rules and regulations. The owner who makes such improvement owns the pier over the water but not the water beneath it.

Title to land beyond the mean (average) high-water mark of navigable waters, as well as to the waters themselves, belongs to the public. Regardless of the property descriptions in owners' deeds, they are only legal owners of property as far as the mean *high-water mark*. High-water mark is defined as the highest elevation of water in the usual, regular, periodic ebb and flow of the tide, not including storms or floods.

AGRICULTURAL LAND PRESERVATION EASEMENT

The Maryland Agricultural Land Preservation Foundation exists to purchase easements on land in certain areas for the purpose of restricting land to agricultural use. Details are contained in the *Agriculture* Article of the Annotated Code of Maryland. The state is actively purchasing development rights and seeking to limit residential subdivision of agricultural land. The purchases are funded in large part by the revenues produced for the State by its real estate transfer tax. Further discussion is found in Chapter 14 of this book.

QUESTIONS

1. Easements to restrict land to agricultural use may be purchased by the

    a. Maryland Land Development Corporation.
    b. Maryland Department of Assessments & Taxation.
    c. Maryland Agricultural Land Preservation Foundation.
    d. Maryland Environmental Department.

2. A person may acquire an easement by prescription in Maryland land over another person's property

    a. after 20 years' continuous use.
    b. after 25 years' intermittent use.
    c. after 30 years' continuous use.
    d. only if it is an easement by necessity.

3. Which of the following is recognized in Maryland?

    a. Dower
    b. Homestead exemption
    c. Curtesy
    d. Easement by prescription

4. Jefferson Thomas owns several acres of land in Maryland. His property is divided by a navigable river. Thomas has the right to

    a. build a pier on one of the riverbanks, subject to state and federal laws.
    b. construct a dam across the river to divert the waters into an artificial lake on his property.
    c. construct a wharf without state approval.
    d. make use only of the dry land.

6

How Ownership Is Held

OVERVIEW

Maryland law recognizes ownership in severalty and various forms of co-ownership: tenancy in common, joint tenancy, tenancy by the entirety, partnership, and trust, as described in the principal text. It also provides for condominium, time-share, and cooperative ownership.

CO-OWNERSHIP

Unless the deed clearly specifies otherwise, a conveyance of Maryland real estate to two or more persons creates tenancy in common. To create a joint tenancy, it is necessary to use such words as " . . . to Fred Donaldson and Sam Roberts, as joint tenants and not as tenants in common." One might also add the phrase " . . . with right of survivorship."

A deed to a husband and wife is presumed to create a tenancy by the entirety unless it specifies tenancy in common or joint tenancy.

In Maryland, only a legally married husband and wife can own property as tenants by the entirety. (Common-law marriages cannot be established in Maryland but are recognized as valid if established in other jurisdictions that recognize and permit them.) Both husband and wife must sign a deed to convey property they hold as tenants by the entirety. Neither spouse who owns Maryland real property as a tenant by the entirety may petition a court for its partition.

Tenants by the entirety may grant their property back to themselves as either tenants in common or joint tenants. Or they can grant the property to one or the other of them. They can do this without having ownership pass through the hands of a third ("straw") party. Legal assistance is still important.

A tenancy by the entirety is terminated by the death of either spouse with the survivor holding the property in severalty. Notice that *severalty* appropriately describes the condition of being *severed* (separated) from others—and owning by oneself.

Although Maryland is not a community property state, the Property Disposition in Divorce and Annulment statute has much the same effect as community property rulings in other states at the time of divorce.

Upon divorce or other legal termination of the marriage, tenants by the entirety are considered tenants in common, by operation of law. But when divorce occurs, causing the former couple's ownership to change in this way, the court may still prevent any partition proceeding (division of the property by one against the other's will) for a period not to exceed three years.

Normally, a tenancy in common, like joint tenancy, can be partitioned at any time by one tenant (owner) without the agreement of the other. The ban on partition after divorce can occur if the property is to be occupied as the "family home" by the custodial spouse together with any minor children.

The provisions of the Uniform Partnership Act apply in Maryland. The statute allows a corporation (as well as an individual) to become a member of a partnership. Also, the real estate investment trust (REIT), a form of unincorporated trust or association, has been recognized in Maryland since 1963. The procedures for forming or dealing with a REIT are legally complex. Brokerage licensees in any way involved with a REIT should strongly urge the use of legal counsel. They, themselves, may be required by law to hold securities licenses to engage in such activities. The Maryland Securities Act, found in the *Maryland Corporations and Associations* Article, requires a securities license for persons engaged in selling securities that are real estate-related.

CONDOMINIUMS

Detailed provisions of the Condominium Act are contained in Title 11 of the *Real Property* Article of the Annotated Code of Maryland. Any licensee involved with condominium sales or development should obtain a complete copy of the law or seek competent legal advice.

Persons developing and selling condominiums are required to hold real estate broker licenses and are therefore subject to the provisions of the Brokers Act. The Condominium Act is enforced by the Division of Consumer Protection in the Office of the Attorney General.

Definitions

A **condominium** is a property subject to a condominium *regime* (plan of organization). It is governed by a **council of unit owners,** which is either an incorporated or an unincorporated nonstock corporation. Persons who subject their property to a condominium regime are called *developers*. A condominium **unit** is a space described in three dimensions in the declaration and on the condominium plat.

Common elements are all the parts of a condominium other than the units. There are two types. **Limited common elements** are identified in the declaration or on the condominium plat as reserved for the exclusive use of one or more, but less than all, of the unit owners. **General common elements** are all the common elements except the limited common elements. The expenses and profits of the council of unit owners are called **common expenses and common profits**.

Converting Property to a Condominium

Those who wish to create condominium ownership in real property must expressly declare their intention to do so by recording a declaration, bylaws, and the condominium plat. These documents must comply with the requirements stated in the statute. Property is then said to be under a *condominium regime*, and the owners are regarded as its developer.

The declaration is indexed on the county records under both the name of the developer and the name of the condominium. The condominium regime must be registered with the Secretary of State before a condominium unit may be sold or offered for sale. The declaration subsequently may be amended within certain limits by the written consent of 80 percent of the unit owners.

Public Offering Statement

A contract for the *initial* sale of a residential condominium unit to a member of the general public is not enforceable by the seller until the purchaser is given a copy of the Public Offering Statement registered with the Secretary of State.

Buyers may make written rescission of a purchase contract, without stating any reason, *within 15 days* after receipt of the Public Offering Statement. They may also rescind that agreement *within 5 days following* receipt of any later amendments

to the Statement made by the seller. Buyers who rescind within these time limits are entitled to prompt return of all deposits.

Buyers who proceed to settlement lose their rights to terminate. However, sellers remain liable to buyers for one year for any damages suffered as a result of the sellers' failure to disclose material facts or their making any false or misleading statements. The purchasers' right to rescind or cancel under the Condominium Act may not be waived in the contract of sale.

Conversion of Residential Rental Facility

Before a residential rental facility is converted to condominium ownership, the tenant must be given a notice in the form prescribed by law. This notice is given after registration with the Secretary of State, along with the Public Offering Statement.

A tenant may not be required to vacate the premises prior to the expiration of 180 days from the giving of notice, except for breach of the lease. However, the tenant may terminate the lease, without penalty for termination, by providing at least 30 days' written notice to the landlord after receiving such notice of conversion.

Ownership of Unit and Interest in Common Elements

In addition to exclusive ownership of a condominium unit, each unit owner has a right to share a defined percentage of the undivided interest in the common elements of the property. The unit owners' undivided interest in the common elements cannot be partitioned or separated from the unit to which that percentage is assigned. All unit owners in a condominium are members of the council of unit owners. It is considered a legal entity even if unincorporated.

Organization: Declaration and Bylaws; Termination

The recorded declaration must contain at least the name by which the condominium is to be identified, including or followed by the phrase "a condominium;" a description of the land and buildings, with a statement of the owners' intent to establish a condominium regime; a general description and number of each unit, its perimeters, location, and other identifying data; a general description of the common elements and the units to which their use is restricted initially; the percentage interest in common areas related to each unit; and the number of votes at meetings of the council of unit owners that go with each unit. These related common elements and voting rights are *appurtenances*—things of value that attach to a property.

At the least, the bylaws must express the form of administration, whether the council is to be incorporated, whether the council's duties may be delegated to a board of directors or manager, and what powers the owners have in their selection and removal; the council's mailing address; the procedure to be followed in council meetings; and the manner of assessing and collecting unit owners' respective shares of the common expenses. By law, the council of unit owners must be established within 60 days after the initial sale of units representing 50 percent of votes in the condominium.

Unless a higher percentage is required in the bylaws, the **Bylaws** may be amended by the affirmative vote of unit owners having at least 66⅔ percent of the votes in the council of unit owners. Addition of and amendments to the **Rules** require 50 percent.

Unless taken by eminent domain, a condominium regime may be terminated only by agreement of at least 80 percent of the unit owners, *or more if so specified in the declaration*. Upon termination of the regime, and *unless otherwise provided in the deed of termination*, the unit owners become tenants in common, with each owning an interest equal to the former percentage interest in the common elements.

Common Expenses, Taxes, Assessments, and Liens

Unit owners are responsible for their percentage share of the common expenses of the council of unit owners. Assessments against unit owners for common expenses become liens on the unit. This lien may be foreclosed in the same manner as a mortgage or deed of trust if foreclosure is brought within three years of recording the lien.

If the condominium is intended for residential use, the council of unit owners is required to maintain property insurance on common elements and units and comprehensive general liability insurance, including medical, in amounts set by the declaration, master deed, or the council.

Each unit is taxed as a separate and distinct entity on the county tax records. A delinquent tax on a specific unit will not affect the title to any other unit on which all taxes and assessments are paid.

Under the Consumer Protection Act of the *Commercial Law* Article of the Annotated Code of Maryland, certain condominium disputes will be investigated by the Division of Consumer Protection of the Office of the Attorney General, which is authorized to administer a program of voluntary mediation of condominium disputes involving unit owners, boards of directors, and/or councils of unit owners.

Resale of Unit

A contract for the resale of a unit by a unit owner other than a developer is not enforceable unless that contract contains, in conspicuous type, a notice in the form specified in the Condominium Act (Section 11-135). The unit owner is required to furnish four things to the purchaser not less than 15 days prior to the closing:

1. A copy of the declaration (other than the plat)

2. The bylaws

3. The rules or regulations of the condominium

4. A certificate containing statements concerning such things as monthly expenses, proposed capital improvements, fees payable by unit owners, financial statements of the condominium, and insurance coverage.

These contracts should contain the required clauses and disclosures to ensure compliance with the Act. Some local real estate boards and associations make available to their members a "Condominium Contract of Sale" and "Condominium Listing Contract." *The contract for resale is voidable by the purchaser for seven days* after the certificate (#4 above) has been provided or until conveyance of the unit has been made, whichever comes first.

TIME-SHARE OWNERSHIP

There are two principal forms of time-sharing: the right-to-use (time-share *license*) method and the purchase-of-fractional-interest (time-share *estate*) method.

In the right-to-use (license) form, owners of interests in vacation properties, including condominiums, hotels, motels, marinas, and boats, may trade their vacation periods and facilities either directly or indirectly through space banks, that are maintained by firms established to help time-sharers swap vacation facilities.

In the time-share estate, widely used in Maryland in the Eastern Shore and western areas, the customers buy fractional interests, for designated time periods, in a resort condominium, either on a rental (estate for years) or permanent (fee simple) basis. The fee simple buyer receives a deed for a share of the property. Mortgages or deeds of trust are accepted for the unpaid portion of the purchase price. Contracts, settlements, and all other matters are similar to purchases of condominium units.

The State Securities Commission requires that anyone offering part ownership or interest in condominiums must disclose the inherent risks of such an investment. Limited-use resort securities must comply with the registration and antifraud requirements of the State Securities Act.

The Time-Sharing Act

The Time-Sharing Act, Title 11A of the *Real Property Article*, provides for the creation, sale, lease, management, and termination of time-share interests; registration of certain documents; registration of time-share developers with the Commission; and certain bonding requirements. Certain advertising and promotional practices are prohibited. Developers are required to prepare Public Offering Statements describing time-share projects regulated by the Secretary of State. Certain protections for purchasers are provided, such as sales contract cancellation periods and disclosures of information, warranties, and exchange programs. Terms generally relating to time-share interests in real estate are defined. The following sections highlight some main points of the Act. Any licensee involved in time-share sales or development should obtain a complete copy of the Act or seek competent legal advice. Time-share developers and persons selling time-share estates are also subject to the provisions of the License Law.

Creating a Time-Share

Time-shares may be created in any condominium unit in existence before January 1, 1985, unless prohibited by a project instrument (condominium document).

Preventing Creation of a Time-Share

The owners of at least 34 percent of the units in a condominium may sign and record a land record document within the county of the project's locale, stating an intent to limit time-shares in the project. Thereafter, no person or other entity may become a developer of more than one unit in the project.

Property owners in a residential community governed by recorded covenants and restrictions may prohibit time-shares on any property subject to recorded covenants and restrictions by amending them with a vote of the owners by majority requirements of said covenants and restrictions.

Public Offering Statement

Upon or before the signing of a sales contract, the developers—or other owner-sellers—who offer time-shares for their own accounts must deliver to each purchaser a Public Offering Statement. This could apply to real estate licensees selling their own time-shares.

The requirements for disclosure under the Time-Sharing Act differ substantially from those required under the Condominium Act.

A time-share owner who is not associated with the developer of a time-share project is exempt from filing and disseminating a Public Offering Statement.

Conversions

A developer desiring to convert a building more than five years old into a time-share project is required to include an engineer's report in the Public Offering Statement and to give any tenant or subtenant at least 120 days' notice of the intention to convert the building to a time-share project.

Cancellation Rights

First purchasers of time-shares have the right to cancel the sales contract until midnight of *the tenth calendar day* following whichever occurs latest: (1) the contract date; (2) the day on which the time-share purchaser received the last of all documents required as part of the Public Offering Statement; or (3) the date on which the time-share unit meets all building requirements and is ready for occupancy, or the developer obtains a payment and performance bond and files the bond with the Commission. The right of cancellation cannot be waived.

Unlike the law concerning condominiums, *no closing on a time-share can occur until the purchaser's cancellation period has expired.* If closing is held prior to the cancellation period, the closing is voidable at the option of the purchaser for a period of one year after the expiration of the cancellation period.

Resale Disclosures

An owner selling his or her time-share is required to furnish to the purchaser before execution of the contract, transfer of title or use:

- a copy of the time-share instrument and

- a resale certificate containing the information required by the Time-Sharing Act.

The purchaser may cancel the contract to purchase at any time *within seven days* after receipt of the resale certificate without reason and without liability and have the return of any deposits made under the contract.

Deposits

All purchase money received by a developer from a purchaser must be deposited in an escrow account designed solely for that purpose with a financial institution whose accounts are insured by a government agency. The funds remain there until the end of the ten-day cancellation period or any later time provided for in the contract. Purchase money may be released to the developer, provided the developer maintains a surety bond. No claim can be made against the Real Estate Guaranty Fund if a loss is covered by that bond.

Warranties

All time-share units sold by developers have implied warranties of three years for common elements and one year for units with respect to structural components and heating and cooling systems. In addition, the developer must warrant to a purchaser of a time-share that any existing use of the time-share unit that will continue does not violate any law.

Sales Contract

The statute requires contracts for the first sale of time-shares to use specific language to disclose cancellation rights. Contracts must also show the estimated completion date of each unit and each common element as well as estimates of the time-share expenses and facility fees. All this is intended to disclose the total financial obligation being incurred by purchasers.

Exchange Programs

The Time-Sharing Act requires detailed information concerning each exchange program a developer makes available for purchasers' use. To comply with the Act, each exchange company offering an exchange program is required to file the required information with the Commission on an annual basis.

Registration

The Time-Sharing Act requires developers, with certain exceptions, to register with the Commission. A developer may not offer a time-share to the public until the developer has received a certificate of registration as a time-share developer. The developer is required to file certain documents and material with the Commission. The Time-Sharing Act gives the Commission the authority to

- issue regulations and orders consistent with the Act;

- investigate possible violations of the Act and subpoena witnesses and documents in connection with the investigations;

- bring suit against violators;

- order violators to correct conditions resulting from the violation; and

- revoke the registration of any developer who is convicted of violating the Act.

In addition, the Secretary of State is authorized to adopt regulations necessary to implement and enforce the provisions of the Act pertaining to Public Offering Statements. A violation of the Act could provide grounds for the suspension or revocation of a broker's or salesperson's license under the Brokers Act.

Project Broker

Developers are required to designate licensed real estate brokers as project brokers for each time-share project. Each time-share project is considered a separate real estate office for purposes of the Brokers Act. Any person who sells, advertises, or offers for sale any time-share must be a licensed broker, associate broker, or salesperson, or be exempt from licensure under Title 17. An unlicensed person may be employed by a developer or project broker to contact, but not solicit, prospective buyers so long as the unlicensed person

- performs only clerical tasks;

- schedules only those appointments induced by others; or

- prepares or distributes only promotional materials.

Time-Share Regulations

Regulations governing time-shares (found in COMAR 09.11.04) require that records be maintained of names and addresses of all personnel retained for sale of time-share estates, including agents, employees, and licensees whether employees or independent contractors. Records must also be made and kept of all sales transactions, of estates conveyed and encumbrances on them and of amounts of purchase money held for such sales. The Commission may require certification of such amounts by a certified public accountant. Developers must also maintain bonding in prescribed amounts for deposit monies being held.

Time-share marketing statements about the characteristics of the time-share project or estate may not be false, inaccurate, or misleading. A developer may not indicate that an improvement will be placed in a time-share project unless the developer has sufficient finances and bona fide intentions to complete the improvement. Statements used in the marketing of time-share estates located in Maryland may not induce a prospective purchaser to leave the State for the purpose of executing a contract for sale when to do so would circumvent the provisions of Maryland law. No one may advertise or represent that the Commission has approved or recommended any time-share project or estate offered for sale.

MARYLAND COOPERATIVE HOUSING CORPORATION ACT

The Maryland Cooperative Housing Act, Title 5-6B of the *Corporations and Associations* Article, Annotated Code of Maryland, provides for conditions, contracts, rights, and requirements relative to the development and sale of interests in cooperatives. Detailed provisions are contained in statutes. A member of the cooperative receives a proprietary lease, an agreement with the cooperative housing corporation that gives the member an exclusive possessory interest in a unit and a possessory interest in common with other members in that portion of a cooperative project not constituting units. It creates a legal relationship of landlord and tenant between the corporation and the member.

MARYLAND HOMEOWNERS ASSOCIATION ACT

This Act sets forth conditions, rights, and requirements regulating homeowner's associations (HOAs) in the State.

For sales contracts to be binding on purchasers, sellers must make disclosure showing that the property is subject to an HOA; listing the rights, responsibilities, and obligations of purchasers; and disclosing purchasers' rights of rescission if the Maryland Homeowners Association Act (MHAA) information is not provided to them by sellers in a timely manner. This information recites factual details pertaining to disclosures that must include liability, warranties, meetings, books, and records. Time periods for rescission vary with the number of lots in the HOA and between initial sale and resale of properties. See Section 11B in the *Real Property* Article.

NOTICE TO TENANTS— MONTGOMERY COUNTY

In Montgomery County, before execution by a tenant of a lease for an initial term of 125 days or more, the owner of any residential rental property *within any condominium or development* is required to provide to the prospective tenant—to the extent applicable—a copy of the rules, declaration, and recorded covenants and restrictions that limit or affect the use and occupancy of the property or common areas, and under which the owner and the tenant are also obligated.

CANCELLATION PERIODS

Because it is important for real estate licensees to know the cancellation periods allowed by law for various types of condominium and time-share sales contracts, they are summarized in Figure 6.1.

Figure 6.1 Cancellation Periods in Various Sale Situations

Type of Sale	Period for Cancellation	After
Condominium by Developer	Within 15 days	Receipt of Certificate
Condominium by Developer	Plus 5 Additional Days After	Receipt of Any Amendments to POS
Condominium Resale	Within 7 Days	Receipt of Resale Certificate
Time-Share by Developer	Within 10 Days	Contract, Receipt of Last Required Disclosure Document or of Occupancy Permit, Whichever is Last
Time-Share Resale	Within 7 Days	Receipt of Certificate
HOA	Varies by Number of Lots and Whether Original or Resale	n/a

QUESTIONS

1. All but which of the following forms of ownership are recognized in Maryland?

   a. Tenancy in common
   b. Community property
   c. Trust
   d. Ownership in severalty

2. In Maryland, a deed that conveys ownership to "Karen and David Maines, husband and wife," but does not specify the form of ownership

   a. automatically creates a tenancy in common.
   b. must be redrawn before the property is sold, specifying the form of ownership.
   c. creates a tenancy by the entirety.
   d. creates an ownership in severalty.

3. Which of the following is NOT true? In Maryland, a tenancy by the entirety

   a. may be held only by a husband and wife.
   b. continues after the death of one of the owners.
   c. gives each individual possession of the entire estate.
   d. may not be partitioned.

4. A time-share developer is required to

   a. register with the State Real Estate Commission.
   b. register with the State Treasurer.
   c. register with the local Board or Association of REALTORS®.
   d. be a licensed real estate broker.

5. The bylaws of a condominium can be changed or altered by

   a. the manager of the property.
   b. a two-thirds vote of the unit owners.
   c. the council of unit owners by majority vote.
   d. a simple majority of unit owners.

6. A developer who proposes to convert a residential rental facility to a condominium regime must register with the

   a. office of the Attorney General.
   b. local Board of REALTORS®.
   c. Secretary of State.
   d. Maryland Real Estate Commission.

7. Tenancy by the entirety is for

   a. husbands and wives only.
   b. cohabiting couples.
   c. any family member.
   d. tenants in common.

8. A developer selling a newly built condominium unit to an original purchaser

   a. is liable for damages as a result of misleading statements for five years after the sale.
   b. is subject to the seller's voiding the contract if the developer fails to deliver a Public Offering Statement.
   c. is protected by the doctrine of caveat emptor from liability for misleading statements.
   d. must file a Public Offering Statement with the State Real Estate Commission.

9. Purchasers of time-shares from a developer

   a. have a right to cancel the contract only if the seller has misrepresented material facts.
   b. have ten days in which to cancel the sale for any reason.
   c. must close the sale within ten days after signing the sales contract.
   d. must obtain a payment and performance bond to ensure their compliance with the contract.

10. A contract for resale of a condominium by its owner (other than its developer) is not enforceable unless the owner furnishes the buyer, not later than 15 days prior to the closing,

    a. a copy of the declaration.
    b. the rules and regulations.
    c. a statement regarding monthly expenses, proposed capital improvements, other fees, financial statements of the condominium, and insurance details.
    d. All of the above

11. Should a dispute develop between a unit owner, Board of Directors, and/or council of unit owners, parties may apply for mediation to the

    a. local Board of REALTORS®.
    b. office of the county state's attorney.
    c. office of the Attorney General.
    d. local Board of Development and Planning.

12. In purchasing a condominium, the most important document to the buyer is the declaration, which in most cases

    a. authorizes a Board of Directors to administer the condominium affairs pursuant to the bylaws and to assess the owners so as to adequately maintain the condominium.
    b. describes the condominium units and the common areas and any restrictions on their use.
    c. establishes the undivided interest percentages.
    d. All of the above

13. The condominium declaration

    a. must be recorded to place the property under a condominium regime.
    b. cannot be rescinded once it is recorded.
    c. can be changed only with the unanimous approval of the council of unit owners.
    d. must be printed in a daily newspaper before changes may be made.

7

Legal Descriptions

OVERVIEW

Two of the methods of property description presented in the student's principal text are in common use in Maryland. They are the **metes and bounds** and **recorded plat of subdivision** methods. The state was never included in the federal government's rectangular survey system.

At the very least, a description that identifies land "with reasonable certainty" is required in a contract for sale of realty. Postal address alone is usually not an adequate legal description except for such short residential leaseholds as one or two years.

EXAMPLES OF LEGAL DESCRIPTIONS USED IN CONTRACTS

Metes and Bounds

- "Beginning at an iron pipe set on the northeast side of Annapolis Street at a point located South 38° 45' East, 200 feet from where the northeast side of Annapolis Street intersects the southeast side of Giddings Avenue—all as shown on Aldridge's Revised and Corrected Plat of West Annapolis recorded among the Land Records of Anne Arundel County in JCB Liber 4, Folio 297; and running thence and at right angles to Annapolis Street, North 51° 15' East, 150 feet to a pipe; thence South 38° 45' East 50 feet to a pipe; thence South 51° 15' West, 150 feet to a pipe on the northeast side of Annapolis Street; thence with same, North 38° 45' West, 50 feet to the place of beginning."

- "That certain parcel of real estate located in Worcester County, Maryland, being on the east side of Farm Lane, north of Jerry Road, being further known as the Arthur R. Jackson property, consisting of one acre, more or less, with the improvements thereon, previously conveyed by deed of Robert Allen, grantor, recorded in FWH Liber 29, Folio 1312, the exact boundaries and acreage to be determined by means of a survey, which has been ordered to be prepared by Johnson and Landsman, surveyors, Snow Hill."

Recorded Plat of Subdivision

- "Lot #16, Block #3 of the Plat of Melville Development Corporation as surveyed by John Walmer, Catonsville, Maryland, August 15, 1968, as recorded in FWH Liber 295, Folio 1720, in the County of Ridge, State of Maryland."

SURVEY MARKERS

Surveyors are governed by the Maryland Professional Land Surveyors Act. They are licensed by the State Board for Professional Land Surveyors. The Board specifies that they use specific types of stakes, markers, monuments, or other landmarks in their work.

It is a misdemeanor—a crime less than a felony, for which a prison term of not more than one year may be imposed—to intentionally move, damage, or obliterate any markers on property belonging to another person if the marker was put in place by a civil engineer, surveyor, real estate appraiser, or members of their teams. The exception is when the marker interferes with proper use of the land. A fine of not more than $500 can be imposed upon conviction.

If there is a dispute over any boundary line or if the bounds mentioned in a document are lost, the circuit court of the county where the property is located may be petitioned to establish the boundary lines or the location of the missing bounds. These experts' fees are considered costs in the proceeding.

LOCATION DRAWINGS AND BOUNDARY SURVEYS

The Office of the Secretary of Licensing and Regulation, through its Board for Professional Land Surveyors, requires surveyors to have a signed election form requesting either a **location drawing** or a **boundary survey** from the party ordering the survey.

The boundary survey identifies property boundary lines and corners sufficiently well to establish the physical position and extent of the boundaries, including visible indications of rights that may arise from prescription or adverse possession. It is needed for an owner having a fence placed or other improvements erected. It reports that monuments have either been located or placed on the property.

A location drawing provides a plat of the property which shows the location of any improvements. It costs less than a boundary survey but is often sufficient for most residential resales and refinancing situations.

A description of each type and of its uses, limitations, and costs appears on the election form. The form electing which survey is being ordered is typically submitted by the title, settlement, or law office preparing for settlement.

SUBDIVISION PLATS

Subdividers must have plats of proposed subdivisions prepared by a licensed surveyor and approved and recorded by local authorities before offering them for sale. Reference to a recorded subdivision plat may be part of a sufficient legal description. No distances on a subdivision plat may be marked "more or less" except those lines that begin, terminate, or bind on a body of water.

QUESTIONS

1. In Maryland, reference to recorded subdivision plats

   a. is permitted in individual lot descriptions if those plats were properly recorded.
   b. must be prepared by licensed real estate brokers.
   c. need not be recorded prior to sale of the lots.
   d. need not have planning and zoning approval prior to recording.

2. A location drawing

   a. is essentially the same as a boundary survey.
   b. is appropriate for typical residential resales.
   c. costs more than a boundary survey.
   d. can properly be used for placing fences and other improvements.

3. Which of the following is most likely to be a sufficient legal description?

   a. 142 Pinehurst Road, Ocean Pines
   b. That lot fronting 100 feet on Pinehurst and being 250 feet deep
   c. That two acres, shown on attached plat of subdivision survey as prepared by Landsman & Co., surveyors of Catonsville, Maryland
   d. 1776-B Liberty St., Snow Hill, Md., being the northern half of a duplex

4. "Beginning at the intersection of the east line of Goodrich Boulevard and the south line of Jasmine Lane and running south along the east line of Goodrich Boulevard a distance of 230 feet; thence easterly parallel to the north line of Wolf Road, a distance of 195 feet; thence northeasterly on a course of N 22 E, a distance of 135 feet; and thence northwesterly along the south line of Jasmine Lane to the point of beginning." This legal description is an example of a

   a. block description.
   b. rectangular survey.
   c. subdivision description.
   d. metes-and-bounds description.

5. Legal real property descriptions in Maryland

   a. employ the rectangular survey system.
   b. consist of the street or mailing addresses of the properties.
   c. are based on recorded plats of subdivision or metes and bounds data.
   d. consist of the post office box numbers.

8
Real Estate Taxes and Other Liens

OVERVIEW

Maryland property taxes are levied by and for the support of the county and city governments, as well as local special taxing districts. A number of counties also impose **impact fees** on developers in addition to property taxes on owners. The impact fees are levied on new residential units to fund additional public facilities and services for the use and benefit of new residents. They increase the initial cost of home ownership since developers have to pass along the cost of the fees to purchasers.

ASSESSMENT

Real property is assessed for tax purposes by the State Department of Assessments and Taxation. There are local offices of that department in Baltimore City and in each Maryland county.

Starting with the tax year beginning July 1, 2001, the assessment ratio became 100 percent of market value, based on the property's most recent triennial, phased-in increments. This increase, for example from 40 percent to 100 percent, was offset by reducing the tax rate by 60 percent. In parts of the state that had 50 percent assessment, the increase to 100 percent was offset by reducing the tax rate by 50 percent.

The net effect in all cases is intended to be *revenue neutral*—to give no more money to government than before the change. The purpose of the change to 100 percent was to make property tax *rates* in the state appear competitive with those in surrounding jurisdictions. This will make the state more attractive to present and prospective residents. See Figure 8.1.

The procedure for assessing property in Maryland, the **triennial assessment,** is based on a three-year cycle in which one-third of all properties are revalued every year for tax purposes.

Each county has been organized into three principal assessing areas to coincide with the years of the assessment cycle. The areas generally have similar density and other common characteristics and are reviewed on a rotating basis. By the end of a three-year period, all properties will have been physically reviewed and valued once; then a new cycle commences.

2001-2002 (Fiscal 2002) County Tax Rates

This information is found at

http://www.dat.state.md.us

Figure 8.1 County Tax Rates

Counties & Baltimore City	Real Property Tax Rate in dollars per $100 of Assessment*	Transfer Tax Rate The Consideration Payable multiplied by this rate**		Recordation Tax Quoted in dollars per $500 of Transaction amount
Allegany	0.984	0.20%	0.002	2.20
Anne Arundel	0.960	1.00%	0.010	3.50
Baltimore City	2.328	1.50%	0.015	2.75
Baltimore County	1.115	1.50%	0.015	2.50
Calvert	0.892	0.00%	0.000	5.00
Caroline	0.952	0.50%	0.005	3.30
Carroll	1.048	0.00%	0.000	3.50
Cecil	0.980	0.50%	0.005	3.30
Charles	1.016	0.00%	0.000	5.00
Dorchester	0.880	1.00%	0.010	3.30
Frederick	1.00	0.00%	0.000	5.00
Garrett	1.018 - 1.036	1.00%	0.010	3.50
Harford	1.092	1.00%	0.010	3.30
Howard	1.044	1.00%	0.010	2.50
Kent	1.012	0.50%	0.005	3.30
Montgomery	0.741	1.00%	0.010	2.20
Prince George's	0.962	1.40%	0.014	2.20
Queen Anne's	0.976	0.50%	0.050	3.30
St. Mary's	0.908	1.00%	0.010	4.00
Somerset	0.980	0.00%	0.000	1.65
Talbot	0.556	1.00%	0.010	3.30
Washington	0.948	0.00%	0.000	3.80
Wicomico	1.070	0.00%	0.000	2.30
Worcester	0.730	0.50%	0.050	3.30

* To this is added any municipal tax

** This is in addition to the State Rate of 0.5%.

An inspection of the exterior premises always accompanies a revaluation. If changes in zoning or use occur, or if additions or extensive improvements to property have been made, the property can be revalued out of sequence.

Real property assessment is further controlled by a **phase-in provision,** designed to take some of the financial sting out of inflation. For the one-third of all real properties reassessed in a particular year, one-third of any increase in value is added in that year, and the balance added in equal increments over the following two years in the three-year cycle. For example, a property increasing in value from $72,000 to $84,000 would have a value for tax purposes of $76,000 the first year, $80,000 the second year and $84,000 the third year.

If, upon completion of the triennial review, the value of a property is found to have changed, the owner is sent a **notice of reassessment** that shows the property's assessment for the next three years; no other notice is sent until the new cycle begins three years later. Taxpayers who believe that their assessments are improper may appeal within 45 days of receiving notice of assessment.

Tax bills mailed after June 30, 2001 reflected the increased assessments and decreased tax rates.

PAYMENT

Taxes on residential property are due and payable twice yearly. Due dates for semiannual payment are July 1—payable without interest by September 30—and January 1—payable without interest by January 31 of each tax year.

One of the intended effects of the recent change to semiannual payment has been to reduce the amount of **ad valorem** tax to be collected in advance at settlement for escrow accounts.

Counties were also required, at the time of setting up this semiannual system, to prepare their data processing systems for quarterly payments, which may be authorized by future legislation.

Lenders who accept responsibility to pay property taxes on the mortgaged properties collect the required funds in expense (escrow) accounts. They are required to pay those taxes within 45 days after the earlier of the following: (1) the first due date after their receipt of the tax bill or (2) after funds collected by the lender are sufficient to pay the amount of taxes and interest due. Lenders who fail to pay taxes as provided above must bear any additional costs of penalties and interest.

PROPERTY TAX RELIEF

The **Homestead Tax Credit** is designed to protect owner-occupied residence assessments from the effects of rapid inflation. It automatically provides a credit against the real estate tax if the assessment on a dwelling increases over the previous year by more than a certain percentage determined by the state legislature. The credit equals the amount by which the reassessment exceeds the established percentage and applies if certain other conditions were met during the previous calendar year.

Because the Homestead Tax Credit does not take into account homeowners' ability to pay, the state legislature devised what is popularly known as the **circuit breaker.** After taking into account homeowners' net worth, gross annual income and assessed value of their property, this program for homeowners of all ages, sets limits on the amount of residential property tax due. This relief must be applied for each year.

The owners of *unsold and unrented* single dwelling units or newly constructed or substantially rehabilitated commercial properties may be entitled to **tax credits** not exceeding the property taxes on the improvements. The credit applies for no more than one year immediately following construction or substantial rehabilitation.

Special provision has also been made for **senior tenants,** age 60 or older, to receive as much as $600 from the State to offset property taxes. Asset and income limits are among certain restrictions that apply.

The residential property *owned* by a veteran with a permanent, 100 percent, service-connected disability, is exempt from property tax. The 100 percent disability may result from blindness or some other disabling cause. This benefit is retained by the un-remarried surviving spouse of the veteran as well. Application for this benefit must be accompanied by documentation of individual's veterans status, 100 percent disability, and ownership of the property.

Assessment on a residence **owned** by an individual who is legally blind is reduced by

$15,000. The property must be the individual's legal residence and not be occupied by more than two families. The un-remarried surviving spouse of the blind individual receives the same benefit.

No individual may claim both the exemption for the blind and the exemption for the disabled veteran.

TRANSFER AND RECORDATION TAXES

Except as discussed in the following paragraph, in every written or oral agreement for the sale or other disposition of property, it is presumed, in the absence of any contrary provision in the agreement or the law, that the parties to the agreement intended that the cost of any recordation tax or any State or local transfer tax be shared equally between the grantor and grantee. This presumption does not apply to mortgages or deeds of trust. Refer to Figure 8.1 on page 92.

First-Time Maryland Homebuyers

The law provides that first-time homebuyers will not pay the State transfer tax. In a transfer involving such a buyer, the State transfer tax of .5 percent is reduced to .25 percent, and must be paid by the seller. Furthermore, unless the parties in such a transaction agree to the contrary, the recordation taxes and local transfer taxes are to be paid by the seller. *First-time homebuyers* are defined in the law as purchasers who have never before owned and occupied a principal residence in this State, will occupy the property as their principal residence, and/or meet certain other requirements.

CORPORATE FRANCHISE TAX

Most corporations are taxed annually on their franchise or right to do business in the State. The annual tax of $40 becomes a general lien on the property or the corporation and can be enforced against it. When a broker files for a real estate license and the brokerage is a corporation, the Commission requires that a copy of the brokerage's Articles of Incorporation be filed also.

PROPERTY TAX ASSESSMENTS, AGRICULTURAL USE

Lands that are actively devoted to farm or agricultural use are favorably assessed on the basis of those uses rather than their probably more intensive highest and best use.

Agricultural Use Assessment

The State Department of Assessments and Taxation establishes criteria for the purpose of determining whether land qualifies for assessment as agricultural use. The State's purpose is to slow the conversion of farm lands to more intensive, nonfarm uses.

Agricultural Transfer Tax

The Agricultural Transfer Tax, ranging from 3 percent to 5 percent of the consideration, funds the state's Agricultural Land Preservation Program. The tax is based on multiple factors: the size of the tract, improvements that may be in place, and the value of the land reflected in the consideration. The tax is waived in a transfer in which the purchaser promises to keep the land in agricultural use for five tax years. The tax is more fully discussed in Chapter 10 of this book.

The Agricultural Transfer Tax is calculated by the Assessments Office and is payable at the time the property transfer takes place. *Negotiation about which party will pay should be reflected in the contract of sale.*

A full discussion of this tax is found at the Maryland State Department of Taxation and Assessment web site.
http://www.dat.state.md.us/ sdatweb/agtransf.html

DELINQUENCY AND REDEMPTION

Taxes are due July 1 and January 1 each year. Taxes that are not paid by September 30, and by January 31 under the two-payment system, are considered delinquent, bear interest as provided by law, and are subject to a real estate tax sale held by the county treasurer.

The dates and rules regarding such sales are made by each county. Tax-delinquent properties sold at a tax sale are not conveyed immediately to the buyer. There is a six-month statutory period of redemption during which the delinquent taxpayer may redeem the property by paying the county treasurer the amount of the delinquent tax plus the accumulated interest in penalty and related legal fees. The rate of redemption is established by law by various jurisdictions.

If no redemption is made during the six-month period, the tax sale buyer may apply to the court for the issuance of a deed to the property. Unpaid taxes create a priority lien on real property.

Ad valorem taxes on a parcel of property that remain unpaid for longer than three years, perhaps because the lien on the property did not sell at tax sales, are no longer collectible. There is a three-year limitation of actions on this tax. Only the most recent three years' taxes remain a lien on any property.

A number of tax program pamphlets are available in each county Tax Assessment Office.

LIENS

Mechanics' liens, as discussed in the main textbook, are provided by state law to protect the rights of contractors, suppliers, and other persons engaged to improve real estate. After the completion of work, contractors or suppliers have six months in which to record a notice of their lien. They then have one year from the date of recording to petition the courts to enforce the lien in the event such petition was not included when the lien was recorded.

It is unlawful for unperformed (executory) contracts between contractors and subcontractors relating to construction, alteration, or repair of a building, structure, or improvement, to contain a provision that waives or requires the subcontractor to waive the right to claim a mechanic's lien.

Buyers purchasing properties that have been recently improved or constructed should seek protection against possible outstanding mechanics' liens. In the usual purchase of real estate, the attorney for the buyer has responsibility to ascertain that the property being purchased is free from unpaid taxes and mechanics' or other outstanding liens.

Release of Lien

When a lien on real property is satisfied, lienholders are required to mail or deliver a release of the lien within seven days after receiving payment. The release may be in the form of the original note, marked "paid" or "canceled." If lienholders fail to provide such a release after demand by the payor, the payor may bring action in the circuit court. In such an action, the lienholders or their agent may be liable for delivery of the release, as well as all costs and expenses of the action.

QUESTIONS

1. In Maryland, real estate taxes are imposed by

   a. cities.
   b. special taxing districts.
   c. counties.
   d. All the above

2. All residential real property in Maryland is

   a. reassessed for tax purposes each year.
   b. assessed for tax purposes at the property's full market value.
   c. reassessed for tax purposes every other year.
   d. reassessed at time of resale.

3. Peter and Jayne Janney own a contracting firm in Maryland. On February 1, 2002, Arch Chandler hired the Janney firm to construct an addition to his five-bedroom house. The Janneys finished work on the project on March 15; it is now April 15, and the Janneys have not yet been paid. Based on this situation, which of the following is correct? The Janneys have until

   a. August 1 to record a notice of lien.
   b. August 1 to enforce their mechanic's lien.
   c. September 15 to record a mechanic's lien.
   d. October 15 to enforce a mechanic's lien.

4. Ollie Akers has chosen to make semi-annual real estate tax payments on the home he occupies. Which of the following statements is false?

   a. Ollie's payments will be due July 1 and January 1 of each tax year.
   b. Ollie's first semiannual payment becomes late if paid after September 30.
   c. Ollie's second semiannual payment becomes late if paid after January 31.
   d. Ollie's second semiannual payment becomes late if paid after March 31.

5. Ted Bolton has never before owned a principal residence in Maryland. He will settle on the purchase of a $100,000 home to occupy here in April. How will the State transfer tax be apportioned at settlement?

   a. Bolton will pay $0 and sellers will pay $500.
   b. Bolton will pay $250 and sellers will pay $250.
   c. Bolton will pay $0 and sellers will pay $250.
   d. The apportionment will be whatever Bolton and the sellers agree in the contract of sale.

9

Real Estate Contracts

OVERVIEW

In Maryland, real estate contracts are used, among other things, for sales, rentals, options, and installment sales. This chapter discusses various requirements, including capacity for valid contracts, the Statute of Frauds, required clauses for residential resales, and limitation of actions on contract enforcement in this state. It also presents the industry-created sales contract now available for REALTOR® use throughout Maryland. Please see Figure 9.1 beginning on page 103. Students who go on to practice real estate brokerage are advised always to obtain and use the latest version of this contract and its addenda.

GENERAL CONTRACT RULES: COMPETENCY, STATUTE OF FRAUDS, LIMITATION OF ACTIONS

Under Maryland law, a person reaches **majority** and has the **capacity** to enter into a valid real estate contract at age 18. However, minors married to persons who have reached the age of majority may enter into valid real estate contracts jointly with their spouses.

To be legally enforceable under Maryland's Statute of Frauds, all contracts for the transfer of any interest in real property for more than one year must be in writing and signed by the parties. Any oral **(parol)** transfer of an interest in real property for more than one year can convey no more than a tenancy at will. Maryland laws require a 30-day notice to vacate under a tenancy at will.

The Maryland Statute of Frauds does not require a lease for a term of one year or less to be in writing to be enforceable. The year is measured from the date the lease is entered into rather than the date on which occupancy begins. Regardless of these interesting facts, all licensees are bound by Commission regulations to reduce to signed, written form **all agreements** that they help negotiate.

Typically, suits to enforce a contract must be filed within three years—the statutory limitation of actions—of a breach of that contract.

CONTRACTS FOR THE SALE OF REAL ESTATE

Real estate sales contracts and other contract forms must always be drafted by attorneys. Licensees are authorized only to insert required information into these forms. Licensees who draft their own clauses or phrases could be accused of the misdemeanor, "unauthorized practice of law."

Although licensees, unless otherwise licensed to do so, cannot act as attorneys in their brokerage activities, they should nevertheless emphasize to buyers and sellers that a signed sales contract is legally binding. Buyers and sellers should obtain legal counsel to interpret and approve the provisions of contracts. It is grossly misleading, and probably an example of the unauthorized practice of law, to give false assurance to the parties such as, "Don't worry; there will be an attorney at settlement," as if that would protect them from errors made in their earlier contract negotiations.

To reduce confusion arising from the use of a wide variety of contract forms, the Maryland Association of REALTORS®, (MAR) working with its member associations and boards throughout the State, prepares a contract form designed to be used by its member brokers in residential sale transactions statewide. The MAR also provides contract language for twenty or more addenda. All these forms are copyrighted by the MAR and may not be altered or modified without the prior written express consent of the Association. MAR member-brokers are free either to use the statewide forms—as long as they make no changes in their wording—or to have counsel draft forms for their particular firms' use. Nonmember-brokers may not use the forms.

Information That Must Be Included In Contracts

In certain circumstances, Maryland statutes require that licensees include specific information in contracts. Unless otherwise specifically agreed, a contract of sale is generally *not* made invalid by omission of required clauses such as those discussed below.

Contracts for the sale of improved residential real property must disclose the estimated cost of any deferred water and sewer charges for which the purchaser may become liable. Violation of this disclosure requirement entitles the initial purchaser to recover from the seller two times the amount of deferred charges the purchaser would be obligated to pay during the five years of payments following the sale.

Licensees acting as sellers or purchasers of real estate must notify the other party of the fact that they are indeed licensees. This notification must be in writing, typically within the contract itself.

A real estate sales contract must indicate whether there is a **ground rent** or a **leasehold interest** involved in the sale. If the ground rent is irredeemable, this fact must be indicated. If the ground rent is to be redeemed at the time of settlement, responsibility for notice, costs of redemption, etc., should be fixed as part of the written agreement. A contract for the sale of real property subject to a ground rent must contain a notice of the existence of the ground rent and notice that if ground rent is not timely paid, the reversionary owner of the ground rent may bring an action for possession against the ground rent tenant and, as a result of the action, may come to own the property in fee.

The Brokers Act requires that every contract for use in the sale of residential property used as a dwelling place for one or two single-family units must contain the following statement in conspicuous type or handwritten:

> Section 14-104 of the *Real Property* Article of the Annotated Code of Maryland provides that, unless otherwise negotiated in the contract or provided by local law, the cost of any recordation tax or any state or local transfer tax shall be shared equally between the buyer and seller.

Notwithstanding the statement above, the First-Time Home Buyers Closing Cost Reduction Act of 1995 reduces the State transfer tax in the case of first-time home buyers, from .5 percent to .25 percent, with that entire amount to be paid by the seller. In such a transaction, the seller must also pay the entire amount of recordation and local transfer tax, unless there is an express agreement between the parties to the contrary. Other details of this issue appear in Chapter 8 of this book.

If the property is subject to a homeowners association (HOA), and to the imposition of mandatory HOA fees, this must be disclosed to purchasers, preferably by reference, within the purchase agreement.

Contracts for the sale of real estate must contain a notice of purchaser's protection by the Real Estate Guaranty Fund in an amount not to exceed $25,000.

A real estate broker must promptly place all earnest (deposit) monies in a special noninterest-bearing account unless directed to do otherwise by both buyer and seller.

The Brokers Act mandates that contracts reveal that buyers of single-family dwellings may not be required to employ specific title insurance, settlement, or escrow companies, or title attorneys, but may choose their own. (See Chapter 1 of this book.)

The seller is also required to notify the purchaser that land being transferred may be subject to **agricultural land transfer tax.** The statewide MAR Residential Contract of Sale provides that sellers who fail to notify buyers as required are liable to those buyers for the agricultural land transfer tax which the buyers will have to pay. This provision can, of course, be removed from the contract language by negotiation before it is signed.

Other Required Clauses

The *Real Property* Article requires that contracts of sale must also include the following notices and disclosures, where applicable:

- Notice pertaining to sale of real property in Prince George's County creating subdivision

- Notice pertaining to resale of condominium unit

- Notice pertaining to initial sale of lot in development containing more than twelve lots

- Notice pertaining to resale of any lot or initial sale of lot in development containing twelve or fewer lots

- Notice pertaining to initial sale of lot not intended to be occupied or rented for residential purposes

- Notice pertaining to initial sale of cooperative interests

- Notice of liability for agricultural land transfer tax

- Notice to purchaser pertaining to sale of certain land in Prince George's County, that the land being sold is subject to a development impact fee, and the unpaid amount of that fee

- Notice pertaining to sale of certain agriculturally assessed land in St. Mary's and Charles Counties

Baltimore City and most counties have various additional contract requirements unique to their jurisdictions. Information about these requirements is available from local boards or associations for use by their members. For example, contracts for the sale of multiple-dwelling property in Baltimore City must contain a clause whereby the seller guarantees that the property being purchased complies with the Baltimore City Multiple-Dwelling Code and that the license will be delivered to the buyer at the time of settlement.

Property in Maryland not served by public sewer and water is subject to the State Department of Health and Mental Hygiene laws and regulations pertaining to individual sewage disposal systems and wells. The licensee must provide the buyer of unimproved land with a notice that if the property being purchased is to be used for residential purposes the buyer, before signing the contract, should ascertain the status of sewerage and water facilities and, if required, whether the property will be approved for installation of a well and/or private sewerage system.

The Department of Veterans Affairs (VA), the Federal Housing Administration (FHA), and many private lenders require an evaluation by the local health department of the sewage disposal system and the water supply on residential property prior to settlement. When this is required, a bacteriological sample must be collected from the well and analyzed by the health department. Consequently, licensees involved in such a transaction must allow sufficient time for these procedures when estimating a settlement date. Assistance and information are available from the Department of Health and Mental Hygiene, O'Conor Building, 201 West Preston Street, Baltimore, MD 21201, or from local health boards.

Contingency and Other Clauses

To express the exact agreements of the parties to a contract and to protect the best interests of their clients, licensees often employ contingency and other additional clauses. They should avoid drafting the language of such clauses and make use of clauses with wording drafted by competent legal counsel. Additional disclosure clauses and contingency language often address such matters as the following:

- Details of financing

- Impact of appraisal

- Buyer's prompt loan application and receipt of lender's commitment

- Lenders' fees and charges and who will receive the benefit of any favorable changes due to market conditions

- Home inspections and their impact

- Sale of purchasers' home and any release *(kickout)* clause

- Existence and extent of any leasehold interests

- Disposition of any agricultural crops

- Party to pay fees for IRS filing

Release from Contract of Sale

When one party is unable or unwilling to consummate a contract of sale and the other party agrees to release that party, the broker should provide a competently drafted release form for both of their signatures. This release should also recite the broker's alternatives in the event of a dispute over the disposition of any earnest money deposit. If the parties cannot agree how to dispose of the deposit, the broker must follow statutory procedures outlined for such a situation in Chapter 3 of this book.

OPTION AGREEMENTS

In Maryland, a **lease option agreement** is defined as any lease agreement containing a clause that gives the tenant some power to purchase the landlord's interest in real property. No lease option purchase of improved residential property is valid in Maryland unless it contains the statement in capital letters "THIS IS NOT A CONTRACT TO BUY" and a clear statement of the option agreement's purpose and effect with respect to the purchase of the property that is the subject of the option.

Even though details of times, prices, dates, financing, prorations, and settlement expenses, etc.—everything needed for a contract of sale—be clearly set forth in the option, it still ". . . IS NOT A CONTRACT TO BUY." It is, rather, a unilateral contract that will become bilateral and binding on both parties only if the option rights are exercised by the optionee.

CONSTRUCTION CONTRACTS

Prior to the signing of a contract for the construction of a single-family dwelling using alternating current (AC) electrical service and a public water system, a builder must, under certain conditions, offer prospective buyers the option of having a sprinkler system installed. Some jurisdictions in the state already require that such systems be installed in new homes in addition to smoke detectors.

Figure 9.1 Maryland Association of REALTORS® Residential Sales Contract (Page 1 of 7)

RESIDENTIAL CONTRACT OF SALE

This is a Legally Binding Contract; If Not Understood, Seek Competent Legal Advice.

THIS FORM IS DESIGNED AND INTENDED FOR THE SALE AND PURCHASE OF IMPROVED SINGLE FAMILY RESIDENTIAL REAL ESTATE LOCATED IN MARYLAND ONLY. *FOR OTHER TYPES OF PROPERTY INCLUDE APPROPRIATE ADDENDA.*

BROKER: _____   BRANCH OFFICE: _____

OFFICE PHONE: _____ FAX: _____   BROKER/AGENT ID: _____

SALES ASSOCIATE: _____ E-Mail: _____   PHONE: _____

ACTING AS: ☐ SELLER AGENT (WHETHER "COOPERATING AGENT" OR "SELLING AGENT"); OR
            ☐ BUYER AGENT; OR
            ☐ INTRA - COMPANY AGENT WITH BROKER AS DUAL AGENT

IN COOPERATION WITH

BROKER: _____   BRANCH OFFICE: _____

OFFICE PHONE: _____ FAX: _____   BROKER/AGENT ID: _____

SALES ASSOCIATE: _____ E-Mail: _____   PHONE: _____

ACTING AS: ☐ LISTING BROKER AND SELLER AGENT; OR
            ☐ INTRA - COMPANY AGENT WITH BROKER AS DUAL AGENT

TIME IS OF THE ESSENCE *UNLESS* BOTH BUYER AND SELLER INITIAL HERE _____ _____   _____ _____

                                                   BUYER   **BUYER**   **SELLER**   **SELLER**

---

1. DATE OF OFFER: _____

2. SELLER: NAME: _____

            ADDRESS: _____ ZIP: _____

3. BUYER: NAME: _____

            ADDRESS: _____ ZIP: _____

4. PROPERTY DESCRIPTION: Seller does sell to Buyer and Buyer does purchase from Seller, all of the following described Property (hereinafter "Property") known as _____ _____ located in _____ City/County, Maryland, Zip _____ together with the improvements thereon, and all rights and appurtenances thereto belonging.

5. ESTATE: The Property is being conveyed: ____ in fee simple or ____ subject to an annual ground rent, now existing or to be created, in the amount of _____ Dollars ($_____) payable semi-annually, as now or to be recorded among the Land Records of _____ City/County, Maryland. If the Property is subject to ground rent and the ground rent is not timely paid, the owner of the reversionary interest (i.e., the person to whom the ground rent is payable) may bring an action of ejectment against the leasehold owner pursuant to Section 8-402.2 of the Real Property Article, Annotated Code of Maryland (as amended). As a result of this action, the owner of the reversionary interest may obtain title to the Property in fee, discharged from the lease.

6. PURCHASE PRICE: The purchase price is _____ Dollars ($_____).

7. SETTLEMENT: Date of Settlement _____ or sooner if agreed to in writing by both parties.

8. SETTLEMENT COSTS: NOTICE TO BUYER: BUYER HAS THE RIGHT TO SELECT BUYER'S OWN TITLE INSURANCE COMPANY, TITLE LAWYER, SETTLEMENT COMPANY, ESCROW COMPANY, MORTGAGE LENDER, OR FINANCIAL INSTITUTION AS DEFINED IN THE FINANCIAL INSTITUTIONS ARTICLE, ANNOTATED CODE OF MARYLAND. BUYER ACKNOWLEDGES THAT SELLER MAY NOT BE PROHIBITED FROM OFFERING OWNER FINANCING AS A CONDITION OF SETTLEMENT. Buyer agrees to pay all other settlement costs and charges including, but not limited to, all Lender's fees in connection herewith, including title examination and title insurance fees, all document preparation and recording fees, notary fees, survey fees where required, and all recording charges, except those incident to clearing existing encumbrances or title defects, except if Buyer is a Veteran obtaining VA financing, those prohibited to be paid by a Veteran obtaining VA financing or except if Buyer is obtaining FHA financing, those prohibited to be paid by a Buyer obtaining FHA financing, which prohibited charges shall be paid by Seller.

The parties acknowledge pages 1 through 7 of this Contract of Sale. _____

                                               BUYER   **BUYER**   **SELLER**   **SELLER**

Figure 9.1 Maryland Association of REALTORS® Residential Sales Contract (Page 2 of 7)

9. **TRANSFER CHARGES:** SECTION 14-104 OF THE REAL PROPERTY ARTICLE OF THE ANNOTATED CODE OF MARYLAND PROVIDES THAT, UNLESS OTHERWISE NEGOTIATED IN THE CONTRACT OR PROVIDED BY STATE OR LOCAL LAW, THE COST OF ANY RECORDATION TAX OR ANY STATE OR LOCAL TRANSFER TAX SHALL BE SHARED EQUALLY BETWEEN THE BUYER AND SELLER. Unless otherwise provided by an addendum to this Contract, the costs of state and local transfer and recordation taxes (other than agricultural land transfer tax) shall be shared equally by Buyer and Seller. (If First-Time Maryland Home Buyer: See Transfer and Recordation Tax Addendum.)

10. **ADJUSTMENTS:** Ground rent, homeowner's association fees, rent and water rent shall be adjusted and apportioned as of date of settlement; and all taxes, general or special, and all other public or governmental charges or assessments against the Property which are or may be payable on a periodic basis, including Metropolitan District Sanitary Commission or other benefit charges, assessments, liens or encumbrances for sewer, water, drainage, paving, or other public improvements completed or commenced on or prior to the date hereof, or subsequent thereto, are to be adjusted and apportioned as of the date of settlement and are to be assumed and paid thereafter by Buyer, whether assessments have been levied or not as of date of settlement if applicable by local law. Any heating or cooking fuels remaining in supply tank(s) at time of settlement shall become the property of Buyer.

11. **TERMITE INSPECTION:** Buyer, at Buyer's expense, (if VA, then at Seller's expense) is authorized to obtain a written report from a Maryland licensed pest control company that, based on a careful visual inspection, there is no evidence of termite or other wood-destroying insect infestation in the residence; and damage due to previous infestation has been repaired. The provisions of this paragraph also shall apply to (1) the garage (2) any outbuildings located within three feet of the residence or garage and (3) a maximum of ten (10) linear feet of the nearest portion of a fence on Seller's Property within three feet of the residence or garage. If there is evidence of present infestation as described above, or if damage caused by present or prior infestation is discovered, Seller, at Seller's expense, shall treat present infestation and repair any damage caused by present or prior infestation. If the cost of treatment and repair of such damage exceeds 2% of the purchase price, Seller may, at Seller's option, cancel this Contract, unless Buyer, at Buyer's option should choose to pay for the cost of treatment and repairs exceeding 2% of the purchase price, then this Contract shall remain in full force and effect. If such report reveals damage for which the cost of treatment and repair exceeds 2% of the purchase price, Seller's decision regarding treatment and repair of damage shall be communicated in writing to Buyer within five (5) days from receipt of the report, after which Buyer shall respond to Seller in writing with Buyer's decision within three (3) days from receipt of Seller's notification of Seller's decision. If Seller does not notify Buyer in writing of Seller's decision within five (5) days from receipt of report, Buyer may, at Buyer's option, pay for the cost of treatment and repairs exceeding 2% of the purchase price. If Buyer does not want to pay for the cost of treatment and repairs exceeding 2% of the purchase price, Buyer may terminate this Contract upon written notice delivered to Seller. In the event this Contract is terminated under the terms of this paragraph, all monies on deposit shall be returned to Buyer in accordance with the terms of this Contract.

12. **CONDITION OF PROPERTY AND POSSESSION:** At settlement, Seller shall deliver possession of the Property and shall deliver the Property vacant, clear of trash and debris, broom clean and in substantially the same condition as existed on the date of Contract Acceptance. All electrical, heating, air conditioning (if any), plumbing (including well and septic), and any other mechanical systems and related equipment, appliances and smoke detector(s) included in this Contract shall be in working condition. Buyer reserves the right to inspect the Property within five (5) days prior to settlement. **EXCEPT AS OTHERWISE SPECIFIED IN THIS CONTRACT, INCLUDING THIS PARAGRAPH 12, THE PROPERTY IS SOLD "AS IS".**

13. **SALE/SETTLEMENT OR LEASE OF OTHER REAL ESTATE:** Neither this Contract nor the granting of Buyer's loan referred to herein is to be conditioned or contingent in any manner upon the sale, settlement and/or lease of any other real estate unless a contingency for the sale, settlement and/or lease of other real estate is contained in an addendum to this Contract. Unless this Contract is expressly contingent upon the sale, settlement and/or lease of any other real estate, Buyer shall neither apply for nor accept a financing loan commitment which is contingent upon or requires as a pre-condition to funding that any other real estate be sold, settled and/or leased.

14. **BUYER RESPONSIBILITY:** If Buyer has misrepresented Buyer's financial ability to consummate the purchase of the Property, or if this Contract is contingent upon Buyer securing a written commitment for financing and Buyer fails to apply for such financing within the time period herein specified, or fails to pursue financing diligently and in good faith, or if Buyer makes any misrepresentations in any document relating to financing, or makes (or fails to take) any action which causes Buyer's disqualification for financing, then Buyer shall be in default, and Seller may elect by written notice to Buyer, to terminate this Contract and/or pursue the remedies set forth under the "Default" Paragraph 16.

15. **SELLER RESPONSIBILITY:** Seller agrees to keep existing mortgages free of default until settlement. All violation notices or requirements noted or issued by any governmental authority or actions in any court on account thereof, against or affecting the Property at the date of settlement of this Contract, shall be complied with by Seller and the Property conveyed free thereof.

16. **DEFAULT:** Buyer and Seller are required and agree to make full settlement in accordance with the terms of this Contract and acknowledge that failure to do so constitutes a breach hereof. If Buyer fails to make full settlement or is in default due to Buyer's failure to comply with the terms, covenants and conditions of this Contract, the deposit may be retained by Seller as long as a release of deposit agreement is signed and executed by all parties, expressing that said deposit may be retained by Seller. In the event the parties do not agree to execute a release of deposit, Buyer and Seller shall have all legal and equitable remedies. If Seller fails to make full settlement or is in default due to Seller's failure to comply with the terms, covenants and conditions of this Contract, Buyer shall be entitled to pursue such rights and remedies as may be available, at law or in equity, including, without limitation, an action for specific performance of this Contract and/or monetary damages. In the event of any litigation or dispute between Buyer and Seller concerning the release of the deposit, Broker's sole responsibility may be met, at Broker's option, by paying the deposit into the court in which such litigation is pending, or by paying the deposit into the court of proper jurisdiction by an action of interpleader. Buyer and Seller agree that, upon Broker's payment of the deposit into the court, neither Buyer nor Seller shall have any further right, claim, demand or action against Broker regarding the release of the

Figure 9.1 Maryland Association of REALTORS® Residential Sales Contract (Page 3 of 7)

deposit; and Buyer and Seller, jointly and severally, shall indemnify and hold Broker harmless from any and all such rights, claims, demands or actions. In the event of such dispute and election by Broker to file an action of interpleader as herein provided, Buyer and Seller further agree and hereby expressly and irrevocably authorize Broker to deduct from the deposit all costs incurred by Broker in the filing and maintenance of such action of interpleader including but not limited to filing fees, court costs, service of process fees and attorneys' fees, provided that the amount deducted shall not exceed the lesser of $500 or the amount of the deposit held by Broker. All such fees and costs authorized herein to be deducted may be deducted by Broker from the deposit prior to paying the balance of the deposit to the court. Buyer and Seller further agree and expressly declare that all such fees and costs so deducted shall be the exclusive property of Broker. If the amount deducted by Broker is less than the total of all of the costs incurred by Broker in filing and maintaining the interpleader action, then Buyer and Seller jointly, and severally, agree to reimburse Broker for all such excess costs upon the conclusion of the interpleader action.

17. MEDIATION OF DISPUTES: Mediation is a process by which the parties attempt to resolve a dispute or claim with the assistance of a neutral mediator who is authorized to facilitate the resolution of the dispute. The mediator has no authority to make an award, to impose a resolution of the dispute or claim upon the parties or to require the parties to continue mediation if the parties do not desire to do so. Buyer and Seller agree that any dispute or claim arising out of or from this Contract or the transaction which is the subject of this Contract shall be mediated through the Maryland Association of REALTORS®, Inc. or its member local boards/associations in accordance with the established Mediation Rules and Guidelines of the Association or through such other mediator or mediation service as mutually agreed upon by Buyer and Seller, in writing. Unless otherwise agreed in writing by the parties, mediation fees, costs and expenses shall be divided and paid equally by the parties to the mediation. If either party elects to have an attorney present that party shall pay his or her own attorney's fees. BUYER AND SELLER FURTHER AGREE THAT THE OBLIGATION OF BUYER AND SELLER TO MEDIATE AS HEREIN PROVIDED SHALL APPLY TO ALL DISPUTES AND CLAIMS ARISING WHETHER PRIOR TO, DURING OR WITHIN ONE (1) YEAR FOLLOWING SETTLEMENT. BUYER AND SELLER AGREE THAT NEITHER PARTY SHALL INITIATE OR COMMENCE ANY ACTION IN ANY COURT OR BEFORE ANY ADMINISTRATIVE AGENCY, WITHOUT FIRST SUBMITTING THE DISPUTE OR CLAIM TO MEDIATION AS HEREIN PROVIDED. IN THE EVENT BUYER AND/OR SELLER SHALL INITIATE OR COMMENCE ANY ACTION IN ANY COURT OR BEFORE ANY ADMINISTRATIVE AGENCY WITHOUT FIRST SUBMITTING THE DISPUTE OR CLAIM TO MEDIATION AS HEREIN PROVIDED, THE PARTY INITIATING OR COMMENCING SUCH ACTION AGREES TO PAY ALL COSTS AND EXPENSES, INCLUDING REASONABLE ATTORNEYS' FEES, INCURRED TO ENFORCE THE OBLIGATION AS PROVIDED HEREIN TO FIRST MEDIATE THE DISPUTE OR CLAIM BY ANY PERSON OR ENTITY WITH WHOM OR WITH WHICH THE PARTY WAS REQUIRED TO MEDIATE. THE PROVISIONS OF THIS PARAGRAPH SHALL SURVIVE CLOSING AND SHALL NOT BE DEEMED TO HAVE BEEN EXTINGUISHED BY MERGER WITH THE DEED.

18. PAYMENT TERMS: The payment of the purchase price shall be made by Buyer as follows:
(a) An initial deposit by way of _____ in the amount of _____
Dollars ($ _____) at the time of this offer. (b) An additional deposit by way of _____ in the amount of _____ Dollars ($_____) to be paid within _____ (_____) days from the date of Contract Acceptance. (c) The purchase price less any and all deposits shall be paid in full by Buyer in cash, wired funds, bank check, certified check or other payment acceptable to the settlement officer at settlement.
(d) All deposits will be held in escrow by: _____

19. FINANCING: This Contract is contingent upon Buyer obtaining a written commitment for a loan secured by the Property as follows:

(Mark)

☐ Assumption Addendum
☐ Conventional Loan as follows:
   Loan Amount $ _____
   Term of Note _____ Years
   Amortization _____ Years
   Interest Rate _____ %
   Loan Program _____

☐ FHA Financing Addendum
☐ Gift of Funds Contingency Addendum
☐ Owner Financing Addendum
☐ VA Financing Addendum

☐ No Financing Contingency

20. FINANCING APPLICATION AND COMMITMENT: Buyer agrees to make written application for the financing as herein described within _____ (_____) days from the date of Contract Acceptance. If such written financing commitment is not obtained by Buyer within _____ (_____) days from the date of Contract Acceptance, this Contract of Sale shall be null and void and of no further legal effect, and all deposits hereunder shall be disbursed in accordance with the terms of this Contract. If Buyer has complied with all of Buyer's obligations under this Contract, including those with respect to applying for financing and seeking to obtain financing, then the release of deposit agreement shall provide that all monies on deposit shall be returned to Buyer.

21. ALTERNATE FINANCING: If Buyer obtains a written commitment for financing in which the interest, terms of payment, amount of loan, or any one of these differs from the financing conditions herein, the preceding financing conditions of the Contract shall be deemed to have been fully satisfied. This alternate financing may not increase costs to Seller or exceed the time allowed to secure the financing commitment as stated herein. Nothing in this paragraph shall relieve Buyer of the obligation to apply for and diligently pursue the financing described in the "Financing" Paragraphs 19 and 20.

Figure 9.1 Maryland Association of REALTORS® Residential Sales Contract (Page 4 of 7)

22. **DEPOSIT:** Buyer hereby authorizes and directs Broker as specified in Paragraph 18-d of this Contract to hold the initial deposit instrument without negotiation or deposit until the parties have executed and accepted this Contract. Upon acceptance, the initial deposit and additional deposit, if any, shall be placed in escrow as provided below and in accordance with the requirements of Section 17-502(b)(1), Business Occupations and Professions Article, Annotated Code of Maryland. If Seller does not execute and accept this Contract, the initial deposit instrument shall be promptly returned to Buyer. Brokers may charge a fee for establishing an interest bearing account. Buyer and Seller instruct Broker to place all deposit monies in: **(Mark One)**

    ☐ A non-interest bearing account.

OR ☐ An interest bearing account, the interest on which, in absence of default by Buyer, shall accrue to the benefit of Buyer.

The deposit shall be disbursed by Broker at settlement. In the event this Contract shall be terminated or settlement does not occur, Buyer and Seller agree that the deposit shall be disbursed by Broker only in accordance with a release of deposit agreement executed by Buyer and Seller. In the event Buyer and/or Seller fail to complete the real estate transaction in accordance with the terms and conditions of this Contract, and either Buyer or Seller shall be unable or unwilling to execute a release of deposit agreement, Buyer and Seller hereby acknowledge and agree that Broker may distribute the deposit in accordance with the provisions of Section 17-505(b)(1), Business Occupations and Professions Articles, Annotated Code of Maryland.

23. **CONVENTIONAL LOAN LENDER FEES/CHARGES:** Buyer agrees to pay loan origination/loan discount fees of ____ % of the loan amount, and Seller agrees to pay loan origination/loan discount fees of ____ % of the loan amount. Buyer shall receive the benefit of any reduction in said fees. All loan insurance premiums as required by Lender shall be paid by Buyer. If the existing loan is to be transferred to/assumed by Buyer, Buyer agrees to pay all fees and charges required by Lender.

24. **INCLUSIONS/EXCLUSIONS:** Included in the purchase price are all permanently attached fixtures, including all smoke detectors. Certain other **now existing items** which may be considered personal property, whether installed or stored upon the property, are included if box below is marked.

INCLUDED	INCLUDED	INCLUDED	INCLUDED
☐ Alarm System	☐ Electronic Air Filter	☐ Intercom	☐ Storm Windows
☐ Built-in Microwave	☐ Exhaust Fan(s) #	☐ Playground Equipment	☐ Stove or Range
☐ Ceiling Fan(s) # ___	☐ Exist. W/W Carpet	☐ Pool, Equip. & Cover	☐ T.V. Antenna
☐ Central Vacuum	☐ Fireplace Screen/Doors	☐ Refrigerator(s) # ___	☐ Trash Compactor
☐ Clothes Dryer	☐ Freezer	☐ w/ice maker	☐ Wall Oven(s) # ___
☐ Clothes Washer	☐ Furnace Humidifier	☐ Satellite Dish	☐ Water Filter
☐ Cooktop	☐ Garage Opener(s) # ___	☐ Screens	☐ Water Softener
☐ Dishwasher	☐ w/remote(s) #	☐ Shades/Blinds	☐ Window A/C Unit(s) # ___
☐ Drapery/Curtain Rods	☐ Garbage Disposer	☐ Storage Shed(s) # ___	☐ Window Fan(s) # ___
☐ Draperies/Curtains	☐ Hot Tub, Equip. & Cover	☐ Storm Doors	☐ Wood Stove

ADDITIONAL INCLUSIONS (SPECIFY): _____

ADDITIONAL EXCLUSIONS (SPECIFY): _____

25. **AGENCY CONFIRMATION:** Buyer and Seller each confirm that disclosure of the agency relationships as described in this Contract conforms with the agency relationships previously agreed to in writing.

26. **BROKER'S FEE:** All parties irrevocably instruct the settlement agent to collect the fee or compensation and disburse same according to the terms and conditions provided in the listing agreement and/or agency representation agreement. Settlement shall not be a condition precedent to payment of compensation.

27. **BROKER LIABILITY:** Brokers, their agents, subagents and employees do not assume any responsibility for the condition of the Property or for the performance of this Contract by any or all parties hereto. By signing this Contract, Buyer and Seller acknowledge that they have not relied on any representations made by Brokers, or any agents, subagents or employees of Brokers, except those representations expressly set forth in this Contract.

28. **ATTORNEY'S FEES:** In any action or proceeding between Buyer and Seller based, in whole or in part, upon the performance or non-performance of the terms and conditions of this Contract including, but not limited to, breach of contract, negligence, misrepresentation or fraud, the prevailing party in such action or proceeding shall be entitled to receive reasonable attorney's fees from the other party as determined by the court or arbitrator. In any action or proceeding between Buyer and Seller and/or between Buyer and Broker(s) and/or Seller and Broker(s) resulting in Broker(s) being made a party to such action or proceeding, including, but not limited to, any litigation, arbitration, or complaint and claim before the Maryland Real Estate Commission, whether as defendant, cross-defendant, third-party defendant or respondent, Buyer and Seller jointly and severally, agree to indemnify and hold Broker(s) harmless from and against any and all liability, loss, cost, damages or expenses (including filing fees, court costs, service of process fees, transcript fees and attorneys' fees) incurred by Broker(s) in such action or proceeding, providing that such action or proceeding does not result in a judgment against Broker(s).

As used herein, the term "Broker(s)" shall mean (a) the two (2) Brokers as identified at the top of Page 1 of this Contract; (b) the two (2) named Sales Associates as identified at the top of Page 1 of the Contract; and, (c) any agent, subagent, salesperson, independent contractor and/or employee of Broker(s). The term "Broker(s)" shall also mean, in the singular, any or either of the named Broker(s) and/or Sales Associate(s) as identified or, in the plural, both of the named Broker(s) and/or Sales Associates as identified.

This Paragraph 28 shall apply to any and all such action(s) or proceeding(s) against Broker(s) including those action(s) or proceeding(s) based, in whole or in part, upon any alleged act(s) or omission(s) by Broker(s), including, but not limited to, any

Figure 9.1 Maryland Association of REALTORS® Residential Sales Contract (Page 5 of 7)

alleged act of misrepresentation, fraud, non-disclosure, negligence, violation of any statutory or common law duty, or breach of fiduciary duty by Broker(s). The provision of this Paragraph 28 shall survive closing and shall not be deemed to have been extinguished by merger with the deed.

29. NON-ASSIGNABILITY: This Contract may not be assigned without the written consent of Buyer and Seller. If Buyer and Seller agree in writing to an assignment of this Contract, the original parties to this Contract remain obligated hereunder until settlement.

30. LEASES: Seller may neither negotiate new leases nor renew existing leases for the Property which extend beyond settlement or possession date without Buyer's written consent.

31. PROPERTY INSURANCE AND RISK OF LOSS: The Property is to be held at the risk of Seller until legal title has passed or possession has been given to Buyer. If, prior to the time legal title has passed or possession has been given to Buyer, whichever shall occur first, all or a substantial part of the Property is destroyed or damaged, without fault of Buyer, then this Contract, at the option of Buyer, upon written notice to Seller, shall be null and void and of no further effect, and all deposits hereunder shall be returned to Buyer in accordance with the terms of this Contract.

32. NOTICE TO THE PARTIES: BROKERS, THEIR AGENTS, SUBAGENTS AND EMPLOYEES, MAKE NO REPRESENTATIONS WITH RESPECT TO THE FOLLOWING:

A. Water quality, color, or taste or operating conditions of private water systems.

B. Location, size or operating condition of on-site sewage disposal systems.

C. The extensions of public utilities by local municipal authorities, existence or availability of public utilities, and any assessments, fees or costs for public utilities which might be imposed by local municipal authorities, should public utilities be extended or available to the subject Property. (Buyer should consult the Department of Public Works to determine the availability of proposed future extensions of utilities.)

D. Lot size and exact location: If the subject Property is part of a recorded subdivision, Buyer can review the plat upon request at the Record Office. If the subject Property is not part of a recorded subdivision, Buyer may verify exact size and location through a survey by a registered engineer or land surveyor, at Buyer's expense.

E. Existing zoning or permitted uses of the Property. Buyer should contact the Zoning Office and/or a licensed engineer to verify zoning and permitted uses.

F. Brokers/agents are not advising the parties as to certain other issues, including without limitation: soil conditions; flood hazard areas; possible restrictions of the use of property due to restrictive covenants, subdivision, environmental laws, easements or other documents; airport or aircraft noise; planned land use, roads or highways; and construction materials and/or hazardous materials, including without limitation flame retardant treated plywood (FRT), radon, molds, urea formaldehyde foam insulation (UFFI), synthetic stucco (EIFS), asbestos, polybutelene piping and lead based paint. Information relating to these issues may be available from appropriate governmental authorities. This disclosure is not intended to provide an inspection contingency.

G. Buyer and Seller each assume full responsibility for selecting and compensating their respective vendors.

33. SINGLE FAMILY RESIDENTIAL REAL PROPERTY DISCLOSURE NOTICE: BUYER IS ADVISED OF THE RIGHT TO RECEIVE A "DISCLOSURE AND DISCLAIMER STATEMENT" FROM SELLER (SECTION 10-702 REAL PROPERTY ARTICLE, ANNOTATED CODE OF MARYLAND).

34. DEED AND TITLE: Upon payment of the purchase price, a deed for the Property containing covenants of special warranty and further assurances, shall be executed by Seller and shall convey the Property to Buyer. Title to the Property, including all chattels included in the purchase, shall be good and merchantable, free of liens and encumbrances except as specified herein; except for use and occupancy restrictions of public record which are generally applicable to properties in the immediate neighborhood or the subdivision in which the Property is located and publicly recorded easements for public utilities and any other easements which may be observed by an inspection of the Property. Buyer expressly assumes the risk that restrictive covenants, zoning laws or other recorded documents may restrict or prohibit the use of the Property for the purpose(s) intended by Buyer. In the event Seller is unable to give good and merchantable title or such as can be insured by a Maryland licensed title insurer, with Buyer paying not more than the standard rate as filed with the Maryland Insurance Commissioner, Seller, at Seller's expense, shall have the option of curing any defect so as to enable Seller to give good and merchantable title or, if Buyer is willing to accept title without said defect being cured, paying any special premium on behalf of Buyer to obtain title insurance on the Property to the benefit of Buyer. In the event Seller elects to cure any defects in title, this Contract shall continue to remain in full force and effect; and the date of settlement shall be extended for a period not to exceed fourteen (14) additional days. If Seller is unable to cure such title defect(s) and is unable to obtain a policy of title insurance on the Property to the benefit of Buyer from a Maryland licensed title insurer, Buyer shall have the option of taking such title as Seller can give, or terminating this Contract and being reimbursed by Seller for cost of searching title as may have been incurred not to exceed 1/2 of 1% of the purchase price. In the latter event, there shall be no further liability or obligation on either of the parties hereto; and this Contract shall become null and void; and all deposits hereunder shall be returned to Buyer in accordance with the terms of this Contract. In no event shall Broker(s) or their agent(s) have any liability for any defect in Seller's title.

35. WETLANDS NOTICE: Buyer is advised that if all or a portion of the Property being purchased is wetlands, the approval of the U.S. Army Corps of Engineers will be necessary before a building permit can be issued for the Property. Additionally, the future use of existing dwellings may be restricted due to wetlands. The Corps has adopted a broad definition of wetlands which encompasses a large portion of the Chesapeake Bay Region. Other portions of the State may also be considered wetlands. For information as to whether the Property includes wetlands, Buyer may contact the Baltimore District of the U.S. Army Corps of Engineers. Buyer may also elect, at Buyer's expense, to engage the services of a qualified specialist to inspect the Property for the presence of wetlands prior to submitting a written offer to purchase the Property; or Buyer may include in Buyer's written offer a clause making Buyer's purchase of the Property contingent upon a satisfactory wetlands inspection.

Figure 9.1 Maryland Association of REALTORS® Residential Sales Contract (Page 6 of 7)

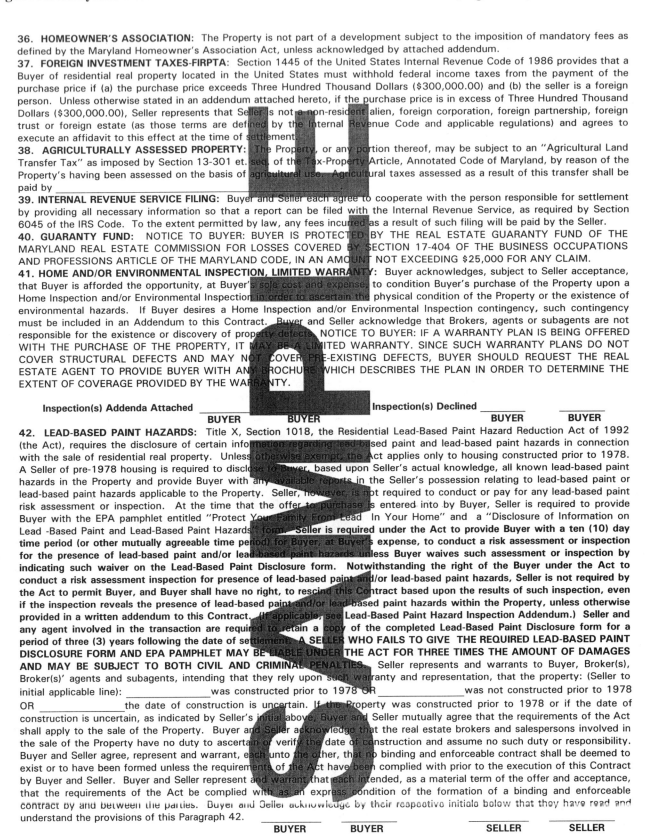

36. **HOMEOWNER'S ASSOCIATION:** The Property is not part of a development subject to the imposition of mandatory fees as defined by the Maryland Homeowner's Association Act, unless acknowledged by attached addendum.

37. **FOREIGN INVESTMENT TAXES-FIRPTA:** Section 1445 of the United States Internal Revenue Code of 1986 provides that a Buyer of residential real property located in the United States must withhold federal income taxes from the payment of the purchase price if (a) the purchase price exceeds Three Hundred Thousand Dollars ($300,000.00) and (b) the seller is a foreign person. Unless otherwise stated in an addendum attached hereto, if the purchase price is in excess of Three Hundred Thousand Dollars ($300,000.00), Seller represents that Seller is not a non-resident alien, foreign corporation, foreign partnership, foreign trust or foreign estate (as those terms are defined by the Internal Revenue Code and applicable regulations) and agrees to execute an affidavit to this effect at the time of settlement.

38. **AGRICULTURALLY ASSESSED PROPERTY:** The Property, or any portion thereof, may be subject to an "Agricultural Land Transfer Tax" as imposed by Section 13-301 et. seq. of the Tax-Property Article, Annotated Code of Maryland, by reason of the Property's having been assessed on the basis of agricultural use. Agricultural taxes assessed as a result of this transfer shall be paid by _____.

39. **INTERNAL REVENUE SERVICE FILING:** Buyer and Seller each agree to cooperate with the person responsible for settlement by providing all necessary information so that a report can be filed with the Internal Revenue Service, as required by Section 6045 of the IRS Code. To the extent permitted by law, any fees incurred as a result of such filing will be paid by the Seller.

40. **GUARANTY FUND:** NOTICE TO BUYER: BUYER IS PROTECTED BY THE REAL ESTATE GUARANTY FUND OF THE MARYLAND REAL ESTATE COMMISSION FOR LOSSES COVERED BY SECTION 17-404 OF THE BUSINESS OCCUPATIONS AND PROFESSIONS ARTICLE OF THE MARYLAND CODE, IN AN AMOUNT NOT EXCEEDING $25,000 FOR ANY CLAIM.

41. **HOME AND/OR ENVIRONMENTAL INSPECTION, LIMITED WARRANTY:** Buyer acknowledges, subject to Seller acceptance, that Buyer is afforded the opportunity, at Buyer's sole cost and expense, to condition Buyer's purchase of the Property upon a Home Inspection and/or Environmental Inspection in order to ascertain the physical condition of the Property or the existence of environmental hazards. If Buyer desires a Home Inspection and/or Environmental Inspection contingency, such contingency must be included in an Addendum to this Contract. Buyer and Seller acknowledge that Brokers, agents or subagents are not responsible for the existence or discovery of property defects. NOTICE TO BUYER: IF A WARRANTY PLAN IS BEING OFFERED WITH THE PURCHASE OF THE PROPERTY, IT MAY BE A LIMITED WARRANTY. SINCE SUCH WARRANTY PLANS DO NOT COVER STRUCTURAL DEFECTS AND MAY NOT COVER PRE-EXISTING DEFECTS, BUYER SHOULD REQUEST THE REAL ESTATE AGENT TO PROVIDE BUYER WITH ANY BROCHURE WHICH DESCRIBES THE PLAN IN ORDER TO DETERMINE THE EXTENT OF COVERAGE PROVIDED BY THE WARRANTY.

Inspection(s) Addenda Attached _____ _____   **Inspection(s) Declined** _____ _____
                                         BUYER   **BUYER**   **BUYER**   **BUYER**

42. **LEAD-BASED PAINT HAZARDS:** Title X, Section 1018, the Residential Lead-Based Paint Hazard Reduction Act of 1992 (the Act), requires the disclosure of certain information regarding lead-based paint and lead-based paint hazards in connection with the sale of residential real property. Unless otherwise exempt, the Act applies only to housing constructed prior to 1978. A Seller of pre-1978 housing is required to disclose to Buyer, based upon Seller's actual knowledge, all known lead-based paint hazards in the Property and provide Buyer with any available reports in the Seller's possession relating to lead-based paint or lead-based paint hazards applicable to the Property. Seller, however, is not required to conduct or pay for any lead-based paint risk assessment or inspection. At the time that the offer to purchase is entered into by Buyer, Seller is required to provide Buyer with the EPA pamphlet entitled "Protect Your Family From Lead In Your Home" and a "Disclosure of Information on Lead -Based Paint and Lead-Based Paint Hazards" form. **Seller is required under the Act to provide Buyer with a ten (10) day time period (or other mutually agreeable time period) for Buyer, at Buyer's expense, to conduct a risk assessment or inspection for the presence of lead-based paint and/or lead-based paint hazards unless Buyer waives such assessment or inspection by indicating such waiver on the Lead-Based Paint Disclosure form. Notwithstanding the right of the Buyer under the Act to conduct a risk assessment inspection for presence of lead-based paint and/or lead-based paint hazards, Seller is not required by the Act to permit Buyer, and Buyer shall have no right, to rescind this Contract based upon the results of such inspection, even if the inspection reveals the presence of lead-based paint and/or lead-based paint hazards within the Property, unless otherwise provided in a written addendum to this Contract. (If applicable, see Lead-Based Paint Hazard Inspection Addendum.) Seller and any agent involved in the transaction are required to retain a copy of the completed Lead-Based Paint Disclosure form for a period of three (3) years following the date of settlement. A SELLER WHO FAILS TO GIVE THE REQUIRED LEAD-BASED PAINT DISCLOSURE FORM AND EPA PAMPHLET MAY BE LIABLE UNDER THE ACT FOR THREE TIMES THE AMOUNT OF DAMAGES AND MAY BE SUBJECT TO BOTH CIVIL AND CRIMINAL PENALTIES.** Seller represents and warrants to Buyer, Broker(s), Broker(s)' agents and subagents, intending that they rely upon such warranty and representation, that the property: (Seller to initial applicable line): _____ was constructed prior to 1978 OR _____ was not constructed prior to 1978 OR _____ the date of construction is uncertain. If the Property was constructed prior to 1978 or if the date of construction is uncertain, as indicated by Seller's initial above, Buyer and Seller mutually agree that the requirements of the Act shall apply to the sale of the Property. Buyer and Seller acknowledge that the real estate brokers and salespersons involved in the sale of the Property have no duty to ascertain or verify the date of construction and assume no such duty or responsibility. Buyer and Seller agree, represent and warrant, each unto the other, that no binding and enforceable contract shall be deemed to exist or to have been formed unless the requirements of the Act have been complied with prior to the execution of this Contract by Buyer and Seller. Buyer and Seller represent and warrant that each intended, as a material term of the offer and acceptance, that the requirements of the Act be complied with as an express condition of the formation of a binding and enforceable contract by and between the parties. Buyer and Seller acknowledge by their respective initials below that they have read and understand the provisions of this Paragraph 42. _____ _____   _____ _____
                                                                    BUYER   **BUYER**   **SELLER**   **SELLER**

Figure 9.1 Maryland Association of REALTORS® Residential Sales Contract (Page 7 of 7)

43. FOREST CONSERVATION AND MANAGEMENT PROGRAM: Buyer is hereby notified that this transfer may be subject to the Forest Conservation and Management Program imposed by Section 8-211 et. seq. of the Tax-Property Article, Annotated Code of Maryland. Forest Conservation/Management program taxes assessed as a result of this transfer shall be paid by   the

_____.

44. FOREST CONSERVATION ACT NOTICE: If the Property is a tract of land 40,000 square feet or more in size, Buyer is notified that, unless exempted by applicable law, as a prerequisite to any subdivision plan or grading or sediment control permit for the Property, Buyer will be required to comply with the provisions of the Maryland Forest Conservation Act imposed by Section 5-1601, et. seq. of the Natural Resources Article, Annotated Code of Maryland, including, among other things, the submission and acceptance of a Forest Stand Delineation and a Forest Conservation Plan for the Property in accordance with applicable laws and regulations. Unless otherwise expressly set forth in an addendum to this Contract, Seller represents and warrants that the Property is not currently subject to a Forest Conservation Plan, Management Agreement or any other pending obligation binding the owner of the Property under said Act; further, Seller represents and warrants that no activities have been undertaken on the Property by Seller in violation of the Forest Conservation Act.

45. ADDENDA: The Addenda marked below, which are hereby attached, are made a part of this Contract:

▢ Affiliated Business Disclosure Notice
▢ Condominium Resale
▢ Disclosure of Licensee Status
▢ First-Time Maryland Home Buyer Transfer & Recordation Tax Addendum
▢ Homeowners Association Notice
▢ Inspection – Environmental
▢ Inspection – Home
▢ Inspection – On-Site Sewage Disposal System
▢ Inspection – Radon
▢ Inspection/Certification - Well
▢ Other Addenda/Special Conditions: _____

▢ Kickout Addendum
▢ Lead-Based Paint Hazard Inspection
▢ Lead-Based Paint and Lead-Based Hazards Disclosure of Information
▢ Local City/County Certifications/Registrations
▢ Local City/County Notices/Disclosures
▢ Notice to Buyer – Maryland Residential Real Property Disclosure/Disclaimer Act
▢ Sale, Settlement or Lease of Other Real Estate
▢ Seller's Purchase of Another Property
▢ Third Party Approval

46. PARAGRAPH HEADINGS: The Paragraph headings of this Contract are for convenience and reference only, and in no way define or limit the intent, rights or obligations of the parties.

47. ENTIRE AGREEMENT: This Contract and any Addenda thereto contain the final and entire agreement between the parties, and neither they nor their agents shall be bound by any terms, conditions, statements, warranties or representations, oral or written, not herein contained. The parties to this Contract mutually agree that it is binding upon them, their heirs, executors, administrators, personal representatives, successors and, if permitted as herein provided, assigns. Once signed, the terms of this Contract can only be changed by a document executed by all parties. This Contract shall be interpreted and construed in accordance with the laws of the State of Maryland. It is further agreed that this Contract may be executed in counterparts, each of which when considered together shall constitute the original Contract.

48. ELECTRONIC DELIVERY: The parties agree that this Contract offer shall be deemed validly executed and delivered by a party if a party executes this Contract and delivers a copy of the executed Contract to the other party by telefax or telecopier transmittal.

_____   _____
Buyer's Signature   Date

_____   _____
Buyer's Signature   Date

_____   _____
Seller's Signature   Date

_____   _____
Seller's Signature   Date

DATE OF CONTRACT ACCEPTANCE: _____

NEW HOME WARRANTIES AND DEPOSITS

Before entering into contracts for sale or construction of new homes, builders must disclose to purchasers on a State-mandated form whether they participate in a new home warranty security plan and the extent of that plan. If builders do not participate in a new home warranty plan, they must disclose, among other things, that without a new home warranty, the purchaser may be afforded only certain limited warranties.

The disclosure must also state that builders of new homes are not required to be licensed by the state and are not licensed in most local jurisdictions. Purchasers who acknowledge by their signature that they have been so informed, then have five working days to rescind their contract and recover all money paid for their purchases. Contracts for purchase or construction of new homes that do not contain this notice are voidable by the buyers.

Any person knowingly misrepresenting the existence of a new home warranty is subject to a fine not exceeding $50,000 or imprisonment for not more than two years, or both, in addition to other penalties provided by the *Real Property* Article.

In connection with the sale and purchase of new, single-family residential units, including condominiums that are not completed at the time of contracting the sale, if the vendor or builder obligates purchasers to pay any sum of money before units have been completed and the realty has been granted to the purchaser, the builder or vendor is required to

- deposit or hold the sums in an escrow account to ensure their return to purchasers who are entitled to them, or

- obtain and maintain a corporate surety bond to provide return of deposits to purchasers who are entitled to them.

The Maryland Custom Home Protection Act, found in the *Real Property* Article, provides protection for buyers of newly constructed homes. This law sets standards for contract payments, surety bonds, contract requirements, mortgage loans, and sales by licensed real estate brokers. Detailed provisions govern brokers' handling of deposit monies.

INSTALLMENT CONTRACTS

Maryland statutes provide protections for purchasers of residential property under installment contracts, which are stronger than protections provided by common law. Maryland requirements concerning installment contracts for the sale of real estate are presented in Chapter 12 of this book. The principal text presents information on installment contracts in its chapters on contracts and on finance.

DISCLOSURE REQUIREMENTS ON CONDOMINIUM SALES

A contract for the initial sale or resale of a condominium unit requires the disclosure of certain information to the purchaser before the execution of the contract. The buyer of a condominium unit has 15 days (for initial sale) or 7 days (for resale) from the signing of such a contract, within which to rescind the agreement. Looking at it from another perspective, the developer must deliver all required papers to the condominium purchaser 15 days prior to settlement. The purchaser cannot waive this requirement.

A settlement performed without meeting this requirement is voidable by the purchaser for up to a year after the settlement date. Refer to Chapter 6 of this book.

A contract for the initial sale of a residential condominium unit to a member of the public must also contain notice of the developer's warranties.

RESIDENTIAL PROPERTY DISCLOSURE AND DISCLAIMER STATEMENT

The required use of the Property Disclosure and Disclaimer Statement is presented in Chapter 4 of this book at **Property Disclosure Requirements.** Be sure to review it. The Disclosure and Disclaimer Statement need *not* be used in

- the initial sale of a single-family residential real property that has never been occupied or for which a certificate of occupancy has been issued within one year before the seller and buyer enter into a contract;

- the transfer of properties exempt from transfer tax under the *Tax-Property* Article (land installment contracts and certain options to purchase require the use of the statement);

- sale by a lender, or affiliate, or subsidiary of a lender, of property acquired by foreclosure or by deed in lieu of foreclosure;

- a sheriff's sale, tax sale, or sale by fore-closure, partition, or by court appointed trustee;

- a transfer by a fiduciary in the course of the administration of a decedent's estate, guardianship, conservatorship, or trust;

- the transfer of a single-family residential real property to be converted by the buyer into use other than residential use or to be demolished; or

- the sale of unimproved real property.

POWERS OF ATTORNEY

Attorneys-in-fact are persons granted authority in documents called *powers of attorney (POAs)* to sell or grant property in a Maryland real estate transaction on behalf of the owner who granted the POA. When a deed or other instrument is signed by an *attorney-in-fact* who is acting under a POA document—properly signed and acknowledged—that document may be recorded either *before*, or *on* the day the deed or mortgage is placed in the public record. It may even be recorded *after* the deed has been recorded if

- the power of attorney was both dated and acknowledged on or before the effective date of the deed;

- the power of attorney had not been revoked up to the time of the recording of the deed; and

- the deed which was recorded contained or was accompanied by an affidavit from the attorney in fact (agent) stating he or she had no actual knowledge that the person who granted the power of attorney had either revoked it, become legally disabled or was incompetent at the time of the agent's signing the deed.

It is prudent, in all cases, for licensees, in preparing for settlement, to check with settlement officers before the scheduled closing to make sure such powers of attorney are in a form acceptable to them and to the lending institutions involved.

DUTIES AND OBLIGATIONS OF LICENSEES

The Regulations of the Commission set forth a number of duties and obligations that the real estate licensee has toward clients, the public and fellow licensees, with respect to contracts. These include

- prompt presentation of all written offers and counteroffers;

- reduction of all agreements to a written form that sets forth all the obligations of the parties;

- seeking proper signatures on all forms; and

- giving and retaining copies of all signed agreements.

EQUITABLE TITLE AND RISK OF LOSS

When a contract of sale has been signed by all parties, the buyers receive **equitable title.** Maryland has not set aside the common law principle that equitable title places the risk of loss due to accidental damage to the premises upon the buyers. This is true unless the sellers cause the damage or the buyers have taken physical possession of the premises. Most contracts, therefore, include a provision that the sellers will maintain until settlement or occupancy—whichever occurs first—full insurance on the property and that the sellers bear the risk of loss due to damage of the property. Licensees should see that this issue is addressed in any contract they negotiate.

RESIDENTIAL SALES CONTRACT PROVIDED STATEWIDE FOR MARYLAND REALTORS®

The residential sales contract form which appears as Figure 9.1 beginning on page 103, is provided to members of the Maryland Association of REALTORS® for their exclusive use. The Association also provides a wide variety of addenda for specific situations and to meet certain legal requirements. Examples are the Lead-Based Paint Hazard Inspection Addendum, required by Federal law in residential sales of structures built before 1978, and the First-Time Maryland Home Buyer

Transfer and Recordation Tax Addendum.

In addition, a form is provided which warns sellers that their providing to the buyers the

Commissions's Property Condition Disclosure/Disclaimer form does not relieve them from affirmative disclosure of material facts relating to the property.

QUESTIONS

1. In Maryland, contracts for the sale of real estate must be

   a. in writing to be enforceable.
   b. on a standard printed form.
   c. signed by the seller only.
   d. signed by the buyer only.

2. Oral contracts for the sale of real estate are

   a. valid.
   b. called *parol* agreements.
   c. enforceable in a court of law.
   d. illegal.

3. Licensees buying or selling real property must

   a. advise the other party of their licensee status.
   b. advise lending institutions of their status.
   c. write to the Real Estate Commission.
   d. advise the Attorney General.

4. Which of the following disclosures will NOT be necessary in a Maryland real estate sales contract?

   a. That a leasehold interest is involved in the sale
   b. That the owner/seller is a real estate licensee
   c. The existence of possible tax charges for agricultural land development
   d. The title insurance company name.

10
Transfer of Title

OVERVIEW

Title to land in Maryland, as elsewhere, can pass by descent, devise, adverse possession, gift, escheat, eminent domain, erosion, foreclosure, and tax and sheriff's sales. This chapter deals with six of the more prevalent ways a title can change hands.

TRANSFER OF TITLE BY DESCENT

Surviving spouses are provided for by The Maryland Law of Descent and Distribution that abolished dower and curtesy. This statute also names other classes of heirs who inherit property owned by decedents who die *intestate* (without a valid will).

Some of the particular situations the law addresses are those in which there is a surviving spouse

- and a minor child: each gets half;

- and no minor children, but there are surviving issue (adult children and perhaps their children): spouse gets $15,000 and half of the residue (rest);

- and no issue (children) but there are parents of the decedent: spouse gets $15,000 and half of the remainder.

- and no surviving issue and no parents of the decedent: spouse takes all.

When the decedent is not intestate but leaves a will giving the spouse less than provided in the situations above—or even nothing—the spouse may renounce the will and elect (choose) to claim the *intestate share* granted by the statute governing descent.

Title to real property of decedents passes immediately to their **personal representatives** (formerly called *administrators* in situations without a valid will). These individuals pay decedents' debts and estate taxes and then distribute the remainder of the estate according to the statute.

Persons who receive property by descent are called **heirs.** Persons who receive property through a will are called **beneficiaries.** Beneficiaries are of two types: **devisees,** who receive real property (a devise), and

legatees, who receive personal property (a legacy).

If the decedent was both intestate and entirely without heirs, the estate is converted to cash and that cash paid to the Maryland Medical Assistance Program if the decedent received long-term care benefits from that program. If that is not the case, the cash is paid to the board of education in the county in which the personal representative was granted authority to administer the estate.

TRANSFER OF TITLE BY ACTION OF LAW

To obtain title to real estate through **adverse possession,** an adverse user must be in actual possession of the property, and that possession, alone or combined with that of previous adverse owners, must have been continuous for 20 years. The possession also must be or have been open, notorious (known to others), exclusive, and hostile (without permission), and—because Maryland law does not recognize "squatters' rights"—under claim of right or color of title. Each of those terms has a very specific legal meaning. Situations involving adverse possession can be very technical and should always be handled with guidance from legal counsel.

TRANSFER OF TITLE BY WILL

There are statutory requirements for a valid will. Persons aged 18 or over, who are of sound mind and are legally competent, may make a will. Wills should be prepared carefully by testators' attorneys and signed

and witnessed as required by law. While surviving spouses can contest wills that grant them less than their intestate share, testators' children do not have this right.

Children born after a testator's will is signed and before the testator's death are said to be **pretermitted** (omitted). This also includes children of the decedent who had not yet been born at the time of decedent's death. Under common law, pretermitted children do not have a share in the decedent's estate. Maryland statute has set aside this aspect of common law and treats pretermitted children as if they were born before the will was signed.

Nuncupative (oral) wills are not recognized in Maryland. Holographic wills (those in the handwriting of the testator) are recognized if they are properly witnessed.

TRANSFER OF TITLE BY DEED

Statutes also set requirements for a valid deed. A deed must be: prepared by an attorney or by one of the parties; in writing; executed by a competent grantor 18 years of age or older; state the actual consideration or be accompanied by an affidavit that does; and give a legally sufficient property description.

Deeds must be typewritten and in English to be recorded, although an accompanying official consular translation into English satisfies this requirement for a deed written in another language.

A deed signed only by the grantor (the one

granting the property) is effective if delivered and accepted by the grantee. It is called a *deed poll.* Transfers of property belonging to a minor and of properties involving corporate sellers or purchasers are situations in which **both** grantees and the grantors are required to sign the deed.

Recordation of Deeds and Mortgages

Maryland law specifies that the transfer of any fee or freehold estate, any declaration or limitation of use, and any estate extending beyond 7 years (such as a deed or a long-term lease) shall be effective only if the deed is executed and recorded. Chapter 13 of this book also points out that leases for more than seven years must be recorded. Title to property passes, as between the parties, upon delivery and acceptance of a valid deed. Consequently, unrecorded deeds are valid between grantors and grantees and also against third persons with actual notice. The law requires deeds to be recorded to alert potential purchasers of land to the possible interests of others. Recording deeds can also protect grantees against third persons without actual notice. The recording of a deed constitutes constructive notice as of date of recording.

Deeds are recorded in the county where the land lies. For land lying in more than one county, the deed must be recorded in each of the counties.

Recordation requires acknowledgment before a notary or other authorized public officer and payment of all required transfer taxes, ad valorem taxes, and special assessments. The deed is considered made (done) on the date it is signed, sealed, and delivered, even though it be acknowledged at a later date and recorded still later.

Mortgages or deeds of trust are exempt from the recordation tax if they secure home loans made for the initial purchase or for renovation of one's residence.

TAXES ON CONVEYANCES

The **documentary stamp tax** (so-called because its payment until several decades ago was indicated by attaching actual revenue stamps to the deed) is a Maryland state tax levied at the rate of $.55 per $500 or fraction thereof on the full sales price of the property. Several cities and counties have added their own stamp tax.

Another state tax is the Maryland **transfer tax.** It is one-half of 1 percent of the full consideration except for transfers to a first-time Maryland homebuyer, as explained in Chapter 8 of this book. Cities and counties collect additional transfer taxes.

Transfers Between Relatives

Transfers between relatives, including in-laws and former spouses, are exempt from recordation and transfer taxes only on the mortgage or deed of trust indebtedness assumed by the transferee.

AGRICULTURAL TRANSFER TAX

The agricultural transfer tax is calculated by the Assessments Office and is payable at the time of property transfer. It is imposed when land subject to agricultural ad valorem tax assessment is sold with nonagricultural use in view. The student is referred to the full discussion and resources given in Chapter 8 of this book.

MARYLAND UNIFORM TRANSFERS TO MINORS ACT

This law authorizes a donor to nominate a custodian to act on behalf of a minor beneficiary. The designation, powers and responsibilities of a custodian and procedures for transfers of custodial property and claims against such property are set forth in the statute. Use of legal counsel is important in such a transfer.

QUESTIONS

1. One requirement for obtaining title to the property of another by adverse possession is that the claimant must

   a. post a sign on the subject property.
   b. notify the original owner in writing.
   c. be in possession of the property for 20 years.
   d. own the adjoining land.

2. The Maryland Law of Descent and Distribution

   a. affects estates of those not leaving a valid will.
   b. assures surviving spouses part of any estate.
   c. can affect both the estates of those leaving a valid will and of those dying intestate.
   d. All the above

3. To be valid between the parties, a deed to Maryland real property must meet all the following requirements EXCEPT that it be

   a. voluntarily delivered during the lifetime of the grantor.
   b. in writing and signed.
   c. signed by a grantor who is competent.
   d. recorded.

4. To be eligible for recordation, a deed conveying Maryland real estate

   a. need only show a nominal consideration.
   b. must be in the handwriting of the grantee.
   c. must have been prepared by an attorney or by one of the parties.
   d. must be witnessed by two persons not mentioned in the deed.

11
Title Records

OVERVIEW

According to Maryland State law, deeds, mortgages, ground leases, and other instruments creating an estate in real estate for longer than seven years must be recorded. This is for the protection of later buyers who need to know who claims to own the property they are considering. Recording gives constructive notice to the world of a grantee's claim of interest in a property. Recording of long-term leases also serves to protect lessees against such third parties as lenders, judgment creditors, etc. After the purchase of real property, the grantee is responsible for recording the deed and paying recording fees.

The law requires subdividers to record plats of subdivision after their approval by state and local authorities. Later documents such as listings, sales contracts, and deeds can refer to the recorded plats by **liber** and **folio** (book and page). Such reference to the recorded plat in a later document can satisfy the need for exact property description.

DETAILS OF RECORDATION

To be eligible for recordation, a deed must state the full, actual *consideration* paid for the property. If the information is not in the deed, it must be stated in an affidavit attached to the deed.

Deeds and mortgages on real estate are recorded by the circuit court clerk of each county and Baltimore City. Recording must take place *in the county or city where the land is located*. If property is located in two counties, it must be recorded in both, with each county receiving a recording fee proportional to the amount of land located in the county, as shown by the tax assessment. Occasionally recordings are made in a county other than that in which the property is located.

It should be noted that Maryland has only one system of recording. The Torrens system, as described in the main text, does not exist in Maryland.

Real estate records are gathered in two indexes: one organized by the names of grantors and one by grantees. Mortgagors are in the grantor index; mortgagees, in the grantee. All references to a previously recorded conveyance should give not only the liber (book) and folio (page) numbers where the conveyance is found but also the name of the grantor and the grantee who were parties to the conveyance.

Purchasers who finance a property purchased with a purchase-money mortgage or deed of trust to a financial institution are the grantees named in their own deed. They will then become grantors shown in the deed of trust they give to a financial institution. In the first instance, their names will be recorded in the grantee index; in the second, in the grantor index.

No deed conveying real estate may be recorded in any county of Maryland until all taxes and other public assessments or charges on the property have been paid and the record of ownership has been transferred on the tax assessment books to the grantee who is named in the deed to be recorded. If the deed transfers all of the real estate owned by the grantor in the county, then, in many counties, all of the grantor's personal property tax must also be paid prior to recording.

In Baltimore City, a deed conveying real estate may not be recorded if there is an unpaid water bill over $50. In Harford County, no deed conveying real estate may be recorded unless the water bill is paid. Licensees preparing for settlement should check requirements in the county or municipality where the property is located that is the subject of the transaction.

The amount of fees charged for the recording of deeds and other documents is set by counties. In many counties, it is $3 per page, or portion thereof, plus $1 for each name to be recorded in the grantor-grantee index. One who records a document takes it to the court clerk's office, pays the proper amount of documentary stamps and transfer tax stamps, pays the recording fee, and leaves the document with the clerk. The clerk's staff then reproduces the document in the public record, stamps the original, to indicate where the information has been recorded, and returns it to the person designated to receive it.

REAL ESTATE BROKERS AND SUBDIVISION LAWS REGARDING RECORDING

Recordation and development of individual lots in a subdivision are regulated on a local level by the county in which the property is located. Licensees should always be sure that the deeds to the individual lots for sale in a subdivision have been properly recorded and that all local laws regarding recordation have been met before advertising the lots for sale. Failure to do so could result in a judicial injunction, which would halt the marketing of the property. In addition, depending on the situation, the licensees may also be in violation of the state license law and subject to suspension or revocation of their real estate licenses.

TITLE EVIDENCE

In Maryland, it is customary for buyers in a real estate transaction to obtain and pay for title evidence. Generally, they will hire attorneys who will usually do one of two things:

1. Have an abstract of title prepared and, based on the abstract, prepare a report (opinion) of title indicating their professional view of the present condition of the title as contained in the public record.

2. Acting as licensed representatives of a title insurance company, personally issue a title insurance policy binder based on examination of the abstract

The attorneys will either deliver this abstract to the purchaser or forward it to the title insurance company so that the company may issue a title policy. The person performing settlement must explain owner's title insurance and make it available to the purchasers.

Note that Maryland law requires that the following notice be given to buyers, printed in bold type in the body of each sales contract presented by licensees: **YOU ARE ENTITLED TO SELECT YOUR OWN TITLE INSURANCE COMPANY, SETTLEMENT COMPANY, ESCROW COMPANY, OR TITLE ATTORNEY.**

PREREQUISITES TO RECORDING

No fee simple deed, mortgage, or deed of trust may be recorded unless it bears a certification that the instrument has been prepared by attorneys admitted to practice before the Maryland Court of Appeals or under the supervision of such attorneys, or by one of the parties to the instrument. There are other requirements imposed by various localities.

UNIFORM COMMERCIAL CODE

The Uniform Commercial Code (UCC) is in effect in Maryland. Two provisions of this code may affect real estate practices.

1. The use of **chattel mortgages** on fixtures or contents has been replaced by use of **security agreements and financing statements.**

2. The **bulk sales provision** applies when a person sells all of the stock in trade when selling a business. The main text contains more information about the UCC.

QUESTIONS

1. Buyers purchased a parcel of real estate that is located in two counties. They should record in

   a. the county with the larger portion.
   b. the county with the smaller portion.
   c. the State capital.
   d. both counties.

2. When a parcel of Maryland real estate is sold, title search is usually ordered on behalf of the

   a. seller.
   b. buyer.
   c. broker.
   d. seller and broker together.

3. Deeds and mortgages may be recorded in each county with the

   a. circuit court clerk.
   b. Torrens system.
   c. tax office.
   d. office of planning and zoning.

4. In Maryland, county real estate records are NOT

   a. indexed under the name of the grantor.
   b. indexed under the name of the grantee.
   c. indexed under the name of the selling broker.
   d. referenced to previously recorded conveyances.

12
Real Estate Financing

OVERVIEW

Most real estate is purchased using borrowed funds. Both the traditional mortgage and the **deed of trust** are common in Maryland and are used both in third-party and in owner financing. The State allows, but stringently regulates, another form of owner financing—the installment land contract.

NOTE TO STUDENT

The deed **of** trust—also called a *trust deed*—is different from a deed **in** trust, which is used to place property into a trust. Both are different from a *trustee's deed* by which property is transferred out of a trust by the trustee. The student should review the discussion of these terms in the principal text.

MORTGAGE AND DEED OF TRUST LOANS

Maryland is considered a **title theory** state as defined in the main text. A lender who records a properly signed and delivered mortgage or deed of trust holds legal title to the real estate pledged. Maryland's mortgage and deed of trust foreclosure and sale laws, however, are similar to those of a **lien theory** state, except that lenders, rather than delinquent landlords, are *allowed to collect rents on investment properties being foreclosed.*

Deeds of trust are widely used throughout the state as financing instruments for real estate. Deed-of-trust financing is a three-party arrangement involving borrower (the trustor), trustee, and lender (beneficiary). This arrangement is so popular in Maryland that it is sometimes called a *Potomac Mortgage.*

Under the deed of trust forms used in Maryland, the **power of sale clause** gives the trustee authority to sell pledged property in the event of borrower's default. In such a case, there is no court action. After giving adequate public notice, the trustee has the property sold at a trustee sale—a public auction.

The money the trustee obtains from the sale is then applied to the principal of the mortgage debt plus the accrued interest and legal costs caused by the sale. Any money left, over and above what is due any lienholder, is returned to the defaulted borrower.

In Maryland, only a natural person and not a corporation or partnership may serve under a deed of trust and sell the property in case of default under the provisions of the document's power-of-sale clause. In some other jurisdictions any person, including corporations and partnerships, may serve.

DEFAULT, FORECLOSURE, AND DEFICIENCY

The parties to a mortgage are the mortgagor (borrower) and the mortgagee (lender). If the borrower defaults, the lender who wishes to foreclose seeks a court order to sell the mortgaged property at public auction, unless there is a power of sale clause in the mortgage. When the funds from a judicial (court-ordered) mortgage foreclosure sale are insufficient to satisfy the debt, a judgment may be issued against the borrower for the deficiency. However, when a deficiency occurs after a nonjudicial foreclosure, either by a trustee or by the mortgagee under a power-of-sale clause, no such judgment is entered. Deficiency actions are not allowed in **Federal Housing Administration** (FHA) loans, and the **Department of Veterans Affairs** (VA) is reluctant to allow them.

INTEREST RATES AND USURY

In Maryland, there is no limit on the rate of interest a lender may charge a borrower in first mortgage loans. The written agreement between mortgagor and mortgagee must specify the rate of interest and cannot require any prepayment penalty. The state interest ceiling on second mortgage loans and land installment contracts is 24 percent.

Violators of the state usury law face penalties requiring the lender to forfeit an amount equal to three times the interest charges collected over the permissible amount or $500, whichever is greater, and pay court costs.

MORTGAGE EXPENSE ACCOUNTS

Maryland savings institutions that require a tax and insurance **expense**—also called *escrow* or *impound*—**account** for mortgage and deed of trust loans must pay interest on these funds at passbook rate, but not less than 3 percent. The interest is computed on the average monthly balance in the escrow account and paid annually by crediting the borrower's account with the amount of interest due. This payment is reported to the IRS on a Form 1099. Loans sold to agencies in the secondary mortgage market are exempt from this requirement.

DISCRIMINATION

Under Maryland law, a lender may not refuse loans to any person based solely on geographic area, neighborhood, race, creed, color, age, sex, disability, marital status, familial status, or national origin. However, a lender may refuse loans based on higher-than-normal risks connected with the loan.

GROUND RENT—FHA/VA LOANS

The Department of Veterans Affairs will guarantee loans only on properties that are subject to ground rent located in Anne Arundel County, Baltimore City, Baltimore County, and the Joppatowne subdivision in Harford County. If a veteran purchases leasehold property located in another part of the state using such financing—often called a "GI" loan—the ground rent must be redeemed on or prior to the date of closing.

For Federal Housing Administration (FHA) loans on Maryland property held subject to a ground rent, the residential mortgage limit must be reduced by the capitalization value of the annual ground rent. Ground rents are discussed in Chapter 13 of this book.

RELEASE OF MORTGAGE LIEN

When a mortgage note has been fully repaid by the borrower, the lender must release the lien of the mortgage. This may be done by a separate form referred to as a **satisfaction of mortgage** or a **deed of release.** If a deed of trust form is used, a separate form of release may be recorded to clear the borrower's title.

In some instances, the mortgagee simply enters the statement of release directly in the margin of the recorded mortgage; then the mortgage form is re-recorded so that the public record will indicate the release. Recording of the release provides public notice that the original mortgage lien has been canceled.

MORTGAGE PRESUMED PAID

A mortgage or deed of trust will be presumed to have been paid and the lien created by that document removed if 12 years have elapsed since the last payment date called for in the instrument or the maturity date. Alternatively, if that date cannot be ascertained and 40 years have elapsed since the date of the document's recording, the mortgage will be presumed paid and the lien extinguished.

FORECLOSURES AND TRUSTEE SALES

The mortgage or deed of trust—but not the note—must be recorded before a lender may start foreclosure proceedings in case of borrower default. State law requires that, in order to record a residential mortgage or deed of trust, a lender must execute and attach an affidavit to each mortgage stating

- that the mortgage document accurately sets forth the amount of the loan, and

- that the entire amount was disbursed when the mortgage was executed or delivered to the lender by the borrower.

When a mortgage does not contain a provision giving the mortgagee the power of sale, a foreclosure sale ordered and supervised by the court is the lender's final remedy for default by the borrower.

Because there is no *statutory right of redemption* in Maryland, a defaulted borrower has to make redemption by paying the necessary funds to the mortgagee *before* the sale has been completed—that is, before the court officer delivers the sale deed to the purchaser.

Mortgagees or trustees are permitted to personally purchase properties in default at the sale rather than sell them to satisfy debts, provided they have diligently attempted to obtain the best possible price for each property on the market.

Holders of subordinate interests in real property may record a request for a notice of sale, requiring holders of superior interests in property to give notice of an impending foreclosure sale. They must file a **surplus money action** to receive any of the proceeds of a scheduled foreclosure sale when they are notified. If holders of such junior liens fail to do these things, their liens will be extinguished, no matter how large the proceeds from the sale.

Note that foreclosure sale under a deed of trust or mortgage in default may terminate any leaseholds on the property that began after the deed of trust was executed and recorded. Leaseholds entered into before the date of the mortgage may survive if they meet any requirements for recordation of leases longer than seven years. Tenants whose leases contain subordination agreements or who have later granted such agreements will not be protected. Strict foreclosure, as described in the principal text, is not recognized in Maryland.

LAND INSTALLMENT CONTRACTS

The state law regarding land installment contract sales of real estate is found in the Annotated Code of Maryland in Title 10 of the *Real Property* Article. Note that this law

applies only to the sale of improved properties, occupied or to be occupied by the purchaser for a dwelling, or of an unimproved, subdivided lot or lots intended to be improved for residential purposes. In other cases, common law rules apply with fewer protections for *vendees* (purchasers).

Land installment contracts should be prepared and processed by attorneys. The purchaser may rescind the contract and demand that all sums paid be returned if the vendor does not record the contract within 15 days of its being signed by all parties. Land installment contract financing also requires cumbersome ongoing processing by the vendor designed to protect the purchaser.

JUNIOR FINANCING

The maximum interest rate a lender may charge in Maryland for a **secondary mortgage** (one that is not a first mortgage) is also 24 percent; the maximum loan origination fee that may be charged is $250 or 10 percent of the proceeds of the loan, whichever is less. Only an actual cost, such as a recording fee or title insurance, may be charged over the origination fee. A lender may refinance a junior loan not more than once in any 12-month period and not more than twice during any five-year period. The *Commercial Law* Article of the Maryland Annotated Code sets forth the details.

The law also permits all fees, discounts, and points allowed or required under federally related second mortgage purchase programs. However, the points and interest rate computed together may not exceed an annual percentage rate (APR) of 24 percent.

Prohibited Practices

Junior (secondary loan) lenders in Maryland are prohibited from certain practices, including the following:

- Attempting to have the debtor waive his or her legal rights

- Requiring accelerated payments, except in case of default

- Having the debtor execute an assignment of wages for payment of the loan

- Charging a fee to execute a release after the loan is paid

Balloon Payments

Maryland Secondary Mortgage Law requires lenders, including private sellers, who take back a second mortgage containing a **balloon clause** (a clause which makes the final payment significantly larger than previous payments) to grant, upon the borrower's request, an automatic, one-time, six-month extension beyond the maturity date. This provision applies in second mortgage loans made for buying residential property for owner occupancy.

RESIDENTIAL PROPERTY LOAN NOTICES

Lenders who make loans on residential property are required to provide prospective borrowers with a written notice informing them of their right to choose an attorney or a title insurance company. This notice must be provided within three days of their application for the loan. They are also required to notify applicants that by completing their loan applications, they are terminating any right they might have had to rescind the contract for lack of a Property Disclosure/Disclaimer statement.

The text of the Secondary Mortgage Loan Law, Title 12 of the *Commercial Law* Article, may be found at
http://mlis.state.md.us/cgi-win/web_statutes.exe
Scroll down to *Commercial Law*.
For "Section", enter *12-401*.
This subtitle of Title 12 extends from 12-401 to 12-415.
Note: In the law, as seen online, each section has a title, but paragraphs and subparagraphs do not. These subtitles are called *catchlines*. They appear in the bound edition of *The Annotated Code of Maryland,* available in libraries. Lexis Publishing™ holds the copyright to all these catchlines.

QUESTIONS

1. Mortgages on Maryland real property

   a. must be recorded to be valid between lender and borrower.
   b. may not be refused to any persons because of their religion.
   c. by law must be for a minimum ten-year term.
   d. may be foreclosed by strict foreclosure if in default.

2. The VA will guarantee a loan on real property in Maryland that is held subject to a ground rent

   a. only in certain areas of the State.
   b. and the loan limit must be reduced by the capitalized value of the annual rent.
   c. only to the in-fee value of the property.
   d. only in Baltimore City.

3. Paul Jennings obtains a loan to purchase a new home from BNN Savings Bank. BNN fails to record the mortgage document. The mortgage does not give BNN the power of sale in case of default. Which of the following is true?

   a. As things stand, BNN Savings Bank will be able to enforce the mortgage in a court of law if Jennings defaults on his loan.
   b. If Jennings defaults on the loan, BNN cannot foreclose on the mortgage in court until the instrument is recorded.
   c. As mortgagor, it is Jennings' obligation to record the mortgage for his own protection.
   d. If Jennings defaults on the loan, BNN could sell the property without foreclosure action.

4. Bonita Harrison needs $165,000 to purchase a new home, and she borrows it from First Maryland Savings Bank. Which of the following security arrangements may First Maryland Savings Bank use?

   a. Mortgage or deed of trust
   b. Real estate trust
   c. Installment contract
   d. Deed of release

5. "CeeJay" Hayward obtains a 30-year loan from Liberty Savings Association to purchase a Baltimore condominium unit. Along with monthly payments of principal and interest, the lender requires Hayward to deposit funds in an escrow account for the payment of taxes and property insurance. Which of the following is true?

   a. Liberty Savings must pay Hayward interest on these escrow deposits when the loan is paid off.
   b. Hayward may require the lender to maintain his escrow account in an interest-bearing depository.
   c. Liberty Savings must credit Hayward's account for passbook rate interest on his escrow deposits annually.
   d. Hayward must pay the lender a minimum of three percent interest for maintaining such an account for him.

6. In Maryland, a land installment contract need NOT

   a. be recorded by the vendor within 15 days after it has been signed.
   b. include all terms of the transaction.
   c. be signed by the vendor and vendee.
   d. be filed with the Real Estate Commission.

13

Leases

OVERVIEW

Leaseholds in Maryland are the four familiar common law estates: (1) leases for a specified time period ("for years"), (2) leases from period to period ("from year to year"), (3) tenancies at will, and (4) tenancies at sufferance. Long-term ground leases, an example of the first type, are common in certain areas.

MARYLAND GROUND RENTS

Ground leases exist in several areas in the State. Some of them may be **redeemed** (freed from ground rent) after specified time periods, while others are irredeemable. The ground lease tenant typically owns the improvements located on the rented ground.

Ground rental is money paid to the landowner (landlord) by a tenant who possesses the landlord's land by virtue of a lease. Such leases usually give tenants possession of land for specific time periods not to exceed 99 years. Possession of the land reverts (goes back) to the fee simple land owner when the lease finally expires, if it is terminated by the tenant's default, or if it is not renewed. Many such agreements have options for renewal for additional time periods either at predetermined graduated rentals or for rentals to be based on reappraisal of the land and improvements at the time of renewal.

Any leasehold interest can be sold, mortgaged, assigned, or subleased. When tenants sell leaseholds, they assign their possessory rights to the purchaser in a document that clearly says that the estate being conveyed is less than a freehold and is, therefore, regarded as personal property rather than real property.

Creation of a Ground Rent

Anyone who owns unencumbered fee simple property can subject the property to ground rent, thus creating a leasehold estate. The **worth of the reversion** (the price to redeem) is based on the capitalized value of the ground rent. Although any amount of ground rental can be charged for a property, the rent typically is kept reasonable to make the property marketable. Ground rent amounts are usually based on rents charged for comparable lots (competitive rents) in the neighborhood or simply "what the market will bear." The student should be aware that capitalization of the annual ground rent amount does not necessarily represent the true value of the piece of land. (Capitalization of ground rent is discussed in the following section.)

Expenses involved in creating a new ground rent include charges for recording the lease, Maryland revenue stamps, and transfer tax based on the capitalized value, notary fees, and legal fees for drawing the lease.

Redemption of Certain Residential Ground Rents—Capitalization

Leases originally executed before April 9, 1884, are irredeemable. Some of those ground rents, having since been periodically renewed, are still in existence today and are still irredeemable.

However, many ground leases made after that date may be redeemed at the costs and the times shown in Figures 13.1 and 13.2.

The *Real Property* Article of the Maryland statutes provides that leases of **residential** land (except apartment and cooperative leases) for periods of longer than 15 years are redeemable at the option of the tenant. This means that tenants may purchase the rented land in fee simple from their ground landlords.

They may demand redemption by giving their landlords one month's notice and then paying them a sum of money equal to the capitalization of the annual rental at rates that do not exceed those shown.

Figure 13.1 Capitalization Rates for Redeeming Ground Leases Longer than 15 Years

Date Lease Executed	Rate to Redeem
Before April 9, 1884	Lease Is Irredeemable
April 9, 1884 to April 5, 1888	4%
After July 1, 1982	12%
At Any Other Time	6%

Example: If the annual rental on a residential lot placed under a lease for 49 years on August 29, 1988 is $240, the capitalization rate is 12 percent. The cost to redeem the property would be $2,000.

Rationale: $240 ÷ .12 = $2,000

Notice that *higher percentage rates* would result in *lower costs* to redeem.

Redemption may be for any lesser sum specified in the lease or for another sum to which the parties may agree at the time of redemption.

The time after which redemption becomes possible depends upon the date on which a lease was created.

In transactions involving ground-rent properties, the licensee should proceed only with the advice of qualified legal counsel when representing either the seller or the purchaser.

Figure 13.2 When Redemption of Reversions in Leases for Longer than 15 Years is Permitted

For Leases Dated	Redemption Is Allowed With 30 Days' Notice
Between April 9, 1884 and July 1, 1969	At Any Time
Between July 1, 1969 and July 1, 1971	Five Years From Date of Lease
On or after July 1, 1971	Three Years From Date of Lease
On or after July 1, 1982	Five Years From Date of Lease

Ground Rent Disclosure

When property subject to ground rent is sold, the contract of sale must inform the buyer that nonpayment of the ground rental may result in

- reversion of the entire property, in fee, to the ground landlord, and

- termination of the buyer's leasehold.

Owners, or licensees representing them, when posting signs announcing property for sale that is already subject to ground rent are required to *show on the sign the amount of annual ground rental and cost of capitalization in numbers as large and clear as the numbers showing the price of the property.*

Land subject to ground rent is not held in *fee simple*. The ground landlord has a *leased fee* and the tenant/occupant has a *leasehold*. Therefore, if a contract of sale for property subject to ground rent does not disclose existence of the ground rent and yet the agreement calls for delivery of fee simple title to the purchaser, the seller must redeem the property before settlement. If the property is irredeemable, the seller cannot deliver fee simple title and will be in breach of contract.

MARYLAND RESIDENTIAL LEASES

In the *Real Property* Article, the Maryland Statute of Frauds provides that, to be enforceable, leases for a year or less need not be in writing. Those whose term is more than one year must be written. The time periods are measured from "the inception of a lease"—the date the lease agreement is made—until the end of its term.

Leases longer than seven years must be **recorded.** Recordation of a document requires acknowledgment before a notary public or similar official. Note, however, that even when such leases have not been properly recorded, they are still valid and binding between the original parties, against their creditors, and against their successors and assignees, who have actual notice of the lease or who acquire the property when a tenant is in actual occupancy.

Possession (occupancy) of property by a tenant under a lease for seven years or less gives **constructive notice** of the tenant's rights. Occupancy at any time under an unrecorded lease that is for longer than seven years, does not give such notice.

Although the law requires any lease for a term longer than seven years to be recorded, a recorded **memorandum of lease** satisfies this requirement.

Post-Settlement Occupancy Excepted

No portions of the *Landlord and Tenant* statute dealing with residential leases apply when, after the sale of an owner-occupied residence, the sellers and purchasers enter into an agreement that sellers may remain in possession for a period of not more than 60 days.

Disclosure of Representation

Licensees must make disclosure of agency representation to both lessors and lessees when negotiating any residential lease for *longer than 125 days*. This disclosure must be made no later than the first scheduled face-to-face meeting between the licensees and any prospective tenant or landlord. Please review the discussion on disclosure of representation in Chapter 2 of this book.

An **application for a lease** must contain a statement explaining the liabilities incurred by the tenant upon signing the application, including the tenant's obligation to take possession if the application is accepted. If the landlord requires any fees other than a security deposit—perhaps a credit check to verify information in the application—and these fees exceed $25, the landlord is required to return the fees in excess of the actual amount spent. This applies to landlords who offer five or more rental units on one parcel of property but not to seasonal rentals or condominiums.

Landlords may not require **security deposits** of more than two months' rent or $50, whichever is more. The landlords must give tenants a receipt for such deposits. Failure to do so makes the landlord liable to the tenant for the sum of $25. Moreover, landlords are liable to tenants for up to three times any security deposit taken in excess of this limit, plus reasonable attorney fees.

Deposit monies must be placed and maintained by landlords or their agents in accounts maintained for this sole purpose in a branch of a federally insured bank or a savings institution licensed to do business in Maryland within 30 days of their being received.

In lieu of such accounts, a landlord may hold security deposits in insured certificates of deposit issued by banks, described above, or in securities issued by the federal government or the State of Maryland. The total of all these deposit accounts, certificates, and securities must be sufficient in amount to equal all the security deposits for which a broker is liable.

Broker licensees' records of these funds must be available for inspection by members of the Commission or its agents during normal business hours.

At the time leases are written, landlords must give tenants written notice of tenants' right, within 15 days of the beginning of the lease, to demand from landlords a written property condition report. A landlord who fails to provide this report to tenants who make the proper request becomes liable to the tenants for three times the amount of any security deposit taken. This amount could be offset (reduced) by amounts due in unpaid rent and tenant damages to the premises.

When a lease is terminated, the landlord must return the tenant's security deposit within 45 days, including simple interest at the statutory rate—presently 4 percent. Interest accrues at six-month intervals from the day the tenant gives the security deposit and does not compound.

Security deposits may be withheld by the landlord to cover

- unpaid rent;

- losses due to breach or violation of lease terms (the landlord is entitled only to the actual financial loss—*damages*—caused by the breach); and

- cost of repairs to leased premises because of damage to the leased premises by the tenants, their families, guests, agents, invitees, or employees, in excess of ordinary wear and tear.

Landlords who wish to withhold deposits to cover damages must present to their tenants, within 45 days of the termination of the lease, a written statement of damages including a written list of repair costs *actually incurred*. Failure to comply with this could make landlords liable to a tenant for three times the amount of the security deposit retained, plus reasonable attorneys' fees. The landlords' right to recover from the security deposit any unpaid rent or rental income lost due to breach of lease can also be lost.

An action concerning security deposits may be brought by tenants any time during tenancy or within two years after its termination.

State law requires that every landlord maintain a **records system** showing the dates and amounts of rent paid by tenants and showing that receipts of some form were given to each tenant for each cash rent payment.

MISCELLANEOUS REQUIREMENTS

Note that Baltimore County and City landlords must give tenants of multifamily dwellings notice when they are located in **floodplain areas.**

Owners of residential rental units in Baltimore City must file an **annual registration statement** with the Baltimore City Commissioner of Housing and Community Development, whether the units are occupied or not, and pay a registration fee. Other jurisdictions also may have registration requirements and conduct periodic inspections.

Owners of multifamily residential rental property are required by State law to post in a conspicuous place a sign listing the name, address, and telephone number of the property owner or managing agent. The information may instead be included in the lease or the rent receipt.

SALE OF LEASED PREMISES

Unless specified to the contrary in the lease, the purchaser of a property occupied by a tenant under a lease is bound by the conditions and terms of that lease just as the original landlord was. A purchaser not wishing to become a landlord should include a clause in the property purchase contract requiring that the premises be delivered unoccupied and vacant at the time of settlement. Baltimore City law requires a landlord to give the tenant the **right of first refusal** before the leased premises can be conveyed to a third party.

TERMINATION OF TENANCIES IN GENERAL

A lease on Maryland real estate may be terminated by any of the following circumstances:

- Expiration of the term stated in the lease

  (Although no additional notice to either party is required by common law, Maryland statutes require a minimum 30-day notice.)

- The lessee's purchase or redemption of the fee simple estate from the lessor or the lessee's acquisition of title to that estate superior to that of his lessor

- Mutual agreement between the lessor and lessee

- Destruction of the premises by fire or unavoidable accident except where the property can be restored by ordinary repairs in a few days or within a stipulated period

  (This termination is effective if the lease is for a term of seven years or less and if the lease did not provide otherwise.) This rule, although statutory, can be set aside by contractual agreement between the parties.

- Cancellations granted by a court of law when there has been a breach of any covenant or condition of the lease

- Eviction of the tenant as a result of litigation

- Foreclosure of a mortgage on the premises that was entered into prior to the leasehold agreement

Termination of Periodic Tenancies

The requirements to terminate **periodic tenancies** differ throughout the State. In all counties except Montgomery County and Baltimore City, the *landlord must give the tenant written notice* to terminate, as follows:

- One week for a week-to-week tenancy

- One month for a month-to-month tenancy

- Three months for a year-to-year tenancy

By contrast, a *tenant's parol (oral) notice* is sufficient to terminate such tenancies. If landlords can prove that the tenants gave such notice, they do not need to give their own notice to those tenants.

In Montgomery County, the parties may agree in writing to longer or shorter notice periods. The local laws of Baltimore City generally require a landlord to give the following written notices to terminate:

- 60 days for a tenancy of less than one year, or at sufferance;

- 90 days for a periodic tenancy; and

• 30 days in all other cases.

A tenant may terminate any of these tenancies by giving the landlord 30 days' notice.

When a landlord consents to a tenant's **holding over** (remaining on the premises), tenant becomes a week-to-week tenant if the lease status was week-to-week prior to the holding over. In all other cases, the tenant becomes a month-to-month tenant unless the lease provides otherwise and this lease provision is initialed by the tenant.

A tenant under a lease who unlawfully holds over beyond the termination of the lease is liable to the landlord for actual damages that may be caused by the holding over.

Landlords' Rights to Summary Dispossession

Landlords who give the required notice or have court orders for termination of tenancy may dispossess tenants and repossess property by simple court suit before a district court judge. The length of notice landlords must give tenants before beginning **dispossession proceedings** is generally one month in renewable monthly tenancies or in tenancies with a fixed term and no provision for renewal. For automatically renewable yearly tenancies, this notice (with certain exceptions) is three months; for renewable monthly or weekly tenancies, it is one month or one week.

Tenant Refusal to Comply

If the tenant or person in possession refuses to comply with the written request to remove from the property, the landlord may make a complaint in writing to the district court of the county where the property is located. The court issues a summons, served by the sheriff to the tenant, to appear before the court, and an attested copy is affixed to the property in a conspicuous place. This is considered sufficient notice.

Back Rent on Renewal of Lease

Tenants or assignees who apply to their landlords for renewal under a covenant in their leases giving them the right to renew must produce vouchers or evidence showing payment of rent accrued for three years preceding this demand and application. If tenants do not provide such proof, landlords, before executing the renewal of the lease, are entitled to demand and recover not more than three years' back rent, in addition to any renewal fine that may be provided for in the lease. This commonly occurs in situations involving ground rent.

Failure to Demand Rent

If there is no demand or payment of rent for more than 20 consecutive years, landlords not only lose the unpaid rental but also the reversion of the property. Landlords under any legal disability when the 20-year period expires have 2 years after the removal of the disability to assert their rights. Landlords' failure to demand rent for 20 years could result in the tenants' receiving fee simple title.

Receipts for Tenants' Rental

In Anne Arundel County, unless the tenant makes payment by check or rents the property for commercial or business purposes, the landlord is required to give the tenant a receipt showing the amount of payment and the time it covers. On conviction of violating this section of the law, any person or agent forfeits the rent for the period in question.

In other counties, when the tenant makes payment other than by check, the landlord or the landlord's agent must give the tenant a receipt.

Surrender of Premises

When a lease contains a covenant or promise by the tenant to leave, restore, surrender, or yield the leased premises in good repair, this does not bind the tenant to erect any similar building or pay for any building destroyed by fire or otherwise if the damage was not due to the negligence or fault of the tenant.

Landlords may ask the district court to seize and sell tenants' personal property for unpaid rent by filing a petition. Landlords may do this only if tenancy has continued for longer than three months (by written lease or periodic tenancy) or was *at will*. Both the landlords' right to and the court's taking of tenants' property are called *distraint*.

A rental agreement must clearly state such information as when tenancy expires, when rent accrues or whether rent is to be paid in advance or in arrears. If it does not, a court may find the agreement's terms too vague and deny the landlord's request for distraint.

PROHIBITED RESIDENTIAL LEASE PROVISIONS

In Maryland, the following provisions are prohibited in residential leases:

- A provision (**cognovit clause**) that authorizes an attorney for the landlord to plead *the tenant* guilty (**confess judgment**) on a claim arising from the lease, especially failure to pay rental

- A provision under which the tenant agrees to waive or forgo any rights or remedies against the landlord as provided by law

- A provision allowing the landlord to charge a penalty for late payment of rent more than five percent of the amount of rent due for the period in which the rent is delinquent

  (In weekly rentals, this late charge may not exceed $3 per week or $12 per month.)

- Any provision under which the tenant waives his or her right to a jury trial

- Any provision under which the tenant agrees to a period for the landlord's **notice to quit** (in the event that the tenant breaches the lease terms) that is less than the period prescribed by law

  (Both parties, however, are free to agree to a period that is longer than is prescribed by law.)

- Any provision authorizing the landlord to take possession of the leased premises or any of the tenant's personal property unless the lease has been terminated by operation of law and such personal property has been abandoned by the tenant

- Any **exculpatory clause** (language in the lease intended to exempt or hold the landlord harmless from liability to the tenant or any other person for any injury, loss, damage, or liability arising from the landlord's omission, fault, negligence, or other misconduct on or about the leased premises in areas that are not under the tenant's control; such areas include stairways, elevators, hallways, and so forth) is contrary to public policy and void

- A provision (not signed or initialed by the tenant) allowing the automatic renewal of the lease term for more than one month

- A requirement that the tenant give the landlord a longer period of notice to terminate the tenancy than the period granted the landlord to similarly notify the tenant

All of the preceding provisions, if included in a Maryland lease, are considered **unenforceable.** Landlords who threaten or attempt to enforce one or more of these provisions may be liable to tenant for actual damages and attorney's fees incurred as a result. There is no penalty for merely including them in a lease.

WITHHOLDING RENT

State law requires that a landlord provide and maintain premises for tenants that are free of defects and do not present substantial and serious threat of danger to the life, health, and safety of the tenants.

Where **hazardous conditions** exist on leased property, a tenant may give the landlord written notice by certified mail of the conditions and wait as long as 30 days. If the hazardous conditions are not corrected within 30 days, a tenant can withhold rent from the landlord or pay it into an escrow account for necessary repairs. Such conditions include fire or health hazards or other defects that may threaten the safety or occupancy of renters, such as

- lack of adequate sewage disposal facilities;

- infestation of rodents in two or more dwelling units; or

- failure to meet the standards set in the *Environment* Article at §6-815 or §6-819 for dealing with lead-based paint hazards. See Chapter 13 in this book..

The Baltimore City Code holds that there is an implied **warranty of habitability** by a landlord that the premises are fit for human habitation. It also provides for remedies for tenants if the premises are unsafe and dirty to the extent that tenants' health is threatened. The warranty of habitability differs from **rent escrow laws** in that tenants have the use of their rent money to make those repairs the landlord has failed to complete. Under the rent escrow law, rent must be paid into an account where it is held until the repairs are made.

The district court can order tenants to pay rents into a **rent escrow account** of the court or administrative agency of the county. If the tenant fails to pay rent accrued or as it becomes due, the court, upon certification of the account, can give judgment in favor of the landlord and issue a warrant for possession. Upon final disposition of the action, the rent escrow account is distributed in accordance with the judgment or hearing.

Note that minor, not dangerous, defects or housing code violations that go uncorrected are not considered just cause for nonpayment of rent.

LEASE AGREEMENT FORMS

A number of lease forms are available from local realty boards or associations, property owner associations, and tenant organizations. Any landlord who offers more than four dwelling units for rent on one parcel of property or at one location and who rents by means of written leases substantially increases the requirements concerning the form of written lease.

RETALIATORY EVICTIONS

A landlord may not evict tenants, increase rent, or decrease any services to which they are entitled for their doing any of the following things:

- Filing written complaints with the landlord or with a public agency against the landlord

- Filing a lawsuit against the landlord

- Joining a tenants' organization

PEACEABLE AND QUIET ENTRY

Landlords are required by law to assure that tenants may peaceably and quietly enter the leased premises at the beginning of the lease. Failure to do so allows the tenant, upon written notice to the landlord before possession is delivered, to recision of the lease, abatement of rent, or actual damages.

SAFETY REQUIREMENTS

Tenant safety is an ongoing concern of landlords and their agents and property managers.

Compliance with Lead-Based Paint and Lead-Based Paint Hazards Reduction Laws

Licensees helping rent older properties must be prepared to protect their clients and their customers by meeting the disclosure requirements outlined in Figure 13.3 on page 138.

Sprinkler Systems

Sprinkler systems must be installed in every newly constructed dormitory, hotel, lodging or rooming house, town house, and multi-family residential dwelling. Sprinkler systems are not required if a dwelling unit is not serviced by a public water supply system.

Smoke Detectors

Smoke detectors must be installed in all multifamily buildings and hotels constructed before 1975 and having four to

Figure 13.3 Lead-Based Paint Disclosure Requirements

Dates	Federal Compliance Requirements
Built Before 1/1/1978	Called "Targeted Property" 1. EPA Booklet *Protect Your Family from Lead in Your Home* 2. Lead Based Paint (Rental) Disclosure Form (Form to be given, signed, and copies kept)
	Maryland Compliance Requirements
Built before 1/1/1950	Called "Affected Property" Must be registered and re-registered annually with the Maryland Department of the Environment 1. Inspection and, if necessary, abatement by owner 2. Maryland Department of the Environment Notice to tenants at beginning of occupancy, whenever the rent changes, and every two years since the last notice

nine units and in all buildings with more than nine units. The landlord is responsible for the installation, repair or replacement of the detectors. The occupant of a one-family, two-family, or three-family residential dwelling constructed before July 1975 is required to equip the apartment with at least one approved smoke detector and to maintain it.

A smoke detector operated both by battery and by alternating current (AC) must be installed in every newly constructed residential dwelling unit. At least one smoke detector must be installed on each level, including basements but not attics.

LEASE OPTION AGREEMENTS

A **lease option** agreement includes any lease that contains a clause giving the tenant the option to purchase the landlord's interest in the property until some specified date. No lease option on improved residential property in Maryland, with or without a ground rent interest, is valid unless it contains the statement "THIS IS NOT A CONTRACT TO BUY" in capital letters. It must also contain a clear statement of the option's purpose and effect with respect to the ultimate purchase of the property.

SOURCES OF ASSISTANCE

Baltimore Neighborhoods, Inc., a private nonprofit civil rights agency working in behalf of fair housing and tenants' rights in the Baltimore area, publishes guides to laws covering tenant/landlord relations in Baltimore City, the counties and the State. These guides, revised annually to incorporate new laws, may be purchased from the organization at 2217 St. Paul St., Baltimore, MD 21218.

MOBILE HOME PARKS

Title 8A of the *Real Property* Article sets forth the rights and responsibilities of mobile home tenants and owners. It addresses such matters as park rules, maintenance, and tenancy.

View Baltimore Neighborhoods, Inc. at
http://www.bni-maryland.org/

Find the text of the Landlord and Tenant Law, Title 8 of the *Real Property* Article, at
http://mlis.state.md.us/cgi-win/web_statutes.exe
Scroll down to *Real Property*
For "Section", enter 8-101. Title 8 extends from 8-101 to 8-604

QUESTIONS

1. Sampson sold a house he owned that was occupied by Rawlins under a one-year lease having six months to run. Therefore

    a. Rawlins must vacate at the closing of the sale.
    b. Rawlins's lease continues until its expiration.
    c. the lease terminates at closing.
    d. the lease is not binding on the new owner.

2. A landlord holding a tenant's security deposit of $500 is required to

    a. credit the deposit account $20 interest per year.
    b. allow the tenant 5 percent simple interest per year.
    c. return the deposit within 30 days after termination of the lease.
    d. give the tenant a receipt or be liable to the tenant for a sum of $250.

3. Which of the following leases need NOT be in writing, acknowledged, and recorded in Maryland?

    a. Seven-year apartment lease
    b. Eight-year residential lease
    c. Nine-year commercial lease
    d. Ten-year residential lease

4. John Builder has just completed a new house, which he is offering for sale at $68,000 with fee simple title. If, to satisfy an immediate buyer, he creates a ground lease requiring $240 a year ground rent at an 8 percent redemption rate, then

    a. the property may not be redeemed for at least 50 years.
    b. he can reduce the price to $65,000.
    c. he can reduce the price to $56,000.
    d. the in-fee price would be $71,000.

5. Arthur Buyer is interested in buying a residence for $40,000 with a ground rent of $180. Arthur will receive

   a. a deed conveying to him a fee simple interest.
   b. a leasehold estate subject to an annual ground rent of $180.
   c. no deed until such time as he redeems the ground rent.
   d. a fee simple deed after paying ground rent for five years.

6. A man who owns and occupies his home and pays a semiannual ground rent owns an estate in real estate that is called a(n)

   a. fee simple estate.
   b. leasehold estate.
   c. estate at will.
   d. estate at sufferance.

7. Ground rents are sometimes originated to

   a. reduce the amount of cash required to purchase a property.
   b. force the tenant to keep the property in good repair.
   c. provide further assurances to the mortgagee.
   d. prevent the lender from foreclosing.

8. The ground rent on a residence is $180 a year, and the lease has been in effect for more than five years. A redemption at

   a. 5 percent will require $3,200.
   b. 6 percent will require $3,000.
   c. 10 percent will require $6,400.
   d. 12 percent will require $6,000.

9. The right of a landlord to have a court seize and sell a tenant's personal property for unpaid rent is called

   a. ejectment.
   b. abandonment.
   c. dispossession.
   d. distraint.

10. Which of the following provisions, if included in residential leases in Maryland, is enforceable?

   a. Tenants agree to pay the landlord a 5 percent penalty for late rent payments.
   b. Tenants agree to let landlords use their passkeys to take possession of tenants' property if tenants fall more than one month behind in rent payments.
   c. Tenants agree to waive or forgo any rights or remedies against landlords provided by law.
   d. Tenants waive their rights to jury trial.

14

Environmental Issues and Real Estate Transactions

OVERVIEW

The State of Maryland, like most states, faces complex environmental challenges. Almost all of them call for balancing economic growth with human safety and quality of life. These tensions can pit the rights of property owners against the wishes of others for preservation or restoration of natural resources. Literally hundreds of statutes, ordinances, and regulations are written statewide each year to address these matters.

> Various resources are available on Maryland Environmental concerns and programs at the Web site of the Maryland Department of the Environment at
> **http://www.mde.state.md.us/**

MULTIPLE CHALLENGES

Some of the greatest areas of environmental concern are loss of woodlands, farmlands, tidal wetlands and nontidal wetlands. These overlap such ecological issues as endangered species, clean air, clean water, fisheries, and other wildlife. Recreation and camping needs are also part of the puzzle.

A variety of hazards to human health are created by auto emissions and other air and/or water pollution, for example, by ozone, asbestos, radon, radium, lead-based paint, wastewater sewerage, industrial waste, leakage from underground storage tanks, and acid rain.

Additional areas of concern are stormwater and nutrient runoff management, post-mining reclamation activities, water pollution near wellheads, and the effects on wildlife and endangered species of dredging and filling of waterways. An ever-increasing problem is disposal of solid waste (garbage and trash) and sludge from water treatment plants and industrial activities.

MEETING THE CHALLENGES

One of the current attempts to balance the conflicting demands of conservation and development is the Governor's *Smart Growth Initiative,* which is designed to motivate local jurisdictions in the State to plan more effectively for growth without sprawl—the wasteful use of space.

> For a better understanding of this and related initiatives, go to the *Smart Growth and Neighborhood Conservation* Web site:
> **http://www.op.state.md.us/ smartgrowth/index.html**

The Smart Growth Initiative is intended to guide growth wisely. It is not a no-growth plan. Even its name is crafted to attract the participation of such diverse parties as environmentalists and developers. Planning for "smart growth" will include all stakeholders—representatives of every side of the issue—in hopes of getting better cooperation from all parties in carrying out the decisions made.

MULTILEVEL APPROACHES

The State reaches upward, outward, and inward in its efforts: upward toward federal agencies, outward toward neighboring states, and inward to subdivisions and municipalities.

To this last group, the State typically grants enabling powers to authorize their participation through zoning and other environmentally related activities. The various subdivisions are authorized to set standards even more rigorous than those set by the State. If they are less strict than the State's, the more rigorous State law will prevail.

Cooperative Approaches

It is rare that an environmental issue can be handled effectively by the Maryland State Government acting alone. Its activities and interests overlap and interact with those of the federal government, neighboring states, Maryland subdivisions and municipalities, and private and corporate citizens.

ENFORCEMENT

Enforcement of standards, set forth in statutes, regulations, and ordinances, is carried out by the Maryland Department of the Environment (MDE), except in cases where county enforcement capabilities and resources are comparable to those of the Department. The Secretary of MDE may delegate enforcement powers to such counties for a two-year period.

THE CHESAPEAKE BAY

The Chesapeake Bay, which is nearly 200 miles long and fed by 48 major rivers, 100 smaller rivers, and thousands of other tributaries, is the largest and most productive estuary in the United States. It covers 64,000 square miles and provides habitat for myriad species of plants and animals. Its 15 million person population is expected to swell to 18 million by 2020.

Chesapeake Bay Critical Area Act

This law identified the "Critical Area" as all land within 1,000 feet of the mean high-water line of tidal waters or the landward edge of tidal wetlands and all waters of and lands under the Chesapeake Bay and its tributaries.

The Buffer

The Act created "The Buffer"—a 100-foot, naturally vegetated, forested zone from the mean high-water line, landward from tidal waters and from the edge of tidal wetlands.

The Buffer's trees filter runoff water returning to the stream and reduce sediments, fertilizers, and toxic substances. Human activities in the area are sharply reduced because of their adverse impact on the nearby waterways and wildlife. No disturbance of the Buffer may be permitted by local jurisdictions unless an applicant can meet strict provisions for a variance.

Land Use Classifications

Within the Critical Area, land is categorized by its level of use. The classifications are Intensely Developed Areas (IDAs), Limited Development Areas (LDAs), and Resource Conservation Areas (RCAs).

In IDAs, among other requirements, new development must use "best management practices (BMPs) so that there is 10 percent *less* runoff of water and pollutants *after* the development than before. This is the "10% Rule."

In LDAs, development must *improve* water quality and not change the prevailing character of land use. It must also preserve, enhance, and encourage the natural habitat of wildlife and plants. Those who build where there was no forest cover must plant 15 percent of the area with trees. If forest cover is cleared, it must be replaced in ratios from 1 to 1 to 3 to 1. Impervious (paved) surfaces may be no more than 25 percent of quarter acre lots and 15 percent of lots a half acre or larger.

RCAs, presently characterized by agriculture, forestry, and fisheries, limit development to one dwelling per 20 acres. Farmers are required to use BMPs to prevent runoff of soil and of fertilizers and other substances that reduce water quality. Timber harvesting must provide protection

of water quality, continuity of habitat, and reforestation of forested area.

A wealth of interesting and useful information on the plan is found at the Web site maintained by the Chesapeake Bay Critical Areas Commission (CBCAC).

> CBCAC Web site:
> **http://www.dnr.state.md.us/**
> **criticalarea/index.html**

FILLING OF WETLANDS RESISTED

Filling wetlands, for whatever purpose, is regarded as one of the most environmentally pernicious of actions. It may be permitted only when no alternative course of action is available or when new areas of wetland to compensate for those being filled will be created by the person seeking a permit. The replacement area ratios range from 1-new-for-each-one-lost to 4.5-new-for-each-one-lost.

When enforced by overlapping bureaucracies, the rules have sometimes proved to be extremely complex for those who apply for approvals, especially for filling operations. For instance, there have even been as many as three different definitions of the term *wetlands* in force at one time.

IMPACT ON RESIDENTIAL REAL ESTATE

Many of these environmental issues directly and indirectly affect availability of residential housing. As a consequence of their efforts to preserve agricultural space and wetlands, various levels of government reduce the amount of land available for development. For instance, the present policy of Maryland is not just to maintain but to increase the number of wetlands.

The State is paying down the Outdoor Recreation Land Loan of 1989 and purchasing more land with part of the State Transfer Tax imposed on most residential real estate transactions. This tax also is applied toward the Agricultural Land Preservation Fund, the Rural Legacy Program, the Heritage Conservation Fund, and the operation of Program Open Space.

In seeking to achieve environmental and public safety goals, the State and its subdivisions impose regulatory and impact fees and increasingly require costly safety measures and techniques that protect both persons and the environment.

By slowing development and imposing fees upon developers—passed along to consumers—and by using settlements as a revenue source, governments make it more costly for people to buy homes.

ENVIRONMENTAL LEGISLATION AND REGULATION

Licensees should become aware of the numerous federal, state, and local environmental land use regulations and agencies and how they affect development. The *Environment* and *Natural Resources* Articles of the Annotated Code of Maryland contain statutes governing waters, soils, forests, and sanitary facilities in the state. Related regulations are made by the MDE.

MARYLAND DEPARTMENT OF THE ENVIRONMENT

The MDE points out the presence of household **radon** in Maryland and cites the danger of continued exposure to it:

> Some Maryland homes have radon levels higher than 200 pico-curies per liter (pCi/l) of air (pico-curies per liter is a measure of radiation). These levels are 50 times higher than the action guidelines set by the U.S. Environmental Protection Agency. By spending your lifetime in a house with radon levels of 10 pCi/l you have a lung cancer risk similar to smoking nearly a pack of cigarettes a day.

The MDE provides basic information about radon on its Web site:
http://www.mde.state.md.us/reference/ factsheets/radon.html

The web site suggests that persons with inquiries about radon contact the EPA (federal) Hotline: 1-800-767-7236.

The MDE is testing for **radium**—a naturally occurring radioactive metal— in wells in portions of Anne Arundel, Baltimore, Cecil, Harford, Kent, Queen Anne's, and Prince George's Counties. It projects the danger from drinking water with radium in it thus:

> (The) Environmental Protection Agency (EPA) estimates that there may be some long-term health risk from drinking water containing radium above EPA standards. According to EPA, if 10,000 people were to consume two liters of this water every day for 50 years, there might be one additional fatal cancer among the 10,000 exposed individuals. Consuming water at

this level is comparable to receiving one routine chest x-ray per year, with the exposure increasing as the concentrations increase.

Air and Radiation Management Administration

Within the MDE, the Air and Radiation Management Administration, among its other duties, sets and enforces standards for **asbestos** removal and encapsulation projects and licenses people who work in that field.

Waste Management Administration

Also within the MDE is the Waste Management Administration which deals with environmental restoration and land redevelopment, oil control, **lead poisoning, solid waste, scrap tires, sewage sludge,** and **hazardous materials.** It oversees aboveground storage tanks for oil and gas and underground tanks for storage of regulated substances. It seeks to identify, prioritize, and abate contaminated sites.

Owners of certain underground storage tanks containing petroleum products must remove or pay for the removal of tanks that leak. MDE regulations set standards for evidence of financial responsibility of owners for costs of cleanup, corrective action, and liability.

Water Management Administration

Among the most important functions within the MDE are those given to the Water Management Administration, which seeks to protect **drinking water.** With its 62 inspectors, it also oversees tidal and nontidal wetlands, floodplains, water appropriations, waterway and floodplain

construction, sediment control, stormwater management, coal mining, and oil and gas exploration.

LEAD PAINT POISONING REDUCTION ACT

The purpose of this law is " . . . to reduce the incidence of childhood lead poisoning, while maintaining the stock of available affordable rental housing." This act, the environmental law that affects more existing residential properties than any other, undergirds Maryland's Lead Paint Poisoning Prevention Program.

> To see the full text of the *Reduction of Lead Risk in Housing Act,* go to
> **http://mlis.state.md.us/**
> **cgi-win/web_statutes.exe**
> For Article, select *Environment.*
> For Section, enter 6-801.

There is broad-based scientific agreement that exposure to lead-based paint can produce devastating results in young children, newborns, and fetuses. This law is an earnest attempt to reduce the exposure of children under age six and of pregnant women to the effects of lead-based paint in residential rental properties built before 1979.

Lead Paint Poisoning Abatement

State and federal legislation concerning lead levels in certain rental properties place substantial responsibilities and burdens on investor-owners of many income properties and their agents. At the same time, these laws allow investors to limit their liability for lead poisoning by following certain procedures.

Children and Mothers Targeted for Protection

Maryland's Lead Paint Poisoning Prevention Plan makes children under age six and pregnant women with EBL (Elevated Blood Lead) levels eligible for specific financial relief for medical treatment ($7,500) and for relocation to lead-safe housing ($9,500). These amounts come either from landlords or the landlords' insurance companies. Investors wishing to limit their liability to their tenants for lead poisoning must bring their property into compliance with "lead-free" or "lead-safe" standards and keep it that way.

Plan Encourages Modest Settlements

The plan doesn't actually limit or "cap" the liability of landlords. Rather, it makes them eligible to present "qualified offers" to their tenants found to have EBLs of amounts up to $7,500 for medical expenses and up to $9,500 for relocation and rent supplement expenses. If tenants with elevated levels of lead in their blood accept the "qualified offer," they give up the right to sue the landlord for larger sums. They get their money as soon as needed and don't have to face the prolonged uncertainty of initiating a lawsuit that may be particularly difficult to win.

Companies insuring residential properties that are, or have been made, lead-free or lead-safe are required to provide liability coverage for lead-paint poisoning up to $17,000—the total of $7,500 and $9,500.

Scope of Program Will Increase

The moratorium (delay) in enforcement of Maryland's requirements on landlords has ended. Moreover, the requirements increase

periodically. Note: *affected properties* are those constructed before 1950 that contain at least one rental dwelling unit; the term also refers to an individual unit within such a multiunit building, as well as *any* residential rental property for which the owner has elected to comply with this law.

- On and after February 24, 2001, owners of affected properties were required to ensure that at least 50 percent of their affected properties have satisfied the risk reduction standard specified in the statute, without regard to the number of affected properties in which there has been a change in occupancy.

- On and after February 24, 2006, owners of affected properties shall ensure that 100 percent of their affected properties in which a person at risk resides, and of whom the owner has been notified in writing, have satisfied the *risk reduction standard*.

- On and after February 24, 2006, an owner of affected properties shall ensure that 100 percent of the owner's affected properties in which a person at risk does *not* reside have satisfied the *modified* risk reduction standard.

Properties To Be Registered

This law divides residential rental properties into three groups, based on dates of their construction:

- Before 1950

- From 1950 through 1977

- 1978 and after

Under this law, effective since October 1994, more than 50,000 rental dwelling properties have already been registered with the MDE. Owners must register every residential dwelling unit built before 1950 and pay an annual fee of $10.

Owners of other properties—those built from 1950 through 1977—who choose not to participate, must pay a fee of $5 per unit per year. Those who do participate pay $10 per unit per year. All registrations must be renewed annually.

Owners of properties built after 1977 are permitted to join the program and submit to its requirements if they choose to do so.

Licensees' Responsibilities

Licensees representing landlords who have affected residential rental properties share their legal responsibilities as their agents. Consequently, they must become familiar with aspects of inspection, lead reduction procedures, property registration, periodic renewal of registration, insurance, and limitation of liability with respect to lead paint issues.

For this purpose, many licensees are taking specialized management courses offered by the Maryland Department of the Environment's Waste Management Administration's Lead Accreditation & Oversight Division and such groups as the Institute for Real Estate Management (IREM) and Business Owners and Managers Association (BOMA) that focus on this law. This is another illustration of the principle that *education and training are a way of life for licensees who are dedicated to meeting their fiduciary responsibilities*.

The "50% Phase-in Requirement"

Under the "Reduction of Lead Risk in Housing" statute, property owners were required to bring at least 50 percent of their affected properties into compliance with the Full Risk Reduction Standard as provided in Maryland Environment Article Title 6, Subtitle 8, §6-815(a), as of February 24, 2001.

This meant that at least 50 percent of affected property rental units had to meet the *full risk reduction standard and be certified* in compliance with the standard by a State-accredited private lead inspector.

"Affected properties" include all residential rental units built before 1950 and rental units built from 1950 through 1977 that the owner has voluntarily elected to bring into compliance with the standard in order to qualify for limited liability.

The standard can be met with an inspection certificate certifying compliance with:

- Full Risk Reduction Standard using either the dust test OR performance of the lead hazard reduction treatments;

- the Lead Free Standard; or

- the Lead Safe Standard.

It is necessary to use accredited contractors and inspectors when performing work to meet the standard.

The State—through its leadership and agencies—is manifesting a determination to pursue the goal of a lead-safe rental environment for the children of Maryland.

The phase-in program is an example of the State's making enforcement seem both reasonable and likely to happen.

FEDERAL LAW ALSO APPLIES

The requirements of Maryland law are in addition to and do not take the place of the requirements set forth in federal law concerning lead in residential properties built prior to 1978. The federal law requires distribution of information in the form of the booklet *Protect Your Family from Lead in Your Home* both to potential tenants and to purchasers of properties built before 1978.

> This booklet can be read and downloaded from the HUD Web site:
> **http://www.hud.gov/lea/leapame.pdf**

Additional HUD/EPA requirements require giving purchasers a form: *Disclosure of Lead-Based Paint and Lead-Based Paint Hazards*. The form becomes a part of the contract to purchase. It allows such purchasers as much as a ten-day interval to secure a lead assessment inspection of the property, and to rescind the contract if sellers will correct any deficiencies that are found. The inspection or risk assessment period can be lengthened, shortened, or waived by mutual written consent between the purchaser and the seller.

It also contains the sellers' disclosure of all known lead-paint hazards in the property and a lead warning statement. It requires the purchasers' signatures about this information, receipt of the EPA/HUD pamphlet, and their decision as to whether they will make use of the maximum ten-day contingency period.

Even owners who sell or rent their own property without the aid of brokerage services are required to provide the form and the pamphlet. The rental form makes no provision for an inspection period, but otherwise contains essentially the same information as the form for sales. It refers, of course, to lessors and lessees rather than to purchaser and seller. Figure 14.1 presents a typical form for sales. Remember: a different form is used for rental transactions that contains no ten-day period for lead inspection and subsequent cancellation.

There is no official federal form, only the requirement that any form used have "substantially the same language" as that prescribed in HUD regulations. Many associations of brokers, therefore, use HUD's language word-for-word.

There is a substantial fine for failure to present the properly completed form. Giving a *purchase* form to a *renter* or a renter form to a purchaser, or failing to respond to every question on the form, or failure to get required signatures of buyers, sellers, and agents would have the effect of not presenting the form at all. When a licensee agent makes any of these mistakes, both the licensee *and* the principal/ homeseller are held responsible. Fines of up to $10,000 may be imposed, and an assessment of treble damages can be levied for deliberate failure. Fines are assessed jointly and severally. (Not proportionately).

Maryland law by contrast, requires inspection and remediation by owners of affected residential rental property built before 1978,

Figure 14.1 Lead-Based Paint Disclosure Form Used When Real Estate Is Sold

Sample Disclosure Format
for Target Housing Sales Disclosure of Information
on Lead-Based Paint and Lead-Based Paint Hazards

Lead Warning Statement

Every purchaser of any interest in residential real property on which a residential dwelling was built prior to 1978 is notified that such property may present exposure to lead from lead-based paint that may place young children at risk of developing lead poisoning. Lead poisoning in young children may produce permanent neurological damage, including learning disabilities, reduced intelligence quotient, behavioral problems, and impaired memory. Lead poisoning also poses a particular risk to pregnant women. The seller of any interest in residential real property is required to provide the buyer with any information on lead-based paint hazards from risk assessments or inspections in the seller's possession and notify the buyer of any known lead-based paint hazards. A risk assessment or inspection for possible lead-based paint hazards is recommended prior to purchase.

Seller's Disclosure (initial)

_____(a) Presence of lead-based paint and/or lead-based paint hazards (check one below):

☐   Known lead-based paint and/or lead-based paint hazards are present in the housing (explain).

☐   Seller has no knowledge of lead-based paint and/or lead-based paint hazards in the housing.
_____(b) Records and reports available to the seller (check one below):

☐   Seller has provided the purchaser with all available records and reports pertaining to lead-based paint and/or lead-based paint hazards in the housing (list documents below).

☐   Seller has no reports or records pertaining to lead-based paint and/or lead-based paint hazards in the housing.

Purchaser's Acknowledgment (initial)

_____(c) Purchaser has received copies of all information listed above.
_____(d) Purchaser has received the pamphlet Protect Your Family From Lead in Your Home.
_____(e) Purchaser has (check one below):

☐   Received a 10-day opportunity (or mutually agreed upon period) to conduct a risk assessment or inspection for the presence of lead-based paint and/or lead-based paint hazards; or

☐   Waived the opportunity to conduct a risk assessment or inspection for the presence of lead-based paint and/or lead-based paint hazards.

Agent's Acknowledgment (initial)

_____(f) Agent has informed the seller of the seller's obligations under 42 U.S.C. 4852d and is aware of his/her responsibility to ensure compliance.

Certification of Accuracy

The following parties have reviewed the information above and certify, to the best of their knowledge, that the information provided by the signatory is true and accurate.

Seller	Date	Seller	Date
Agent	Date	Agent	Date
Purchaser	Date	Purchaser	Date

and delivery of the Maryland Department of Environment Notice to tenants when such properties are next rented and each later time the properties "turn over."

The requirements for distribution of lead-based paint literature by both the Federal Government and Maryland are outlined in Figure 14.2.

Figure 14.2 Federal and Maryland Requirements for Residential Structures Lead Paint Poisoning Disclosure Literature

Built (Dates are Inclusive)	Lease	Sale	Federal Requirements	MD Requirements
1/1/1979 and forward (Fed) 1/1/1978 and forward (MD)	✔	✔	n/a	n/a
1950-1978 (Fed) 1950-1977 (MD)	✔	✔	EPA Booklet & Rental Disclosure Form	n/a
Before 1/1/1950	✔		EPA Booklet & Rental Disclosure Form	MD DOE Notice
Before 1/1/1950		✔	EPA Booklet & Sale Disclosure Form	n/a

15
Fair Housing

OVERVIEW

Competent real estate licensees realize that fair housing compliance is very demanding. It requires knowledge of applicable federal, state, and local laws, each of which often has its own list of protected groups and of prohibited and required activities. In chapter 15, we see their overlapping similarities and some differences.

In this chapter, the term *Commission* refers to the State of Maryland Commission on Human Relations.

COMMISSION ON HUMAN RELATIONS

The Human Relations Commission is comprised of nine members who are appointed by the Governor for staggered six-year terms. Its chairman is chosen from among its members, and it is served by an Executive Director and Deputy Director. The Executive selects an attorney to serve as the Commission's General Counsel. The body meets monthly with additional special meetings on five days' notice to the members.

In addition to their work with fair housing, the Commission works to reduce discrimination in employment and in public accommodations.

In addition to receiving complaints from the public, the Commission may also take the initiative and generate complaints when at least three of its members agree to do so.

The Commission is also subject to the very law from which it receives its authority. That is because all state agencies, departments, boards, and their employees, are subject to Article 49b, the Human Relations Commission law.

PROCESSING COMPLAINTS

Complaints *to the Commission* must be made within one year of the alleged discriminatory action or the end of such action, whichever is later. Complaints must be made in writing and under oath.

When a complaint is received, the Executive Director considers it and refers it to staff for investigation. Copies of the written staff report submitted to the

Executive Director are then sent both to the *complainant*—the aggrieved party making the complaint, and to the *respondent*—the party accused of discriminatory behavior. If the respondent is also a real estate licensee, a copy of the report is sent to the state Real Estate Commission.

If the report concludes that a discriminatory act has probably been committed, staff members seek to deal with the matter by conference, conciliation, and persuasion. If no agreement is reached between complainant and respondent, a report of that fact is sent to all parties.

If the initial conclusion of staff is that there is no *probable cause,* their report is considered a "final order" appealable by the complainant to a circuit court in the county where the alleged violation occurred.

When there has been found to be probable cause and no agreement is reached, all findings are certified to by staff and a written notice is sent in the name of the Commission to the respondent requiring an answer to the charges at a public hearing before a hearing examiner, to be held in the county of the alleged violation.

If conciliation is productive, a *conciliation agreement* is written and signed by the parties. Its terms are made public unless the parties request they not be **and** the Commission determines such disclosure would not serve the purposes of the statute.

Up to this point, all proceedings are non-public and held in strict confidence. Indeed, a Commission member, or one of its staff members, who violates this confidentiality can be punished by a fine of not more than

$1,000 and a term of not more than one year in prison!

At a public hearing, the General Counsel makes the case in support of the complaint. Respondent may make written answer, be heard in person, call and examine witnesses, and be represented by counsel.

If hearing examiners find (conclude) that respondents have engaged in a discriminatory practice, they may order the respondents to:

• cease and desist;

• take positive action to remedy the situation;

• reinstate or rehire (in an employment dispute); or

• provide any other appropriate equitable relief.

If the finding is that there was no discriminatory practice, the examiner shall issue and file an order of dismissal. False and/or malicious complaints are punishable by a fine of not more than $500 and/or one year in prison.

If a respondent fails to do what is ordered, the Commission may sue to enforce compliance with any order within its authority.

ALTERNATIVE COMPLAINT PROCEDURE

Whereas complaints to the Human Relations Commission must be made within one year, the complainant may apply *to a court* for relief at any time up to two years from the time of the alleged discriminatory event or breach of a conciliation agreement.

During the early stages of, or instead of, the processing of a complaint by the Commission, a civil action (suit) may be initiated against the respondent in a circuit court in the appropriate county. If this happens, the administrative hearing process on the same alleged discriminatory practice must stop immediately. Complainant is required to notify all parties of initiating civil action.

FAIR HOUSING LAWS

Persons who believe they have been discriminated against in a property transaction—whether it be of real property or of personal property—because of their race, may petition a federal court to order an end to the discrimination, by virtue of the 1866 Civil Rights Act.

They may choose, however, to file a complaint with the Maryland Human Relations Commission if they have experienced discrimination in a "residential real estate-related transaction."

Aspects of a real estate-related transaction that would be covered include not only selling and brokerage, but also appraisal, insuring and lending, either for purchase or improvement and repair of a home.

Because Maryland has laws and enforcement mechanisms that have been adjudged "substantially equivalent" to the Federal Fair Housing Law of 1968, as amended, residential discrimination complaints are handled by State agencies and by State courts.

> The Federal Fair Housing Act of 1968 as amended in 1988 may be found at: Section 801 [42 United States Code 3601]
> **http://www.usdoj.gov/crt/housing/ title8.htm**

Those seeking help under the Maryland law—§19, and following, of Article 49b,—will find that the protected categories are similar to, but go beyond, those in the Federal law. In addition to the usual categories of race, color, religion, sex, familial status, national origin, and disability, **marital status** is included.

In addition, **sexual orientation** was added to the list of protected categories by the Antidiscrimination Act of 2001, which was passed by the General Assembly and signed into law by the Governor, only to be challenged by a referendum to submit the matter to the voters of the state. This challenge has itself been challenged, based on the validity of the required signatures which accompanied it. At the time of this writing, the immediate outcome is unclear. The Act defines *sexual orientation* as "identification of an individual as to male or female homosexuality, heterosexuality, or bisexuality."

The General Assembly, with the Governor's approval, created a law in the Year 2000 Session requiring all uses of the word *handicapped* throughout the Maryland Annotated Code, to be replaced with the phrase *individual with a disability*.

Exceptions

The Maryland law has exceptions to its antidiscrimination requirements that parallel those in the 1968/88 Fair Housing Act.

An individual may discriminate in the sale or rental of a single family dwelling if the property is sold or rented without the help of any broker, or of any person in the business of selling or renting dwellings, or of any agent of either of these. The property must also be marketed without the use of discriminatory advertising. Unlike the Federal law, Article 49B makes no requirement about the number of properties such seller may own or how many were sold in a recent time period.

The statute, as amended by the 2001 law, would allow owner-occupants of a principal residence to reject tenant applicants for *rooms* based on sex, marital status, and/or sexual orientation.

Building owners *who occupy one of the units in a multifamily dwelling* may also reject those three categories of persons if their building has no more than 5 *rental* units. This contrasts with the Federal law's standard of a *total* of 4 units, one of which the owner occupies as a principal residence.

Maryland's other exceptions closely follow those in the Federal Fair Housing Act by granting specified relief or handling in each of several situations.

• Religious organizations

• Private clubs

• Persons convicted of manufacture or distribution of illegal drugs

• Housing for elderly—two kinds:

  1. All residents age 62 and above

  2. One person 55 or above in each apartment, plus special accounting and reporting rules

• Reasonable occupancy standards set by local government units

Counties, municipalities, and other local governments are also empowered to enact ordinances and extend protection to additional groups.

Additional Protected Groups

All jurisdictions include the Federal "core" of protected categories: race, color, religion, national origin, sex, handicap (*disability,* in Maryland), and familial status. The State and some counties and cities have added others. *Marital status* is added by the State of Maryland and most of its jurisdictions; *sexual orientation,* by the counties of Montgomery, Prince George's, and Howard and the City of Rockville; *occupation* and *personal appearance*, by Howard and Prince George's Counties; and *source of income* and *ancestry,* by Montgomery County.

Sources of law relating to enforcement include the Civil Rights Act of 1866; The Fair Housing Act of 1968, as amended; Article 49B of the Maryland Code; §16-526 of the *Business Occupations and Professions* Article of the Maryland Code; Chapter 27 of the Montgomery County

Code; Title 12, Subtitle 2 of the Howard County Code; Division 12, Subdivision I of the Prince George's County Code; and Chapter 13 of the Laws of Rockville. The list is not comprehensive, but it is suggestive of the number of laws governing and protecting the people of Maryland in the area of fair housing.

DISCRIMINATION IN HOUSING

Examples *listed in the Maryland statute* of unlawful discriminatory housing practices against protected groups include:

- refusing to sell, rent, or negotiate after a bona fide offer;

- making unavailable or denying a dwelling, or representing that a property is not available for inspection, sale or rent when it is in fact available;

- discriminating in terms, conditions, privileges of sale or rental of a dwelling;

- discriminating in the provision of related service or facilities;

- making or ordering to be made any publication, notice or statement concerning properties for sale or rent indicating any preference, limitation or discrimination; and

- seeking, *for profit,* to induce any person to sell or rent a dwelling by making representations regarding the entry of a protected group into an area.

Special Provisions for Individuals with Disabilities

In addition to protections for those persons with disabilities as mentioned in the previous list, the following details are added on their behalf:

- Discrimination against an applicant with a disability or a non-disabled applicant who will have a person with a disability residing in the dwelling after it is sold, rented, or made available

- Discrimination in sale, rental, or availability of a property

- Discrimination in terms, conditions, or privileges of sale or rental or in connection with the dwelling after sale or rental

- Refusal to permit reasonable modifications of existing premises occupied or to be occupied by individuals with disabilities (These modifications are those necessary to give the disabled person full enjoyment of the dwelling and are made at tenants' expense and with the tenants' agreement to restore the premises to their condition before the modification.)

- Refusal to make reasonable accommodations in rules, policies, practices, or services when such accommodations are necessary to give persons with disabilities equal opportunity to use and enjoy a dwelling

- Failure to design or construct a multifamily dwelling for first occupancy so that the public use and common areas are readily accessible to and usable by persons with disabilities; all doors for passage into and within all premises within the dwelling are wide enough to accommodate wheelchairs; and all premises have suitable adaptive design features (for example, an accessible route into and through the dwelling; light switches, electrical outlets, thermostats, and other environmental controls in accessible locations; reinforcements in bathroom walls to allow later installation of grab bars; and kitchens and bathrooms designed so that individuals in wheelchairs can maneuver about the space.)

Real Estate Industry Groups

The law forbids any person or business entity that engages in real estate related transactions

- to discriminate against any person in making available a transaction or in the terms or conditions of a transaction because of membership in a protected group, or

- to deny access to, or membership in, or participation in a multiple-listing service, brokers' organization, or other service, organization, or facility relating to the business of selling or renting dwellings, or to discriminate in the terms or conditions of membership or of participation based on protected group status.

Threats, Coercion, Intimidation, etc., Against Persons Seeking Housing and Against Others Who Encourage Them

The statute makes it unlawful to coerce, intimidate, threaten, interfere with, or retaliate against persons who seek to exercise the rights granted by this law or persons who encourage others to exercise such rights. Persons guilty of such actions may be fined not more than $1,000, or suffer imprisonment for not more than one year, or both. If the violation results in bodily injury, penalties may range up to $10,000 and ten years in prison; if it results in death, imprisonment for any term of years or for life.

Enforcement of Agreements

The Commission may sue to enforce an agreement that a respondent has breached.

At the time a complaint is first received, the Commission may also authorize a civil action in circuit court of the county where the property is located for relief of the complaining party. Having done this, the Commission may still proceed with its administrative proceedings.

If an aggrieved party initiates a civil action under federal or State law seeking relief for a discriminatory housing practice, the Commission may review the complaint and refer the matter to the State Attorney General, but may not continue further on the same charges.

Anyone who deliberately submits false information to the Commission as it investigates, or who fails to make full disclosure, or who changes previous records, reports, or accounts shall be fined not more than $100,000 or imprisoned for not more than one year, or both.

Aggrieved persons may begin civil actions in an appropriate State court not later than two years after the discriminatory action. They may file no such civil actions, based on the same discrimination, after the Commission or a State or local agency has succeeded in producing a conciliation agreement that the aggrieved parties agreed to, except to enforce such agreement.

Relief granted in a civil action may not set aside any lease or sales contract to other bona fide purchasers or tenants who did not have actual notice of the filing of a complaint with the Commission or of the civil action.

Pattern of Discrimination

When the Commission believes there is a pattern of discrimination or resistance to the rights granted by this law, it may commence a civil action in circuit court. The court may award preventive relief or grant temporary or permanent injunctions and restraining orders against those responsible for violations. It may also award, in addition to attorney's fees, monetary damages to aggrieved persons in amounts not to exceed $50,000 for a first violation and $100,000 for subsequent violations.

COMMERCIAL PROPERTY

Neither the owners or the operators of commercial property, their agents and employees, nor any persons licensed or regulated by the State may discriminate against an individual in the terms, conditions, or privileges of property leased for commercial usage, or in the provision of services or facilities in connection with the property, because of the individual's race, color, religion, sex, age *(sic)*, physical disability, marital status, or national origin.

THE REAL ESTATE BROKERS ACT

The Brokers Act also addresses discrimination against protected groups.

Whether or not acting for monetary gain, a person may not knowingly induce or attempt to induce another person to sell or rent a dwelling or otherwise transfer real estate or knowingly discourage or attempt to discourage another person from purchasing real estate:

- by making representations regarding the entry or prospective entry into a neighborhood of individuals of a particular race, color, sex, religion, or national origin;

- by making representations regarding the existing or potential proximity of real property owned or used by individuals of a particular race, color, sex, religion, or national origin; or

- by representing that the existing or potential proximity of real property owned or used by individuals of a particular race, color, sex, religion, or national origin will or may result in the lowering of property values; a change in the racial, religious, or ethnic character of the block, neighborhood, or area; an increase in criminal or antisocial behavior in the area; or a decline in the quality of schools serving the area.

This contrasts with both Human Relations Commission Law and Federal Fair Housing Act which require *the profit motive* for such blockbusting.

A person may not provide *financial assistance* by loan, gift, or otherwise to another person if the person has actual knowledge that the financial assistance will be used in a transaction that results from a violation of these prohibitions.

Solicitation of Residential Listings

If one of the purposes of the solicitation or attempted solicitation is to change the racial composition of a neighborhood, a person may not solicit or attempt to solicit the listing of residential properties for sale or lease by in-person, door-to-door solicitation, telephone solicitation, or mass distribution of circulars.

Baltimore City law prohibits the solicitation of residential properties for purchase or sale by general door-to-door solicitations, in person or by telephone, or by the mass distribution of circulars. There are no exceptions to the law. Solicitations as a result of personal referrals, general knowledge that a property is for sale, or offerings by an owner also constitute violations of the law. The court has added that any uninvited call or visit could constitute a violation of this ordinance.

Baltimore County law provides several methods of **canvassing** that are not

considered solicitation. They include advertisements in bona fide newspapers of general circulation, radio or television; literature distributed through the U.S. mail; legitimate personal referrals; contacts with property owners resulting from the owners' having personally advertised the property for sale; and solicitation for the purpose of obtaining information for appraisals or similar collection of general sales or market data.

Violation of either the Baltimore City or Baltimore County law is punishable as a misdemeanor, with penalties, upon conviction, of a fine, imprisonment, or both.

Laws concerning solicitation vary from jurisdiction to jurisdiction. It is the responsibility of licensees to be familiar with the local laws.

Conservation Areas

The Brokers Act empowers the Real Estate Commission to identify and designate certain localities as **conservation areas.** In these areas and for limited time periods, all advertising of properties for sale and the use of "For Sale" signs is suspended. Brokerage firms may not solicit listings from owners of such properties but may list them when approached by their owners. This is done for the purpose of preserving racial stability in the affected locality in the event of a threatening volume of real estate transactions.

Requirements for establishing such areas are presently so cumbersome that not one such area has been identified for more than a decade.

ENFORCEMENT

A person, aggrieved by a fair housing violation, may have to decide the avenue through which to seek redress—whether it will be by local, county, State, or federal agencies.

Federal Laws

In the area of race, aggrieved persons may go directly to federal district court for injunctive relief. For race and other matters, they may sue in local courts for damages. They may complain to HUD, but HUD will refer the matter to the Maryland Human Relations Commission, because Maryland laws are "substantially equivalent" to the federal Fair Housing Laws.

State Enforcement

Complaints made, or referred, to the Maryland Human Relations Commission are investigated, mediated, and resolved by agreements enforceable in the courts.

Financial Penalties Available to the Maryland Human Relations Commission

If the Human Relations Commission, after proper investigation and hearing, concludes that a **respondent**—the person against whom the charge was brought—has engaged in any of the unlawful practices listed above, it may seek an order assessing a civil penalty against the respondent not exceeding $500 for a first offense. If it is the second offense within five years, the penalty can be in an amount not more than $1,000. If there were two prior offenses within the last seven years, the maximum penalty would be $2,500.

If the respondent is a natural person—an individual rather than a firm or organization—the penalty may be imposed without regard to the time periods between previous violations.

Fair housing provisions of the Brokers Act may be enforced administratively by the State Real Estate Commission or judicially by the Office of the Attorney General. Courts and other governmental agencies finding licensees guilty of discrimination are required to report their findings to the Commission.

Local Laws and Their Enforcement

Chartered counties are empowered to enforce fair housing law violations with fines or penalties not to exceed those provided in the federal Fair Housing Act Amendments of 1988 and 1993. Many counties have Human Rights or Human Relations Commissions as possible alternatives to court enforcement.

DISCRIMINATION IN FINANCING

It is unlawful for any bank, savings and loan institution, credit union, insurance company, or other creditor to deny a housing loan or credit to persons who apply or to discriminate against them in the fixing of the down payment, interest rate, duration, or other terms or conditions of such a loan because of the race, color, religion, creed, marital status, familial status, sex, national origin; or physical or mental disability of such person or of any member, stockholder, director, officer, or employee of such person; or of the prospective occupants, lessees, or tenants of the dwelling for which the loan application is made.

HUD FAIR HOUSING ADVERTISING GUIDELINES

Brokers are urged to obtain any available current version of **Fair Housing Advertising Guidelines** from the Department of Housing and Urban Development. Although withdrawn in 1996, the former Code of Federal Regulations 24 CFR Part 109 apparently still reflects the position of HUD on advertising.

Check out HUD's fair housing advertising guidelines at:
http://www.fairhousing.com/ hud_resources/hudguid2.htm

See also the detailed **Achtenberg Memo** of January 1995, concerning what phraseology will and will not trigger prosecution when used in advertising.

For the Achtenberg Memo, go to this Web address:
http://www.fairhousing.com/ legal_research/regs/

THE STATUTE

Maryland's fair housing law, §49B, has been found to be "substantially equivalent" to the federal Fair Housing Act of 1968 as amended. It is of central importance and is the source of much of the material in this chapter.

The entire text of §49b, The Human Relations Commission Article, may be found at:
http://mlis.state.md.us/cgi-win/ web_statutes.exe
Scroll down to *Human Relations Commission*—(49b). For "Section," enter 19.
The portion of Article 49b dealing with housing discrimination runs from Section 19 to Section 42.

EDUCATIONAL REQUIREMENTS

Real Estate Commission General Regulations 11, 14, and 17 require that all license applicants be instructed in the human relations aspects of the practice of real estate, including study of fair housing laws and the effects of such undesirable practices as exploitation, steering, block-busting, prejudicial solicitation, discriminatory practices, misleading advertising, and other related activities. This instruction is mandated in the prelicense education requirements for salesperson and for broker.

QUESTIONS

1. James and Frances Miller, who are African American, tell the real estate salesperson that they need a three-bedroom house in the $120,000 to $130,000 price range that is within walking distance of an elementary school. The salesperson, after identifying the Millers as genuine prospects, finds a house on Judson Street that meets all the Millers' requirements, but the salesperson knows that the residents of the neighborhood are unhappy about African Americans moving into the area. The agent should

   a. refrain from telling the Millers about this particular house.
   b. tell them about the house but suggest that they would be happier in another neighborhood.
   c. file a complaint with the Human Relations Commission.
   d. inform the Millers about the availability of the house and arrange to show them the listing.

2. With respect to fair housing, all persons engaged in real estate transactions

   a. must be familiar with all applicable federal, state, and local antidiscrimination statutes and ordinances.
   b. carry E&O insurance to be protected.
   c. may refuse to be held liable.
   d. have the right to decide what is best for their customers and clients.

3. Two salespersons are working on a residential listing in a neighborhood that was formerly all white. They

   a. are proper in not showing this listing to white prospects.
   b. violate Maryland and federal laws when they determine whether or not to show a listing based on a prospect's race.
   c. need not introduce into the neighborhood anyone not of the predominant race of the neighborhood.
   d. should have a salesperson of the same race as the prospect show the property.

4. A broker approaches homeowners seeking to list their property for sale. They had not been thinking of selling, but the broker tells them, "The time to sell is now," because the neighborhood is experiencing a large minority group influx and that the value of their property, ". . . is sure to drop," if they wait any longer. This broker's behavior illustrates

   a. blockbusting.
   b. steering.
   c. blind advertising.
   d. redlining.

5. A private club, by limiting the rental or occupancy of its lodgings to club members, as long as the club is not operated as a commercial hotel, is violating

   a. the federal Fair Housing Act of 1968.
   b. the Maryland Fair Housing Law.
   c. the Real Estate License Law.
   d. no state or federal laws.

16
Closing the Real Estate Transaction

OVERVIEW

Whether it is called *settlement*, *closing*, *going to escrow*, or some other name, this event is the culmination of real estate brokerage activities. At this event, legal title to property passes from sellers to purchasers and then, usually, to the lender. As a result of the closing, purchasers take on long-term debt and sellers get equity funds from the sale of their property. From these funds, sellers typically pay commissions to their listing broker and satisfy outstanding mortgages or other liens against the property sold.

Listing brokers may divide their commissions with in-house affiliates who *assisted* purchasers; intra-company agents who *represented* buyers and sellers; or other brokers who either assisted or represented buyers.

EVIDENCE OF TITLE

In Maryland, it is customary for buyers to authorize a title search and a **binder** (interim commitment) for mortgagee title insurance at the time of entering into a purchase contract. In most cases, the settlement officers or attorneys for the lending institution order the preparation of an abstract of title from the public records and then prepare from this abstract an opinion of the marketability of the title. Some attorneys issue their own certificates of title. Typically, an abstract may be used by a title company attorney as the basis for offering title insurance.

Lenders typically require *mortgagee* (lender's) *title insurance* for the protection of their position. State law requires that purchasers be offered homeowner (buyer) title insurance by the settlement officer at every residential closing. Buyers who decline homeowner title insurance are asked to confirm their refusal in writing.

SETTLEMENTS

Most purchase contracts and sale agreements are closed in the office of a title insurance company, the buyer's or seller's attorney, the mortgage lender, or the real estate broker. Closing in Maryland is usually performed at a meeting involving buyers, sellers, agents, and a settlement officer. *Closing in escrow,* as described in the principal text, is generally not practiced in Maryland.

CLOSING AND TAX STATEMENTS

The buyers' or sellers' attorney or a settlement company officer will prepare the necessary closing statement. Licensees should know how these statements are calculated in order to estimate accurately sellers' expenses of sale and net proceeds from the transaction. They should also be able to estimate for purchasers the amount of additional cash needed at closing to complete the purchase. They should be able to understand every entry on the typical settlement sheet, HUD Form #1.

Closing costs are apportioned according to statute, where applicable, and/or by contractual agreement. Typically, the seller is responsible for such property charges on the day of closing as ad valorem taxes, special assessments, and utilities.

Real estate brokers or their salespersons normally are present at settlement, although the interaction is—and should be— principally among the officer conducting the settlement, the parties to the agreement, and any attorneys present. Licensees are present for whatever nonlegal services they may be asked to render, provide personal support for their clients, and, of course, to receive the commission for their companies.

By federal law, all owner/sellers must provide the closing agent with their forwarding addresses and Social Security numbers. Corporate sellers must provide their corporate tax identification numbers.

All persons must sign an affidavit as to the accuracy of information they have given that will be reported to the IRS. Typically, the person conducting settlement will request photo IDs of the principals. Copies of these IDs are maintained in the title company's records. Licensees should make sure that their sellers are prepared to provide all the required information at the time of settlement. The closing agent or title company can answer any questions that may arise.

EVIDENCE OF RELEASE

Persons responsible for disbursement of funds in connection with a settlement at which a transfer of title occurs must mail or deliver to the sellers, within 30 days, evidence of recorded release of mortgage. If the recording of release is delayed beyond the 30-day period for causes beyond their control, they must mail or deliver to the sellers a letter explaining the delay. They must send another letter for each additional delay of 30 days. Failure to follow these rules may subject them to audit of their accounts by the court.

If persons conducting closing properly disburse all funds entrusted to them in the closing procedure within five days, no such evidence is required unless specifically requested by purchasers or vendors. Vendors and purchasers are to be informed in writing of these requirements before the deed is delivered at closing.

Appendix A
Maryland Real Estate License Examinations

OVERVIEW

Passing the state licensing examination is a major challenge for persons seeking a real estate license. Every applicant would like to pass the exam on the first try, not only to speed up the licensing process but also to reduce the cost of reexamination, minimize inconvenience, and avoid embarrassment.

The 1998 Maryland General Assembly established the present standard of 60 hours of prelicense instruction. A total of 135 additional hours is required before the broker examination.

Candidates for broker or salesperson licenses must meet the required educational requirements *before* taking their examination.

The goal of regulation, as of any exercise of the police power of the state, is *to protect the public interest. The public interest* refers not only to consumers but also to the brokerage business community. The salesperson education requirement has ranged from 33 hours to 90 hours during the last 30 years. The length of today's educational course requirement is a com-promise designed to protect users of brokerage services and, at the same time, keep a steady supply of new workers coming into the brokerage industry in this state.

THE REAL ESTATE LICENSE EXAMINATION

Psychological Services, Inc., (PSI), of Glendale, California, an independent testing service under contract with the Commission, prepares and administers the - licensing examination. PSI's testing program is adapted to each state's real estate license laws and practices and to the priorities of its licensing agency.

PSI reports two applicant scores for the examination: the Maryland portion score and the Principles and Practices score. The passing grade set by the Commission is currently 75 percent. One must achieve at least that score on each section to qualify for licensure.

The *Principles and Practices Section* of the examination contains 80 questions based on general real estate information. Subjects include Property Ownership, Laws of Agency, Contracts, Real Estate Mathematics, Valuation and Real Estate Economics, Financing, Land Use Controls and Regulations, and Specialty Areas. Students must answer at least 60 of these questions correctly to pass this section.

The *Maryland Portion* contains questions based on Title 16 of the Maryland Code of *Laws* (the Brokers Act) as well as questions relating to *Regulations* set forth by the Maryland Real Estate Commission. There are 30 state-specific questions on the salesperson examination and 40 on the broker. The minimum to be answered correctly are 23 and 30 questions, respectively. Applicants are allowed 120 minutes to take the salesperson exam, and broker candidates also get 120 minutes for their exam.

Test questions deal with duties and powers of the Commission, licensing requirements, and conduct of the brokerage business. Each of these subjects has been discussed in this book.

Because tests are not preprinted, they can be generated daily from a computer database. Thus they can be continually updated and revised.

APPLICATION PROCEDURES

Students obtain the **Application Bulletin,** containing instructions and application forms for the examinations from the school where they take their class.

Those ready to take the examination should mail the application form, together with

evidence of passing the prelicense course, as well as the testing fee, and any other required documents, to

> PSI Examination Services
> Attention: Exam Registration
> 100 West Broadway, Suite 1100
> Glendale, CA 91210-1202.

Failure to follow the instructions on the registration form may result in students not being scheduled promptly for the examinations they request.

The registration fee for taking a Maryland Real Estate Licensing Examination (either broker or salesperson) is $46. Payment can be made to PSI by personal check, money order, company check, or cashier's check.

Candidates who have previously been sent PSI certification of eligibility, may register with PSI by mail or through *Express Registration.* These applicants may be persons who failed all or part of a previous exam, or those whose initial application form was incomplete but was accompanied by proper proof of their completion of the education requirement. Express Registration, which may be done by phone or FAX, using a valid VISA or MasterCard, costs an additional $10—for a total of $56.

First-time applicants are to send their Registration Forms and the necessary documents directly to PSI. In response, PSI will mail them (within two weeks) a Registration Confirmation Notice. This notice explains how to make an examination appointment.

Once this appointment, including place, date, and time for examination, has been set, applicants may still request a change in that appointment. They may do this by calling 1-800-733-9267, three or more days before their scheduled testing date. All examinations—even if delayed—must still be taken within 90 days of registration, or the candidates must reapply and pay another registration fee. The expiration date is shown on each student's Confirmation Notice.

The Registration Form asks for information that will be relayed to the Commission so it can process the license applications when candidates pass their test. It also asks for certification that the candidate has successfully completed the mandatory educational hours. In addition, it contains a statement of *irrevocable consent,* which is required of all out-of-state applicants.

Applicants must answer the application questions to the best of their ability. The form is signed as an affidavit, subject to the penalties of perjury.

TESTING PROCEDURES

Candidates may take an examination at any of the several testing centers located throughout the State. All candidates must bring positive identification to the testing site.

PSI uses a computerized testing system approved by the Commission. Upon conclusion of the testing session, the computer will show candidates whether they passed or failed. Official notification of examination results, however, will be mailed to candidates. The computerized real estate examinations are administered every business day during the week at most locations. There is no "walk in" testing.

Candidates take their examinations seated at specially designed computer work stations. Onscreen instructions provide a 15-minute to 20-minute tutorial in the use of the keyboard. Only eight keys are used. Taking the test requires no computer skills. Instructions appear on the screen to guide the candidate through each step of the test. The testing period is 120 minutes. There is an onscreen clock for the candidate to watch.

Applicants with disabilities should make written request for special testing arrangements, describing any specific accommodations needed, when first submitting their registration form. This special request will then be forwarded by PSI to the Commission. At present, PSI presents the examination in English only.

When candidates first take the real estate exam, they answer mixed general and State-specific questions. Candidates who have already taken the exam but only passed one of its two sections are permitted to retake the group of questions—state or general—they still need to pass. Candidates must pass both sets of questions to be eligible for a Maryland real estate license.

TYPES OF QUESTIONS ON THE EXAM

The tests use multiple-choice answer format. An incomplete statement or a question is presented and is followed by four possible choices. Applicants are sometimes asked to *find the one correct answer.* At other times, they must find the *one wrong answer.* Here are examples of each:

Example 1

Which one of the following agreements is most likely to be valid?

a. Owners orally agree to take their house off the market as a result of an expected offer from a potential buyer, whose spouse has not seen the house.

b. Owners of a large house in a university town agree to rent a room to a 17-year-old college student for $450 per month.

c. Owners have a signed agreement to sell their house in return for a down payment plus monthly payments over a 15-year period.

d. Owners agree to rent their house to a coach for $750 for two days, to hold a beer keg party for the high school football team.

Example 2

A Maryland real estate licensee may take all of the following kinds of listing agreements EXCEPT one that

a. allows the sellers also to list their home with other brokers.

b. allows the broker to keep all sales proceeds in excess of a stated amount.

c. allows the sellers to find their own buyers and avoid paying the promised commission.

d. allows the broker to collect a commission regardless of who sells the property during the listing period.

The PSI testing approach is designed to test reasoning processes as well as factual real estate knowledge. In the examination, there are questions on general real estate information, the Brokers Act, and COMAR, as well as math problems and several kinds of comprehensive problems. Examples of such questions and problems have been included in most chapters of this book so that you will become familiar with them and be better prepared for the examination.

In answering these types of questions, consider all answers carefully and eliminate the least likely ones instead of randomly selecting an answer. However, it is better to guess than to give no answer at all. The purpose of the examination is to provide a measure of your knowledge of real estate and thereby allow you to demonstrate your qualification for licensure. You should try to answer all questions without spending too much time on any one question.

Here are the answers to the model questions:

1. a b c d
   [] [] [x] []

2. a b c d
   [] [x] [] []

Applicants may use calculators without an alphabetic keyboard for both the broker and the salesperson license examination. They may use PSI-provided scratch paper at the computer testing table. The fourth answer/choice to each math test item is typically "None of the above." Do not be surprised by it.

MORE HELP IN PREPARING FOR THE LICENSE EXAMINATION

We have tried to prepare you for the Maryland Real Estate License Examination by including in this book the kinds of items usually found on the test. Familiarity with the test items in this book, however, will not in itself ensure a passing score. Your most important preparation for this examination involves thoughtfully studying real estate principles and practices and brokerage laws and regulations.

Concentrate on learning the material by studying the main text and this supplement. When using the tests and exercises in these books, be sure that you find *and understand* the correct solutions for any questions you miss. Use the Answer Key in the back of this book thoughtfully.

Dearborn™ Real Estate Education publishes other instructional materials in addition to *Modern Real Estate Practice* and *Maryland Real Estate: Practice & Law,* which are especially designed to aid you in passing the licensing exam: *Mastering Real Estate Mathematics,* by Ventolo, Tamper, and Allaway; *Study Guide for Modern Real Estate Practice;* and *Guide to Passing the PSI Real Estate Exam,* by Sager. If copies of these books are not available through your local bookseller, you may purchase them directly from the publisher at the following Web address:

---

www.dearbornRE.com

Practice with the *interactive software* for the Sager book will give you the experience of answering onscreen questions similar to State exam questions while seated at a computer keyboard—the way you will take your test.

Another very effective way to *master* the basics for the general exam is to use the *SuccessMaster™ Software.* Although it is not designed to *teach* test-taking, its thousands of questions, multiple-choice, yes-or-no, true-or-false, and fill-in-the blanks, are designed to build *fluency and mastery* in the use of all basic real estate terminology and concepts. Such fluency and mastery are fundamental to successful test-taking.

TYPICAL MARYLAND-SPECIFIC TEST ITEMS

The Maryland-related questions throughout this book are similar to those found on the real estate licensing exam. Use them to identify strengths and weaknesses in your knowledge.

List the items you miss and use that list as a guide to further intensive study of the text. Sometimes you may want to test yourself on an entire list of questions. Other times, you may wish to attempt the items one by one, checking your answers as you go. Decide why every correct answer IS correct. In items that ask you to find the WRONG answer, do so; but then try to learn all you can from the three CORRECT answers to the same questions. Make intelligent use of all practice questions and the answer keys.

Figure A.1 Summary of Facts about Examinations

Exam	Portion	Number of Questions	Total Time Allowed in Minutes	Number Correct To Pass	Fee Regular	Fee Express
Salesperson	National	80		60		
	State	30		23		
	Both	110	120	n/a	$46	$56
Broker	National	80		60		
	State	40		30		
	Both	120	120	n/a	$46	$56

PRACTICE QUESTIONS

1. When unlicensed salespersons negotiate a sale of real property, the commission is payable to

    a. the broker only.
    b. no one.
    c. the salesperson only.
    d. the broker and the salesperson.

2. If a salesperson license is issued on September 20, 2001, it will expire

    a. on September 20, 2003.
    b. on September 20, 2002.
    c. on April 30, 2000.
    d. on April 30, 2002.

3. When prospective purchasers first arrive at a brokerage office to inquire about real estate assistance, what is their status under the Brokers Act?

    a.. Customers
    b. Clients
    c. Agents
    d. Factors

4. Salespersons' licenses must be

    a. kept in a safe place by the salespersons.
    b. carried by the salespersons.
    c. displayed in their brokers' offices.
    d. maintained in their personnel files by their brokers.

5. The maximum amount that a claimant may collect per claim from the Guaranty Fund is

    a. unlimited.   c. $25,000.
    b. $250,000.   d. $10,000.

6. When the license of a broker is suspended or revoked, the broker's salespeople **MUST**

    a. find a new broker-employer.
    b. continue listing and selling.
    c. stop listing and selling with that broker.
    d. obtain a broker's license.

7. Membership on the State Real Estate Commission includes

   a. only licensed salespersons.
   b. only licensed brokers.
   c. unlicensed persons and licensed brokers and salespersons.
   d. those persons appointed by the Attorney General.

8. Real estate licenses are issued

   a. by the Real Estate Board.
   b. to all applicants who have successfully passed required educational courses.
   c. to all brokers who have successfully passed required education courses.
   d. by the Real Estate Commission.

9. Ethical standards that must be observed by all Maryland real estate licensees are set by the

   a. National Association of REALTORS®
   b. State Real Estate Commission.
   c. Maryland Association of REALTORS®
   d. local Boards or Associations.

10. When a broker provides brokerage services through a partnership, which of the following statements is FALSE?

    a. The broker is responsible for the real estate brokerage activities of the partnership.
    b. The broker must have a contractual or employment agreement with the partnership.
    c. The broker must be one of the partners.
    d. The broker must be designated by the partnership as its broker of record.

11. If builders sell houses they have built and own, which of the following is TRUE?

    a. They need not hold real estate licenses.
    b. They must be licensed if they sell more than six per calendar year.
    c. They must be licensed brokers.
    d. They may be licensed as salespersons and not affiliated with brokers.

12. A developer desiring to convert a building that is more than five years old into a time-share project in Maryland must

    a. give each tenant 180 days' notice.
    b. give each tenant 120 days' notice.
    c. not give tenants any prior notice.
    d. notify each tenant within 10 days after filing the Public Offering Statement.

13. The responsibilities of real estate licensees do NOT include

    a. fair treatment of third parties.
    b. competence in performance of duties.
    c. duty to give legal interpretations.
    d. loyalty to their principal.

14. In what states are lenders allowed to collect the rents on income properties during the foreclosure process?

    a. Title theory states
    b. Lien theory states
    c. Modified lien theory states
    d. Trust theory states

15. Under the Maryland Real Estate Brokers Act, the Commission may impose a penalty per violation. The penalty is

    a. not more than $500 and/or one year in jail.
    b. not more than $5,000.
    c. not more than $2,000.
    d. not more than $1,000 and/or one year in jail.

16. The amount of commission set in a listing agreement is determined by

    a. state law.
    b. the local Board or Association of REALTORS®.
    c. mutual agreement.
    d. the Real Estate Commission.

17. Earnest money received by salespersons must be

    a. deposited in their trust accounts.
    b. given to the sellers of the property.
    c. placed in their broker's safe.
    d. given to their broker for deposit in the firm's trust account.

18. Which of the following is NOT true about tenancy by the entirety?

    a. If husband and wife divorce, it is terminated.
    b. Both spouses' signatures are required to sell such property during both spouses' lifetimes.
    c. Upon death of either spouse, it converts to tenancy in common.
    d. In Maryland, only a legally married husband and wife can own property under it.

19. When a broker receives a less-than-full-price offer from a prospect and at the same time a full-price offer through another firm, the broker should present

    a. only the full-price offer.
    b. only the offer from the broker's customer.
    c. both offers.
    d. the first offer received and if it is rejected, present the other offer.

20. The Maryland law requiring certain contracts to be in writing in order to be enforceable is its

    a. written instrument law.
    b. parol evidence law.
    c. statute of limitations.
    d. statute of frauds.

Appendix B
Complaint Procedure

Possible Steps in Handling Complaints Against a Licensee

1.	Complaint is received by Commission (REC).
2.	Complaint is reviewed by REC designee, usually the Executive Director.
2.1.a	OR: If complaint is deficient in form, i.e., unsigned or not made under oath, it is returned to Complainant as rejected with explanation for the rejection.
2.1.b	OR: If complaint lacks facts alleging prima facie case, it is returned to Complainant as rejected with that reason given.
3.	Complaint is adjudged by REC designee to be in good form and contain facts which suggest that a violation of Brokers Act or REC Regulations has taken place.
4.	REC designee refers complaint to a hearing panel of the REC.
4.1	REC informs Complainant that the complaint is being processed.
5.	Hearing panel examines the complaint and if they find it is worthy of action, refers the matter to Investigative Services for investigation.
5.1	OR: Panel concludes that the facts do not warrant further pursuit of the complaint. Complainant is notified of this finding of insufficient grounds and that the complaint is rejected. There is no right to appeal to this finding of an investigative panel.
6.	Licensee who is being complained about (the Respondent) and Respondent's broker are informed of the complaint and asked by the panel for written comment.
7.	Investigative Services investigates and reports its findings to the hearing panel.
8.	Hearing panel examines the report from Investigative Services and the responses from the Respondent and Respondent's broker. Panel concludes that Respondent has violated law or regulation they **set the matter in for** (schedule) a hearing.
8.1	OR: Panel concludes that the facts do not warrant further pursuit of the complaint and that the complaint is rejected. Complainant is notified of this decision. There is no right to appeal of this finding of an investigative panel.
9.	Panel notifies Respondent and Respondent's broker of the scheduled hearing and informs them of their rights to be present, to respond, to be represented by counsel, and to have witnesses subpoenaed (at Respondent's expense). They are also informed what the charges are and the possible penalties that could be imposed. Respondent must have 10 days notice prior to the hearing. Complainant is also notified.

10.	In almost every case, the hearing is held before an Administrative Law Judge (ALJ). It is open to the public. Written and/or oral Testimony is given. An Assistant Attorney General (AAG) presents the Commission's case. Respondent has opportunity to be heard in defense or mitigation. ALJs base their conclusion on **preponderance of evidence**. **Hearsay evidence** is admitted but weighed with discretion. The AAG and the Respondent's attorney may both rebut testimony and give summations. No decision is announced at the hearing. Hearing is conducted according to the Rules of Procedure of the Maryland Office of Administrative Hearings. [COMAR 28, Subtitle 02.01—a 16-page document]. Some days after the conclusion of the hearing, the **proposed decision** of the ALJ is sent to the REC.
11.	A *new* hearing panel is given the proposed decision to review along with the case record. Panel adopts (or modifies) the proposed decision and sends it to the Respondent and the Complainant, giving each one notice of the right to file an **exception** within 10 days.
12.	If either Complainant or Respondent takes exception within 10 days, the panel sets a date for a hearing at which the parties can present arguments against the decision and rebut each other's argument. Parties must have 14 days advance notice of this hearing.
13.	The same panel that sent out the proposed decision hears the arguments taking exception to the decision. The panel reaches a decision.
14.	Some days later the panel notifies parties of its decision rejecting the exception and issues a **final written order.**
15.	Parties submit to the decision contained in the final written order.
15.1	OR: A party **appeals** to the **circuit court** (The appeal alone does not create a **stay** of the decision for a licensee.)
15.1.a	AND: Appellant (one who is appealing), if a licensee, petitions the circuit court for a stay of the decision (perhaps delaying the suspension or revocation of appellant's license). Court usually grants this request and seeks a bond not exceeding $50,000.
15.1.b	AND: Circuit court denies the appeal and lets final order stand.
15.2	BUT: Appellant carries appeal to Court of Special Appeals
15.2.a	AND: Court of Special Appeals affirms the final order.
15.3	BUT: Appellant carries appeal to Court of Appeals
15.3.a	AND: Court of Appeals sustains the final order.
15.1.2.or 3	OR: Any of the three courts could have granted the appeal and set aside the final order.
16.	Appeals are exhausted; final order will be executed by the REC.
	End of Case
	Note: This case addresses a violation of the statute or the regulations in which no financial damages were experienced and no reimbursement was sought from the Guaranty Fund.

Appendix C
Maryland Real Estate-Related Web Sites

KEEPING UP-TO-DATE

Print materials such as this volume are up-to-date when written and printed. Changes in laws, regulations, and in the business environment are constant. In various chapters of this book, Web site addresses (URLs) have been given for specific topics. Here, in Appendix C, the author lists several "master" Web sites of great value. They can aid students in meeting their responsibility to remain current on all real estate matters. These sites are veritable "springboards" into a wealth of information for the student of Maryland Real Estate Brokerage. Most are listed according to the entity that maintains them.

The Maryland General Assembly

> **http://mlis.state.md.us/**

This is the main source of information for everything that happens in the Legislative Branch of Maryland Government. It gives the dates for the annual sessions, the number of Senators, Delegates, and Districts. It enables its readers to identify their Legislators by giving their own ZIP codes and to contact any State Legislator by e-mail.

It lists all bills that have been introduced during current as well as the most recent session of the Legislature as well as those in session from 1996 to 2000. It gives the status of current bills and the ultimate disposition of all bills from previous sessions. Bills are indexed by Subject, Statute affected, Sponsor, and Bill Number. When asked to choose a topic, select *Agents and Brokers, Real Estate Brokers,* or *Real Property.*

The site also sets forth the Order of Business for both the Senate and House, their current agendas, and hearing schedules. It lists all the bills either signed or vetoed in the most recent session. In the case of a veto, a link is given to the letter in which the State Governor explains the veto.

In every instance above, the actual texts of bills can be brought to the screen and then printed out or saved to disk.

The Maryland State Archives

> **http://www.mec.state.md.us/**

This site, *The Maryland Electronic Capital,* gives links that connect the student with the Executive Branch, the Maryland Judiciary, the Maryland State Law Library, Maryland State Departments, Agencies, Boards, and Commissions, and important links to the Federal Government. It links to each Maryland county for local government information and business developments.

Office of the Secretary of State Division of State Documents

> **https://constmail.gov.state.md.us/comar/dsd_web/default.htm**
> (Notice that in this URL, *http* is followed by the letter *s.*)

This Web site provides links to two valuable resources for the student of Maryland Real Estate. One is COMAR—the Code of Maryland Regulations, which offers the entire text of every State Agency Regulation together with tips on how to search. The other is *The Maryland Register*—the official publication for the State Government for publishing proposed changes and approved changes to all agency regulations. Its current issue and several past issues are kept available. They can be searched, read, and downloaded.

The Maryland Real Estate Commission

> **http://www.dllr.state.md.us/license/occprof/recomm.html**

At this site, the student is shown the names of Commission members, their terms, and the area of the state that the licensee members are from. Here the Commission makes available forms for complaints against licensees and forms for license renewal. It provides a means of inquiring about licensees by name. It contains information about licensing requirements, examinations required, license reciprocity, continuing education, and requirements for reinstatement of expired licenses. It also gives direct access to the current year's new laws and administrative changes which impact real estate licensees.

Maryland Statutes Text

> **http://mlis.state.md.us/cgi-win/web_statutes.exe**

This site gives the text of every Maryland Statute. It does not, however, give the *catchlines*—the section and paragraph titles which appear in the bound volumes. Nor does it provide the commentary and explanations found in *The Annotated Code of Maryland*. It is not indexed, but if students know generally where a certain statute is located, they can read it and download it, one small section at a time.

The State Department of Assessments and Taxation

> **http://www.dat.state.md.us/**

Billed as "Maryland's Largest Source of Real Estate Data," this site not only gives information about Homeowners' Tax Credit, Homestead Tax Credit, and Renters' Tax Credit, it also provides the assessment of every parcel of real estate in Maryland. It also explains the new full-value assessment with its consequent lower tax rates, as well as the semiannual payment schedule.

The site also provides average sale prices of residential properties sold by county and by quarter for the last several years. Rates for Transfer Tax, Recordation Tax, and Tax Stamps are also provided county by county.

The Maryland State Archives

> **http://www.mdarchives.state.md.us/msa/mdmanual/html/mmtoc.html**

The Maryland Manual On-Line is a complete guide to Maryland government. It contains links to the three branches of Maryland State Government as well as to county and federally-related agencies. It is updated daily.

PSI Examination Services Information and Tutorial

> **http://www.psiexams.com/**

At this Web site go to the information about Maryland by clicking on the state name in the navigation bar near the top of the screen. Scroll down and click on *Real Estate Commission*. On the screen, click on *Maryland Real Estate Licensing Bulletin*. For the Tutorial, return to the PSI home page and click on Examination Experience near the top of the screen.

Appendix D
Documentation Required in Maryland Residential Real Estate Sales Transactions

While prospects are asking assistance in locating property to purchase or lease:	No document is in play at this point, but the law presumes that a licensee represents prospects and owes them such *fiduciary duties* as confidentiality and loyalty. The prospects have no financial obligation for this service.
While marketing (or locating) property:	Commission's agency relationship information form, *Understanding Whom Agents Represent,* is to be presented at the first scheduled face-to-face meeting of the licensee with the buyer (or lessee) and the seller (or lessor). This is a disclosure form, not a contract to represent any party.
First written agreement:	A written Agency Agreement to represent either buyer (or lessee) or seller (or lessor). This may require an amended (new) *Understanding Whom Agents Represent* form in situations where buyer representation and/or dual agency are undertaken and were not stated in the original form. When the licensee is acting as a cooperating agent of the seller, no buyer representation or dual agency forms are necessary.
When brokerage firm represents both opposing parties, i.e., is performing dual agency:	Commissions's *Consent for Dual Agency* form, signed by buyers (or lessees) and sellers (or lessors). An additional *Consent for Dual Agency* form is required for each property to be shown under dual agency, since the forms are both property-specific and owner-specific.
Prior to submitting a written offer:	Purchasers are to be given the following before the offer to purchase is signed: 1. The *Property Condition Disclosure/Disclaimer* form properly completed and signed by sellers. This is the duty of all sellers which must be assured by the licensee representing them, by a cooperating agent assisting the buyer, or by the licensee representing the buyer. A buyer not receiving this form prior to ratification of contract may rescind the contract at any time prior to applying for financing; and 2. The *Lead-Based Paint Disclosure Statement;* together with the booklet *Protecting Your Family from Lead-Based Paint Hazards* are to be given to purchasers of property built before 1978, prior to the time the offer to purchase is fully signed.
At time of contract:	Copies of, or receipts for, disclosures given to all parties are to accompany the signed contract. These include *Understanding Whom Agents Represent, Consent for Dual Agency, Property Condition Disclosure/Disclaimer* and, if applicable, the federally-mandated *Lead-Based Paint Disclosure Statement* and information booklet *Protecting Your Family from Lead-Based Paint Hazards*.

Answer Key

These answers are given for each chapter in order to help you make maximum use of the tests. If you did not answer a question correctly, restudy the course material until you understand the correct answer.

Chapter 1

1.	c	(3)
2.	b	(10)
3.	d	(14)
4.	a	(25)
5.	b	(4)
6.	c	(9)
7.	c	(7)
8.	b	(6)
9.	c	(6)
10.	c	(23)
11.	d	(20-21)
12.	d	(3)
13.	b	(5)
14.	b	(7-8)
15.	b	(1)
16.	c	(5)
17.	c	(23)
18.	a	(19)
19.	b	(6)
20.	b	(5)
21	a	(21)
22.	d	(9)
23.	b	(3)
24.	a	(7)
25.	a	(5)
26.	a	(14)
27.	b	(21)
28.	d	(4)
29.	b	(7)

Chapter 2

1.	b	(34)
2.	c	(35-36)
3.	d	(36)
4.	b	(46)
5.	d	(42)
6.	d	(45-46)
7.	d	(34)
8.	c	(46)

Chapter 3

1.	b	(56)
2.	a	(56)
3.	d	(54)
4.	d	(50)
5.	a	(56)
6.	b	(50)
7.	a	(56)
8.	b	(57)

Chapter 4

1.	a	(61)
2.	c	(61)
3.	b	(68)
4.	b	(61)
5.	a	(72)
6.	c	(71)
7.	c	(60)
8.	d	(68)
9.	a	(69)
10.	c	(60)

Chapter 5

1.	c	(75)
2.	a	(74)
3.	d	(74)
4.	a	(74)

Chapter 6

1.	b	(76)
2.	c	(76)
3.	b	(76)
4.	a	(83)
5.	b	(79)
6.	c	(78)
7.	a	(76)
8.	b	(78)
9.	b	(85)
10.	d	(80)
11.	c	(80)
12.	d	(79)
13.	a	(78)

Chapter 7

1.	a	(89-90)
2.	b	(89)
3.	c	(89)
4.	d	(88)
5.	c	(89)

Chapter 8

1.	d	(91)
2.	b	(91)
3.	c	(96)
4.	d	(95)
5.	c	(94)

Chapter 9

1.	a.	(98)
2.	b	(98)
3.	a	(99)
4.	d	(100)

Chapter 10

1.	c	(115)
2.	d	(114)
3.	d	(116)
4.	c	(115)

Chapter 11

1.	d	(118)
2.	b	(119-120)
3.	a	(118)
4.	c	(118)

Chapter 12

1.	b	(123)
2.	a	(124)
3.	b	(124)
4.	a	(122)
5.	c	(123)
6.	d	(125)

Chapter 13

1.	b	(132)
2.	a	(131)
3.	a	(130)
4.	b	(129)
5.	b	(130)
6.	b	(130)
7.	a	(128)
8.	b	(129)
9.	d	(135)
10.	a	(135)

Chapter 15

1.	d	(155)
2.	a	(151)
3.	b	(160)
4.	a	(157)
5.	d	(154)

Appendix A

1.	b	(6)
2.	a	(7-8)
3.	b	(42)
4.	c	(13)
5.	c	(19)
6.	c	(10)
7.	c	(5)
8.	d	(3)
9.	b	(6)
10.	c	(50)
11.	a	(5)
12.	b	(82)
13.	c	(99)
14.	a	(122)
15.	b	(6)
16.	c	(69)
17.	d	(57)
18.	c	(76-77)
19.	c	(112)
20.	d	(98)

Index

A

Abstract of title, 120
Acquired immunodeficiency syndrome, 67
Ad valorem tax, 93, 96
Administrative law, 2
Administrators, 114
Adverse possession, 74, 115
Advertising, 55-56
Affiliates, 3-4, 10-11
  arrangements, 51
  ownership control and, 50
  termination, 14
Agency, 33-37
  disclosure, 42-44
  relationship, 34, 38-39, 45-46
Agency Relationship Disclosure, 70
Agreement, termination of, 69
Agricultural Land Preservation Fund, 144
Agricultural land transfer tax, 95, 100, 116-17
Agricultural use assessment, 95
Agriculture Article, 75
Air and Radiation Management Administration, 145
Ancestry discrimination, 154
Anne Arundel County, 124
  rent receipts, 134-35
Annotated Code of Maryland, 15, 28, 33, 75, 77, 80, 84, 100, 125, 126, 153
Annual percentage rate, 125-26
Annual registration statement, 132
Answer key, 178
Application Bulletin, 165-66
Application for lease, 131
Appurtenances, 79
Arbitration, 54
Asbestos, 145
Assessment, 79, 91, 93
Associate broker, license, 8
Attorney general, 80, 159
Attorney-in-fact, 111-12

B

Back rent, 134
Balloon payments, 126
Baltimore City

annual registration statement, 132
  brokerage, 27-28
  Commissioner of Housing and Community Development, 132
  floodplain areas, 132
  ground rent, 124
  Multiple Dwelling Code, 101
  requirements, 101
  solicitation ban, 158
  warranty of habitability, 136
  water bill, 119
Baltimore County
  canvassing, 158
  floodplain areas, 132
  ground rent, 124
Baltimore Neighborhoods, Inc., 138
Beneficial owner, 56, 57
Beneficiaries, 114-15
Blind owner, 94
Bona fide purchaser, 74
Boundary survey, 89
Branch office, 55
Broker
  cooperation, 70
  disclosure/disclaimer, 68
  license, 8
Brokerage, 33, 49
  Baltimore City, 27-28
  commission disputes, 54
  organization of, 50-51
  personal assistants, 52-53
  place of business, 54-55
  supervision, 51-52
  worker's compensation, 54
Buffer, 142-43
Building inspections, 28-29
Bulk sales provision, 120
Business Occupations and Professions Article, 29, 154
Buyer representation, 34-35, 37
Buyer representation agreements, 37, 60
Buyer's market, 67
Bylaws, 79

C

Cancellation

period, 85
  rights, 82
Canvassing, 158
Capacity to contract, 98
Capitalization, 129
Chattel mortgage, 120
Chesapeake Bay, 142-43
Chesapeake Bay Critical Area Act, 142
Circuit breaker, 94
Civil monetary penalties, 159
Civil Rights Act of 1866, 2, 153, 154
Claim of right, 74
Client-level service, 34
Closing statements, 163
Code of Ethics, 28, 46, 62, 70
Code of Maryland Regulations, 17, 33, 49, 84
  advertising, 55-56
Coercion, 156
Cognovit clause, 135
Color of title, 74
Commercial Law Article, 80, 125
Commercial property, 157
Commissions, 69-70
Common elements, 77-79
Common expenses, 78
Common law, 1, 76
Competency, 98
Competitive market analysis, 28
Complaint, 151-53
  procedure, 172-73
  processing, 15-18
Condominium, 77-80
Contract of Sale, 80
  declaration, 79
  disclosure requirements, 110-11
  Listing Contract, 80
  regime, 78
Confess judgment, 135
Confidentiality, 42, 44-45
Consent for dual agency, 37, 40-41, 43
Conservation areas, 158
Construction contracts, 102
Constructive notice, 130
Consumer Protection Act, 80

Continuing education, 11, 12
Contract, 61
    contingency, other clauses,
        101-2
    general rules, 98
    necessary information, 99-
        100
    release from, 102
    sale of real estate, 99-102
Conversions, 82
Conveyance taxes, 116
Cooperating agent, 36, 37
Cooperative environmental
    approaches, 142
Co-ownership, 76-77
Corporation franchise tax, 95
Council of unit owners, 77
County tax rates, 92
Customer-level service, 34
Customers, 34

D

Deceased broker license, 14
Declaration, 79
Deed
    recordation, 116, 118-19
    transfer of title by, 115;16
Deed in trust, 122
Deed of release, 124
Deed of trust, 122
Default, 123
Deficiency, 123
Delinquency, 95-96
Department of Veterans Affairs,
    101, 123, 124
Deposits, 82
Developers, 77
Devisees, 114
Disabled persons, 153, 154,
    155-56
Disabled veteran exemption, 94
Disclosure, 46
    condominiums, 110-11
    ground rent, 130
    home warranties, 110
    lead-based paint, 137, 138,
        148-50
    representation, 131-32
    resale, 82
    residential property, 111
Discrimination, 123
    in financing, 159-60
    in housing, 155-57

Dishonored checks, 11
Dispossession proceedings, 134
Distraint, 135
Division of Consumer
    Protection, 80
Documentary stamp tax, 116
Documentation, 177
Drinking water, 145
Dual agency, 35
    option, 70
Dual agent, 37, 45

E

Earnest money deposit, 56-57,
    100
Easement by prescription, 74
Elderly housing, 154
Enforceable, 70
Environmental issues, 141-42
Environmental legislation, 144
Environmental Protection
    Agency, 144-45
Environment Article, 136
Equitable title, 112
Escrow account, 123
Escrow company, 100
Eviction, 137
Evidence
    of release, 163
    of title, 162
Exchange programs, 83
Exclusive agency, 60
Exclusive buyer agency, 35
Exclusive seller agency, 35
Exclusive-right-to-sell, 60
Exculpatory clause, 136
Expenses, 79

F

Fair housing, 151-60
    enforcement, 156-57, 159
    laws, 153-55
Fair Housing Act, 154, 160
    Amendments, 159
Fair Housing Advertising
    Guidelines, 160
Fairness, 46
Federal Deposit Insurance
    Corporation, 57
Federal Fair Housing Act, 153,
    154, 158
Federal Housing
    Administration, 101, 123, 124

Federal Savings and Loan
    Insurance Corporation, 57
Fee payments, 45-46
Felonies, 24
Fiduciary duties, 42
Financial assistance, 158
Financial institution, authorized,
    57
Financing, 122-26
    discrimination, 159-60
    statement, 120
First-time homebuyers Closing
    Cost Reduction Act, 100
First-Time Maryland Home
    Buyer Transfer and
    Recordation Tax Addendum,
    94, 113
Floodplain areas, 132
Folio, 118, 119
Foreclosure, 123, 124-25

G

General common elements, 77-
    78
Ground lease, 56
Ground rents, 99, 124, 128-30
Guaranty Fund, 7, 10-11, 19-21,
    100

H

Harford County, water bill, 119
Hazardous condition, 136
Hazardous materials, 145
Hearings, 16-17, 20
Heirs, 114
Heritage Conservation Fund,
    144
Holdover tenancy, 134
Holographic wills, 115
Home inspections, 29
Homeowner's association, 84,
    100
Homestead Tax Credit, 93-94
Housing and Urban
    Development, 148, 160
Howard County, 154
Howard County Code, 155
Human immunodeficiency
    virus, 67
Human Relations Commission,
    151-60

I

Implied agency, 45
Impound account, 123
Industry groups, 156
Installment contracts, 110
Interest rates, 123
Internal Revenue Service, 3-4,
    52, 54, 123, 163
Intestate, 114
Intestate share, 114
Intimidation, 156
Intra-company agent, 34-35, 37
Irrevocable consent, 8, 15

J-K

Joppatowne subdivision
    (Harford County), 124
Judicial review, 18
Junior financing, 125-26
Kickout clause, 102

L

Land installment contract, 125
Landlord rights, 134
Landlord and Tenant statute,
    131
Land use classifications, 143
Lead-based paint, 137, 138,
    148-50
Lead-Based Paint Hazard
Inspection Addendum, 112
Lead Paint Poisoning Reduction
    Act, 145-48
Lead poisoning, 145
Lease, 128-39
    agreement forms, 137
    assistance sources, 138
    ground rent, 128-30
    option agreement, 102, 138
    prohibited residential
        provisions, 135-36
    renewal, 134
    residential, 130-32
    safety requirements, 137-38
    sale of premises, 132-33
    tenancy termination, 133-35
Leasehold interest, 99
Legal descriptions, 88-90
Legatees, 115
Legislative (statutory) law, 1
Letter of protest, 58
Liber, 118, 119

License
    certificates, 10
    certificate status, 13
    deceased broker, 14
    dishonored checks, 11
    educational requirements, 160
    examination, 164-69
    exchange of, 10-11
    experienced licensees, 12-13
    fees, 9
    general rules, 8, 10
    inactive status, 13
    law
        changes, 29
        sources, 1-2
    levels of, 3, 7-8
    lost, destroyed, 13
    name change, 13
    out-of-state applicants, 15
    reciprocity, 10
    return to commission,
        affiliation termination, 14
    revocation, 17
    suspension, 18
    transfer of, 11-12
Licensee
    duties, obligations of, 112
    responsibilities, 61-62, 147
Liens, 79, 96
Lien theory state, 122
Limited common elements, 77
Limited development areas, 143
Limited liability company, 50
Listings, 60
    solicitation, 158
Location drawing, 89

M

Majority, 98
Marital status, 153, 154
Maryland Agricultural Land
    Preservation Foundation, 75
Maryland Association of
    REALTORS®, 99, 112
    residential sales contract,
        103-9
Maryland Cooperative Housing
    Act, 84
Maryland Corporations and
    Associations, 77
Maryland Credit Union
Insurance Corporation, 57

Maryland Custom Home
Protection Act, 110
Maryland Department of
Environment, 142, 144-45
Maryland General Assembly,
    174
Maryland Homeowners
Association Act, 84
Maryland Human Relations
Commission, 159
Maryland Law of Descent and
    Distribution, 114
Maryland Medical Assistance
    Program, 115
Maryland Real Estate Brokers
    Act, 1-2, 33, 49, 56-57, 77
    acts punishable by
        imprisonment, 24-27
    advertising, 55-56
    commissions, 69-70
    conservation areas, 158
    fair housing, 157-58
    prohibited acts, 21-24
    trust money, 57
    scope of, 4-5
Maryland Real Estate
Commission, 5, 49, 54, 175
    duties, powers of, 6-7
    personal assistants, 52
Maryland Register, 2, 29
Maryland Securities Act, 28
Maryland State Archives, 175,
    176
Maryland Statutes Text, 176
Maryland Uniform Transfers to
Minors Act, 117
Material facts, 62, 67
Mechanics' liens, 96
Memorandum of lease, 130
Metes and bounds, 88
Ministerial acts, 61
Mobile home parks, 139
Montgomery County, 71, 154
    Code, 154-55
    tenant notice, 85
Mortgage
    expense accounts, 123
    lien release, 124
    loans, 122-23
    presumed paid, 124
    recordation of, 116
    release of, 163
Mortgagee title insurance, 162

Multiple listing service, 62, 71

N

Name change, 13
National Association of
REALTORS, 46
National Credit Union
Administration, 57
Natural persons, 3
Net agreements, 61
New home warranties, deposits,
110
Nonemployee status, 3-4
Notice, 16, 57-58
to buyer, 20
to quit, 135
of reassessment, 93
tenant, 85
Nuncupative wills, 115

O

Occupancy, post-settlement,
131
Occupational discrimination,
154
Office, 54-55
location, change in, 55
sign, 55
Office of the Secretary of State
Division of State Documents,
175
Open agreement, 60
Option agreements, 102
Oral transfer, 98
Out-of-state listings, 72
Outdoor Recreation Land Loan,
144
Owner, 56, 57

P

Parol transfer, 98
Peaceable and quiet entry, 137
Periodic tenancy, 133-34
Personal appearance
discrimination, 154
Personal assistants, 52-53
Personal representatives, 114
Persons, 3
Phase-in provision, 93
Place of business, 54-55
Plat of subdivision, 88, 89
Pocket cards, 10

Potomac Mortgage, 122
Power of sale clause, 122-23
Powers of attorney, 111-12
Premises
sale of, 132-33
surrender of, 135
Prescriptive term, 74
Preservation easement, 75
Presumed buyer's agent, 37, 42,
43
Presumed client, 44
Pretermitted, 115
Prince George's County, 154
Prince George's County Code,
155
Professional member, 7
Profit motive, 158
Program Open Space, 144
Prohibited acts, 21-24
Project broker, 83
Property Condition Disclosure
and Disclaimer Statement, 62,
63-66, 67-68
Property conversion, 78
Property Disclosure and
Disclaimer Statement, 111
Property insurance, 79
Property loan notices, 126
Property tax
assessments, agricultural use,
95
relief, 93-94
Proposed order, 20
Prospective buyers, 68
*Protect Your Family from Lead
in Your Home*, 148
Psychological Services, Inc.,
164-65
Public offering statement, 78,
81-82, 83

Q-R

Qualified real estate agent, 54
Radium, 144
Radon, 144
Real estate, 4
Real Estate Appraisers Act, 28
Real estate broker, 2
Real estate brokerage, 2
Real estate investment trust
(REIT), 77
Real Estate License Law, 83

Real Property Article, 77. 81.
100-101, 110, 129, 130, 139
Realtist, 55
REALTOR®, 55, 71
Reciprocity, 10
Record keeping, 58, 132
Recordation, 130
of deed, 116
details of, 118-19
of mortgage, 116
prerequisites to, 120
subdivision laws, 119
tax, 94
Recorded plat of subdivision,
88, 89
Red flags, 29
Redemption, 95-96, 124-25,
128, 129-30
Regime, 77
Registration, 83
Release of lien, 96
Renewal, 11-12
Rent
escrow account, 136-37
failure to demand, 134
withholding, 136-37
Representation
categories, 37
disclosure, 131-32
Resale
condominium unit, 80
disclosures, 82
Residential brokerage
agreements, 60-62
Residential land, lease, 129,
130-32
Residential Property Disclosure
and Disclaimer Statement, 61
Residential real estate
environment and, 143-44
rentals, 146-47
Residential sales contract, 103-9
Resource conservation areas,
143
Revenue neutral, 91
Right of first refusal, 133
Riparian rights, 74-75
Risk reduction standard, 146,
147
Rockville, 154
Rockville Laws, 155
Rules, 79
Rural Legacy Program, 144

S

Sales commission disputes, 54
Sales contract, 83
Salesperson, license, 8
Satisfaction of mortgage, 124
Scrap tires, 145
Secondary mortgage, 125-26
Secondary Mortgage Loan Law,
   126
Security agreement, 120
Security deposit, 131-32
Self employed, 54
Seller's agent, 37
Sellers' market, 67
Senior tenants, 94
Settlement company, 100
Settlements, 162-63
Severalty, 76
Sewage sludge, 145
Sexual orientation, 153, 154
Sheriff's sale, 111
Signatures, 70-71
Single agency, 35
Smart Growth Initiative, 141-42
Smoke detectors, 137-38
Solid waste, 145
Sprinkler systems, 137
State Commission of Real
   Estate Appraisers and Home
   Inspectors, 29
State Department of
Assessments and Taxation,
   95, 176
State Department of Health and
   Mental Hygiene, 101
State Government Legislative
   Reference, 2
State of Maryland Deposit
   Insurance Fund Corporation,
   57
State Real Estate Commission,
   159
State Securities Commission, 81
Statute of frauds, 98, 130
Stigmatized property, 67
Straw party, 76
Strict construction, 2
Subagents, 37
Subdivision
   laws, 119
   plat, 89-90
Summary actions, 17
Supervision, 51-52

Surplus money action, 125
Survey markers, 89

T

Tax bill payment, 93
Tax credit, 94
Taxes, 79-80
Tax sale, 111
Tax Property Article, 111
Tax statements, 163
Tenancy at will, 135
Tenancy termination, 133-35
Tenant
   Montgomery County, 85
   receipts for rental, 134-35
   refusing to vacate, 134
Term, 11-12
Termination agreement, 69
Testing procedures, 166
Threats, 156
Time-share ownership, 80-84
Time-Sharing Act, 81
Title evidence, 119-20, 162
Title insurance, 162
Title insurance company, 100
Title records, 118-20
Title theory state, 122
Torrens system, 118
Trade name, 56
Transfer
   between relatives, 116
   of title, 114-17
      by action of law, 115
      by deed, 115-16
      by descent, 114-15
Transfer tax, 94, 116, 144
Triennial assessment, 91
Trustee sales, 124-25
Trustee's deed, 122
Trust fund violations, 18
Trust money, 56-58

U

*Understanding Whom Real
   Estate Agents Represent*, 42
Unenforceable provisions, 136
Uniform Commercial Code, 120
Uniform Partnership Act, 77
Unit, 77
Unit ownership, 78-79
Usury, 123

W

Warranties, 82
Warranty of habitability, 136
Waste management
administration, 145
Web sites, 174-76
Wetland preservation, 143
Worker's compensation, 54
Worth of the reversion, 128